EDUCATION IN LATIN AMERICA:

Policies and Recommendations

Education in Latin America
© 2023 Ejiro U. Osiobe
© 2021 Ane Osiobe International Foundation.
All Rights Reserved.

Paperback: ISBN: 978-1-64318-118-9
Hardback: ISBN: 978-1-64318-119-6
Ebook: ISBN: 978-1-64318-120-2

703 Eighth Street
Baldwin City, KS, 66006
www.imperiumpublishing.com

EDUCATION IN LATIN AMERICA:

Policies and Recommendations

Ejiro U. Osiobe

Baker University Assistant Professor
Founder of The Ane Osiobe International Foundation

IMPERIUM PUBLISHING
CREATE YOUR STORY

PREFACE

This book's primary contribution to the existing literature on education in many Latin American countries is that it delves into each nation's education policies and compares relevant economic indicators with the aggregate trends of Argentina, Bolivia, Brazil, Chile, Colombia, Costa Rica, Honduras, Mexico, Nicaragua, Panama, Peru, El Salvador, Uruguay, and Venezuela. The book is among a few studies that have examined Latin American educational policies and compared them to the stated countries, making this book unique and of great value to economists, educationalists, and the economic development departments in each nation and globe.

CONTENTS

Education and Human Capital	1
Understanding Human Capital	23
United Mexican States	51
El Salvador	67
Honduras	79
Nicaragua	95
Costa Rica	109
Panama	123
Columbia	135
Venezuela	151
Brazil	167
Peru	183
Bolivia	199
Chile	215
Argentina	231
Uruguay	249
Cointegration	263
Causality	289

EDUCATION AND HUMAN CAPITAL

INTRODUCTION

The book examines the relationship between human capital and economic growth within the selected countries and the aggregate of the nations. Each chapter analyzes datasets from previous works, reviews previous literature, and draws some conclusions on human capital and economic growth. The book summarizes books and academic articles on human capital in terms of:

(i)   The theoretical framework of economic growth theory.

(ii)   The neo-classical growth model.

(iii)   The Solow growth production function.

(iv)   The new endogenous theory.

(v)   Empirical evidence on the relationship and causal link between human capital and economic growth.

1

Assessing the literature on human capital and economic growth will serve as a comprehensive guide to policy formulation and implementation in the short and long run, creating developmental goals for any region not limited to Latin American nations.

Latin American countries have evolved over the years. Still, after years of military reign, socioeconomic-instability, and civil wars, the region has been known for its anti-hegemonic economic growth (educational-policies) strategies. Researchers have long investigated Central and South America's educational system theoretically and empirically. The transition of its education system through the introduction of centralized, liberalized, and populist ideology has sparked many researchers' interest. The book and its chapters aim to understand and compare 14 Latin American countries' education orientations. The investigation uses a matrix table to visualize the qualitative finding.

"Human capital" can be described as human abilities and skill sets. The United Nations (2009) expands on the definition of productive wealth embodied in labor, skills, and knowledge. Integrated with humans, this expertise is acquired partly through formal and informal education. The human capital theory focuses on education and the individual's health as an input to economic production. In contrast, human capital development (expenditure on education or training as a proxy) refers to the acquisition and increase in the number of person's skills, knowledge, and work experience critical for a country's economic growth (Adelakun, 2011). The book and its chapters' primary contribution to the literature on economic growth, development, and stability focuses on providing a comprehensive summary of the literature on the topic.

A sustainable economic growth path incorporating environmentally sound development is a more critical macroeconomic objective (United

Nations, 2015) because it ensures the continuity of renewable resources and the optimal use of non-renewable resources. The continuity and optimal use of these resources build on Arrow et al. (2004) definition of development as "meeting the needs of the present without compromising the ability of the future generation to meet their own needs;" [after all], *our resources are not gifts to our children, they are loans from them.* For this to occur, human capital is an essential ingredient. Both theoretical and empirical economic literature has provided evidence that education is significant to economic growth. Klenow and Rodriguez-Claire (1997), Hall and Jone (1997), and Easterly and Levine (2001) built on the ideas of Adam Smith and other 18th-century philosophers and economists who advocated that labor productivity helps create a surplus of wealth. They asserted that technological change is the primary source of growth and that differences in the rate of technological change are the principal causes of income disparity among countries. Nelson and Phelps (1996), Romer, P. (1989, 1990), and Abramovitz (1986) posited that to achieve technological change, a country must engage in innovation or imitation activities that use mainly human capital as their input of interest.

The endogenous growth theories primarily emphasize the role of human capital (e.g., Mankiw, Romer, and Weil (1992) and Lucas (1988)). Common recommendations from these models are for an economy to invest in its educational system; fight poverty; create more labor market participation and economic growth opportunities, and facilitate socio-economic development. The logic is that if a national economy spends more on education, the country will experience long-term economic growth. Thus, investment in education would have a positive effect on both the individual human capital and the overall economy: it will fight poverty; reduce the number of children that go to school hungry; address government-sponsored job fears, training, and open networking sections; create more interdisciplinary opportunities in the economy; and promote socio-economic growth.

Hanushek and Woessmann's (2008) theoretical contributions emphasized two main mechanisms through which education affects economic growth. The first, based on Uzawa (1965) and Lucas (1988), is human capital, an input in the production process, implying that there is a relationship between human capital and economic growth. The second is the assumption that human capital is the primary source of productivity growth (Nelson & Phelps, 1966). This implies that improving education quality at all levels is imperative for regional development.

Interdisciplinary opportunities and trade liberalization are essential for increasing global economic growth. Increased imports and exports from countries have diversified their economies, encouraging capitalism to grow and resulting in rapid economic growth. Although the relationship between trade liberalization and economic growth has been analyzed extensively, it remains a controversial topic among policymakers and economists because of the diversity in the empirical findings noted by Chaudry and Rahman (2009). However, there is a greater consensus that trade policies promoting openness, surplus trade balance, and high trade volume to Gross Domestic Product (GDP) have positively affected economic growth (United Nations, 2009, 2015). Trade openness can increase the level and efficiency of investment and the market size in countries with liberal trade policies; hence, developing countries liberalize their economies to attract more foreign capital.

Human capital determines the ability of an economy to manage its other factors of production, and it is necessary for innovation. Adopting existing technologies, technological advancement, and catch-up processes contribute to an economy's growth rate. Amaghionyeodiwe (2009), Chaudry

4

and Rahman (2009), Liap, Du, Bing, and Yu (2019), Khembo and Tchereni (2013), and Akpolate (2014) have supported the notion that the growth of any economy is influenced by its level of physical and human capital. Hence, no country can achieve a sustained economic development path without a substantial investment in human capital (Kanayo, 2013).

Some economists argue that higher formal educational attainment leads to more economic growth. Lucas (1988) suggests that human capital accumulation translates into sustained economic growth and that education is the primary driving force through knowledge accumulation. Romer P. (1989, 1990, 1994) showed that human capital stimulates economic growth and can drive innovation. As documented in the econometric literature, Romer, P. (1989) and Rostow (1960) show that education also provides spillover effects, improves the adaptation speed of entrepreneurs to disequilibrium, and boosts research productivity.

However, there is mixed evidence in the empirical literature regarding the relationship between human capital and economic growth. Temple (1999) and Bills and Klenow (2000) reported a weak correlation between the two, while Levine and Renelt (1992) showed that education (human capital) has no significant statistical impact on economic growth, and Dessus (1999) argued that Temple's (1999) findings might have been caused by specification bias. Dessus's (1999) results suggested that as the education enrollment level increases, the standard of education decreases. As a result, educational investment in developing countries fails to generate higher growth.

While most developing countries in Africa and Asia have achieved a noticeable improvement in terms of physical and human capital, which is empirically supported by Macham (2015) and De Gregorio and Lee (2003), most Latin American countries still need more development programs to

5

facilitate their human capital and capital stock growth. These Latin American nations can benefit from increased human capital (OECD, 2017; OECD/ECLAC/CAF, 2016). Rostow (1960) argued that necessary investment must be made in three key economic sectors—technology, infrastructure, and transportation systems—for rapid economic growth. The importance of physical capital in enabling an environment for growth and development cannot be overemphasized, and the impact of human capital and infrastructure on economic growth is a well-established issue (Rahman, 2011; Holden and Biddle, 2017; Sharma and Sahni, 2015; Mehrara and Musai, 2013). For instance, a positive influence exists from human capital to economic growth, meaning economies with high-skill populations, such as Estonia, Switzerland, and the United States of America, have led the world in state-of-the-art human ingenuity. Infrastructure also contributes to the development of a country in various ways, connecting states and countries by building broadband, seaports, airports, intercountry and interstate roads to facilitate the exchange of goods, services, and information faster (Diaz, 2013).

CHRONICLES

Most people believe that individuals with a higher level of education and more working experience earn more money than those with less (Weiss, 1995). In most developing countries, the net marginal social returns of expenditure on primary education are higher than tertiary education. Statistics have shown that people with higher education generally earn more, have higher earning potential, and are more capable of improving the quality of their lives and better able to improve the quality of their lives than those with less education (UNESCO, 1997).

Human capital, or skilled labor, was first incorporated into economic analyses in the 1960s and 1970s. Goode (1959), Mincer (1958), and Becker (1975, 1962) expressed different views on human capital, likely since a broad spectrum of factors can directly or indirectly influence the formation and exploitation of human capital. These factors include positive or negative intensive or extensive effects on the economy at the macroeconomic or microeconomic level. The exogenous or endogenous influencers are sometimes grouped into demographic, social, socio-demographic, economic, and ecological categories. The interest in human capital grew as the endogenous growth theory developed. Mankiw, ROnner, and Weil (1992), Romer, P. (1989, 1990), Uzawa (1965), and Lucas (1988) each created models where the output level is defined as human capital. They argue that the quality of education may lead to an economy's long-lasting and continued growth.

Theories of Economic Growth

The framework of the economic growth theory is appropriate for analyzing the effect of human capital on economies. Education directly impacts human capital, measured by the Human Development Index (*HDI*), and influences income distribution (Gini Index). According to Solow (1956), the physical capital stock will increase per capita income. Still, based on his neo-classical growth theory, long-term growth will not be sustainable from inputs in education due to the assumption of the law of diminishing marginal returns, which is associated with excess spending on education. Therefore, an increase in the expenditure on education will increase education enrollment and the quality of education to a certain point; then, as enrollment continues to grow, the quality of knowledge begins to decrease.

7

Education generally impacts economic growth by increasing innovation and technological/knowledge spillover. According to Romer, P. (1994), improved technology and knowledge skills will translate into increased productivity, leading to short and long-term economic growth. A discussion of educational expenditures broadens the topic to include two significant theories of economic growth: the neo-classical growth theory and the new endogenous growth theory.

Neo-classical Growth Model

In 1950, Robert Solow and Trevor Swan developed the exogenous neo-classical growth model (Dimand & Spencer, 2011). The Solow growth model states that long-run growth is achieved through capital accumulation, skilled labor, population growth, and technological progress (Solow, 1956). The model is based on four variables that are used to determine long-term growth, including output (Y), capital (K), labor (L), investment (I), or savings (S). In Solow's growth theory, the output is a capital, labor, investment, and technology function. Solow had four critical assumptions in his model: the first and second, he assumed that labor force growth and technology are exogenous factors, which means that labor force growth is constant; third, the Solow growth model assumes capital and labor to have a constant return to scale; fourth, the model assumes a diminishing return of its variable factor $GDP_{per\ capita}$.

The Solow Growth Production-Function

$$Y = F(K, L) \qquad (1)$$
$$y = f(k) \qquad (2)$$

8

With the constant return-to-scale assumption, the Solow growth production-function becomes *equation* (1) and *equation* (2), where *y* is output per labor and *k* is capital per labor. Based on *equation* (2), as capital per labor increases, output per labor will also increase. Hence, as the capital-labor ratio grows, output peaks and diminishes; thus, the law of diminishing marginal returns initiates. Therefore, balance can be achieved when savings and investment are at equilibrium with the capital-labor ratio, which will result in a steady-state of the economy:

$$s f(k *) = (\delta + n) \, k * \qquad (3)$$

Where: *s* is the savings rate, *k* is capital per labor, δ is depreciation, and *n* is the population growth rate.

The New Endogenous Theory

The neo-classical growth model assumes that the accumulation of capital (savings) in an economy and how people utilize this capital is vital for economic growth. This model shows the relationship between capital and labor and how capital and labor translate to output. The model has some weaknesses, such as the exogenous determination of technology. It assumes that all countries will converge at the same steady-state. Romer, P. (1994) and Stonier and Hague (1972) agree with Solow's assumptions, arguing that technology should be an endogenous determinant rather than exogenous because investment, research and development, knowledge, and capital accumulation translate to long-term economic growth. An investment that concentrates on physical and human capital encourages more economic growth, reinforcing the idea that at the steady-state, growth is a direct result of the level of human capital (Romer P., 1990, 1994).

This stated shortcoming led to the creation of the new endogenous growth theory. This model is founded on three main assumptions:

1) Technological change results from the "animal spirit" optimism and pessimism of the market, which determines long-run economic growth.

2) Technological change causes labor to be efficient, improving output per capita, and 3) the cost of production of new inventions is incurred once as a fixed-sunk cost. The endogenous growth theory makes technology endogenous and, as a result, addresses the flaws associated with the neoclassical growth model.

Liew (2004) provides a guideline for using the Lag Selection Criteria (LSC) to determine the autoregressive lag length. The study provided the following information: first, Akaike's Information Criterion (AIC) and Final Prediction Error (FPE) are superior to the other criteria when studying data sets that are between 0-60 observation because the AIC and FPE minimize the chance of underestimating while maximizing the possibility of recovering the actual lag length; second, these criteria managed to pick up the correct lag length at least half of the time in a small sample; third, the performance increases substantially as the sample size increases; fourth, with relatively large sample size, the HQC is a better estimator of the autoregressive lag length.

Empirical Evidence of the Relationship and Causal Link Between Human Capital and Economic Growth

According to Weiss (1995), those with a higher level of education and more working experience earn more money than those with less. In most developing countries, the net marginal social returns of expenditure on primary education are higher than tertiary education. The relationship between education and poverty is defined: people with a higher degree of education earn more or have higher earning potential and are better able to improve the quality of their lives than those with a lesser educational background (UNESCO, 1997).

Human capital, or skilled labor, was first used in the 1960s and 1970s. Goode (1959), Mncer (1958), and Becker (1962, 1975) had differing views on human capital because many factors, directly and indirectly, influence the formation and exploitation of human capital. As the concept of human capital kept growing based on the endogenous growth theory, Mankiw, Romer, and Weil (1992), Romer, P. (1989, 1990), Uzawa (1965), and Lucas (1988) each created models where the output level is defined as human capital. Using human capital in the production-function model to support their argument for human capital investment in the economic growth theory, they argued that the quality of education might lead to long-lasting and continued growth of an economy.

Alexious (2009) and Kim (2010) argued that education is the first step in economic development, finding that education plays a crucial role in building a nation's human capital capacity and promoting economic growth. High age-dependency ratio, the undergrowth of *GDP* and *GDP*$_{per\ capita}$, high unemployment, low *HDI* index percentage, and Gini Index numbers are common problems in emerging economies. Pedroni (2002) and Psacharopoulos and Patrinos (2004) analyzed the effects of educational investment on countries. They found that the impact of these expenditures is higher in African, Asian, and Latin American countries and is less in the OECD countries.

In contrast, Benhabib (1994) measured the effect of human capital investment on economic growth and found a negligible or somewhat negative correlation between education investment and economic growth and development. Quiggin (1999, 2002) also asserted that education has zero monetary or economic benefits, resulting in a decline in economic growth. Due to evidence presented by economists like Benhabib (1994) and Quiggin (1999, 2002), some governments have cut their spending and budgets for the education sector. Devarajan (1996) also found that education spending harms or is insignificant to economic growth, supporting Benhabib and Quiggin's findings.

Riihelaninen (2013) analyzed the relationship between government education expenditure in the European Union during the Economic Crisis and found a temporary positive effect of educational spending on economic growth. In South American studies, Kiran (2014) analyzed the impact of educational expenditure on economic growth for 18 Latin American countries and found a cointegration relationship between economic growth and educational spending. Blankenau et al. (2007) analyzed 23 developed countries and found a positive relationship between education expenditures and long-term economic growth.

Engelbrecht (1997) argued that human capital is essential to the new growth theory. Sinnathurai (2013), in his study, found that a country with low labor productivity per capita will have low economic growth, high unemployment, and a high poverty rate. In Asia, Africa, and Latin America, over 1.3 billion people earn less than 1 USD per day, and citizens from these continents suffer from malnutrition (Vijayakumar, 2013). The high dependency ratio in a family leads to low labor force productivity in that economy, thus proving the negative relationship between poverty and economic growth.

Schultz (1963, 2009) found that increasing the educational level of the labor force significantly boosted economic growth in both developing and developed countries. This researcher determined that a higher economic growth rate opens the path to a sustainable steady-state increase in productive capacity, wealth accumulation, and employment opportunities, increasing productivity. When a country increases its human factor (L) and factors of production ($Y = F(K, L)$), they gain more workers in production and affiliated activities, which will lead to a decrease in the unemployment rate in that economy.

Hawkes and Ugur (2012) argued that the ingenuity of human capital has a broad spectrum of benefits for the national economy, communities, and individuals. Hence, quality education, healthcare systems, low crime rates, and environmental protection laws and policies are significant economic growth and development determinants. Researchers from the OECD (2017), OECD/ECLA/CAF (2016), and UNESCO (1997) argue that the Millennium Development Goals (MDG), specifically Universal Primary Education (UPE), can't be achieved by only implementing UPE. Education is a significant determinant for developing countries and encourages an environment that attracts investment in human capital stock. The MDG and the Sustainable Development Goals provide a sustained economic development path (United Nations, 2009). Using Kazakhstan as a case study, the United Nations (2015) found that countries with high economic growth rates are more likely to experience an exponential decline in their poverty rate. Hawkes and Ugur (2012) posited that this poverty reduction would lead to an increase in employment rate and higher income.

Rehman et al. (2015) analyzed the relationship between education and economic growth, finding that a nation couldn't develop without investing in education. The authors stated that education reduces poverty by increasing productivity per capita. The study also showed strong linkages between poverty-education and education-economic growth. Wolf et al.

(1993) analyzed the relationship between higher education level and the labor productivity index. They found a high correlation between university enrollment in science and technology and labor productivity growth. The study found that the more scientists and engineers graduate, the more opportunities for economic growth there are within the country. Therefore, as Sen (1999) argues, education is essential to human capital and a country's sovereignty.

Kim et al. (2010) argued for the importance of a well-educated labor force in the diffusion and adoption of new technology and production methods. Wedgwood (2007) analyzed how secondary education accessibility is limited to those who can supplement education through the private sector. The author found that some issues of post-primary education are more of a quality sustainability problem than an initiation one. Using Tanzania as a case study, Wedgwood (2007) found the secondary education system in Tanzania is not graduating quality students to supply and support the demand for primary school teachers in the country, making a strong case for government investment in secondary schools. Dahal (2006) found that higher education encourages economic growth and creates employment opportunities and argues that the quantity and quality of an education system influence the labor force, governance, and working conditions of a nation. Hick (1980) researched the net private and social benefits of education investments in the workplace and found a significant increase in the growth rate when the investment was directed to human capital/resources.

Bloom et al. (2006) studied the positive impacts of research, higher education, and innovation on economic activities. Still, his study focused on the financial returns generated through personal income tax and less on educational gains in the economy. Abbas and Foreman-Peck (2008) and Tilak (1997) estimated the relationship between human capital and economic growth using the *OLS* technique. They argued that human capital was responsible for almost 40% of the increase in a nation's *real GDP*. The two studies concluded that only little to no investment in the educational system of an economy could cause low investment and zero economic growth in an economy. The papers found that the higher the educational attainment of a region's population, the less likely its members are to be considered poor or live below the United Nations' 1 USD per day mark because education impacts knowledge and skills, encouraging growth and development. Barro and Lee (1993) found that an increase in productivity is directly correlated with an increase in the average duration of education. A study by Njong (2010) found that primary education in a poor learning environment, minimal secondary education, and limited higher education reduce economic growth and development. Njong (2010) stated the absence of a current/updated curriculum and a lack of skills/qualified instructors, administrative assistants, and management personnel have a linear relationship between education and earnings.

Abdullah et al. (2015) used the meta-regression analysis (MRA) method to revisit earlier works on the effect of education on aggregate income share and income inequality. The study assessed the average impact of education on inequality and modeled the heterogeneity in the empirical estimates. The authors analyzed 64 econometric studies that collectively reported 885 estimates of the effect of education on inequality. They aimed to re-examine later works on the impact of education on inequality using a comprehensive MRA and found that education affects the two tails of the distribution of income, reduces earning from the top earners, and increases the percentage of the bottom earners. Education has been instrumental in reducing inequality in Africa. It appears to have a stronger effect in reducing inequality at the secondary level than at the primary level or higher education. Abdullah et al. (2015) state that the differences in the specification of the econometric models and measures of inequality and education could explain the heterogeneity in reported estimates.

Anyanwu (2014) highlighted deep, underlying factors that have promoted or hindered African economic growth and drew lessons from the experience of China. The author used five non-overlapping three-year averages of cross-sectional data from 53 African countries between 1996 and 2010, where the *real GDP* was the dependent variable, the elasticity of growth concerning initial *real GDP$_{per\ capita}$* is $\beta1$, the elasticity of growth with respect to government consumption expenditure as a percentage of *GDP* is $\beta2$, the elasticity of growth with respect to investment rate is $\beta3$, and the vector of elasticity of the control variables was "X." "X" represents other control variables ($\beta4......n$), including official development aid (*ODA*), which is a percentage of *GDP*; Foreign Direct Investment, which is a percentage of *GDP*; trade openness (total trade as a percentage of *GDP*); external debt, which is a percentage of *GDP*; level of education (secondary school enrollment); inflation rate; policy-2 (institutionalized political regime); government effectiveness; urban population; domestic credit to the private sector (as a percentage of *GDP*); agricultural materials price index; metals price index; oil price index; industrial materials price index. The author's analysis showed that higher domestic investment is significantly correlated with higher economic growth in Africa, consistent with Abamann (2008) but contrary to Haacker et al. (2009), who found significant adverse effects. Initial real per capita income has a positive but insignificant coefficient. Hence, the cross-country data does not support the hypothesis of absolute convergence during the analysis period.

Other results showed that foreign aid impacts economic growth in Africa. Net *ODA* has a positive and statistically significant impact on

16

economic growth. On average, a 1% increase in net *ODA* as a percentage of *GDP* will lead to a 0.437%-point rise in economic growth in Africa. Education positively affects economic growth in Africa, concluding that secondary education is significantly related to economic growth. Hence, a 1% increase in secondary education enrollment would increase economic growth by 0.309%-point, meaning, for Africa, education is good for boosting economic growth, and credit to the private sector has an insignificant negative effect on economic growth.

Drucker (2007) reviewed different approaches for examining the influence of research universities on regional economic development outcomes. The authors used four methods to examine the impacts of universities on regional economic development. The first method was the impact of individual universities or university systems, which was done using growth accounting, regional input-output modeling, estimation of Keynesian multipliers, or a broader regional economic forecasting model. This method estimates the direct and indirect impact of a region's university spending, investment, and employment. The limitation of this approach is that studies of individual universities cannot be generalized to other universities, regions, or economic situations. Another shortcoming is that it is difficult to assess the indirect impact of a university, such as regional productivity gains or increases in innovative regional activities that depend on a host of interacting factors apart from the university itself. The second approach is based on surveys. This methodology aims to overcome the weakness of the single-case approach by producing results that can be generalized beyond institutions or regions. The limitation of the survey questions aimed at the attribution problem(s) is that they suffer from noticeable validity threats, such as respondent ignorance or bias. The third approach is the production-function estimations and the fourth is the cross-sectional or quasi-experimental designs. These involve selecting a sample from a sampling frame and then analyzing the empirical relationships between the variables using regression-based statistical methods. The advantage of the cross-sectional approach is its flexibility, but one disadvantage is its susceptibility to sampling issues and omitted variable bias.

Heckman (2002) analyzed the importance of cognitive and non-cognitive skills and how they translate into social and economic success. He identified formal (academic institutions) and informal (family culture and workplace) sources of learning as a unique and independent environments for acquiring knowledge. After evaluating a human capital investment strategy, he found that skill begets skill and learning begets learning; hence, early investments in education are effective. The author concluded that it is essential to consider the entire policy portfolio of interventions together, including training programs, school-based policies, school reform, and early interventions, rather than focusing on one type of policy in isolation from the others. The paper also explored the relationship between primary and secondary school quality and economic growth. The author used a 20-year data set from Malaysia, using the Gini Index to measure educational inequality at the primary and secondary levels and *GDP* as the dependent variable. The author used a Cobb-Douglas production-function to show the relationship between labor and overall economic production. Their model included

$$Y_t = K^\alpha H^\beta (AL)^{1-\alpha-\beta} \tag{4}$$

Where Y_t is per capita income, H is the stock of human capital, L is Labor, K is capital, and A is the growth coefficient.

The research goals of Boyce et al. (2010) were two-fold: first, to examine cognitive, dispositional, and motivational precursors of the propensity to engage in leadership self-development, and second to explore the role of organizational support and the relationships between self-development propensity and reported self-development activities. A survey was designed to test a structural model used in the study of leader self-development. A random sample of over 400 junior-military leaders participated in this study, and the results indicated that a person with characteristics related to mastery, work, or career growth ethics displays the intuition to perform leadership roles and self-development and is more skilled at performing instructional and self-regulatory processes. The authors concluded with implications for future research on and practice of leader self-development activities.

Soumare (2015) recognized the chicken-and-egg dilemma of education and economic development. Education needs to be sponsored. Developed countries can easily fund education programs that translate into economic growth and development, and emerging economies lack the funding to begin the cycle. The study assessed the impact of Foreign Direct Investment (*FDI*) on North African welfare using the *HDI* and *GDP*$_{per\ capita}$ as welfare measures. The author examined the relationship between FDI inflow and welfare improvement in North African countries in the study. He also explored whether *FDI* contributes to improved welfare in the North African region, examining whether *FDI* has; long-term welfare-improving impacts in some North African countries than others and drew policy recommendations from their findings. (Soumare, 2015) used *HDI* and an alternative *real GDP*$_{per\ capita}$ as indicators to measure welfare improvement, *net FDI* $_{per\ capita}$, and an alternative *net FDI inflow* to *GDP ratio* to measure *FDI*. The author used the Granger causality test and found a unidirectional causality between *FDI* and *HDI* for the entire region. But, when *real GDP*$_{per\ capita}$ was used as a welfare variable, he found bidirectional causality between *FDI* and *real GDP*$_{per\ capita}$. The dynamic panel regression model analysis indicated that *FDI* positively impacted welfare in North Africa and the differing relationships between different countries in the region. In general, *FDI* contributes to economic growth in North Africa, which generates additional government revenues for the region through fiscal policies and job creation. Soumere (2015) also found that government spending, infrastructure development, institutional quality, and better governance amplify the positive effects of *FDI* on welfare in the region, and it is essential for the governments in the area to continue investing in social infrastructure while improving the quality of their institutions and their governance.

Mehrara (2013) investigated the Granger causal relationship between education and *GDP* in a panel of 11 oil-exporting countries. The author's results showed a causality between oil revenue and economic growth and education. Still, education did not significantly affect *GDP* in the short or long run. The implication suggests that oil revenue drives education and not vice-versa. The authors added that oil revenue primarily contributes to human capital and economic growth, but as enrollments increase, the educational system's quality declines. Mehrara & Musai (2013) also assessed a similar test, using only developing countries, and the results supported the view that higher economic growth leads to higher education expenditures, but the reverse did not hold.

Akpolat (2014) analyzed the long-run impact of human and physical capital on *GDP* from 1970 to 2011. The author analyzed 13 developed and 11 developing countries and found that physical capital investment and education expenditures increased *GDP* in developed countries more than in emerging economies. In contrast, life expectancy at birth was more efficient in increasing *GDP* in developing countries than the developed ones. Edrees

(2016) investigated the causal relationship between human capital, infrastructure, and economic growth in the Arab world. The study found a feedback relationship between human capital and infrastructure and economic growth in the full sample (rich and non-rich). The author found a unidirectional movement running from economic growth to human capital in rich countries. He also found a unidirectional movement from economic growth to infrastructure in non-rich countries. The results suggest that these causal relationships are not uniform at different income levels. For example, economic growth Granger causes human capital in all groups bidirectionally.

Rahman (2011) investigated the causal relationship between Bangladesh's health expenditure, education expenditure, and GDP. The study found a bidirectional Granger causal relationship between healthcare expenditure and education, education expenditure and *GDP*, and a unidirectional relationship between healthcare expenditure and *GDP*. In contrast, (Pelinescu, 2015) highlighted the importance of human capital in promoting economic growth. The study showed a positive relationship between $GDP_{per\ capita}$ and innovative capacity of human capital (number of patents) and the qualification of employees (education attainment [secondary education and above]). The analysis indicated a negative relationship between education expenditure and $GDP_{per\ capita}$.

Sharma and Sahni (2015) explored the Granger causal relationship between human capital investment (education and healthcare investment) and India's economic growth. The analysis showed that investment in education and health care is essential and has a positive significant long-term effect on $GDP_{per\ capita}$ growth, asserting that healthier people who live longer have stronger incentives to invest in skill development, which increases workforce productivity by increasing work capacity and efficiency with new technology. The cointegration test results confirmed that education investment, health investment, and *GDP* are cointegrated, which indicates a long-run equilibrium relationship between the variables of interest. The findings of Khembo and Tchereni (2013) agree with that of Sharma and Sahni (2015) that education has a positive statistically significant effect on *GDP* $_{per\ capita}$.

UNDERSTANDING HUMAN CAPITAL

INTRODUCTION

Most Latin American and Caribbean Countries (LAC) are exposed to some of the world's ills and inhumane conditions (Aman & Ireland, 2015). This chapter builds on the literature on Latin America's socio-economic, political, and educational transition. The study presents descriptive statistics of our Selected Latin American Countries (SLACs), such as the educational policies that have moved SLACs forward, identifying their differences and similarities, and proposing recommendations for some of the SLACs to improve their nations' human capital.

The concept of human capital emerged from the recognition that the investment in human capital by an individual, firm, or country has an increasing return to scale on productivity. Human capital can be split into three concepts: talent (natural-given ability), acquired qualifications, and expertise. The term human capital was first used in the late '50s and early '60s (Holden & Biddle, 2017). Before the '50s and '60s, the word was a suggestive phrase in economics and played no role in the decision-making algorithm when recommending, passing, and implementing educational policies. Upon empirical and practical evidence that there was a high return on quality education and that it helped promote a country's national goals, new ideas on public spending on education as a form of domestic investment were advocated by academics, policymakers, and economic development practitioners.

Human capital is labor used to produce other goods and services. Schultz (1961) defined human capital as a value measuring human potential. Smith (1776) stated that "the improvement to human capital through training, education, and experience make the individual enterprise more profitable, but also add to the collective wealth of the nation." While Osiobe (2020) defined human capital to be education and training (formal, informal, and cultural); knowledge; labor; skills (general, industry, firm, job, and task-specific); experience. Human capital is the collective wealth of a nation in terms of judgment, skills, training, knowledge, expertise, and talent for a population ((Schultz, 1963), (Schultz, 1961), and (Osiobe, 2020)).

In a standard growth economic model (Romer, 1989), (Solow, 1956), and (Mankiw et al., 1992), the accumulation of human capital is a private and public investment undertaken to promote economic growth and development. The principle of opportunity cost is implemented in the model where the individual gives up some proportion of income during the period of education and training in return for increased future earnings. Hence, an individual will only undergo additional schooling or training if the future reward (return on education) exceeds the instant gratification.

Figure 1: Latin America

Author's creation (Google Earth, 2019)
*Grey countries are the selected countries for the study

In the last decades, LACs have achieved remarkable social and economic success. The middle-class population in the LACs has grown to historic levels; the poverty rate has been reduced by almost half; access to education, electricity, and health care has expanded at moderate levels; property rights are enforced. As a result, most countries in the LACs region have now achieved emerging market status, but according to (Sanguinetti 2016), more work is needed.

Suppose a country intends to move toward sustained and inclusive economic growth for its members. In that case, it will have to address some

Table 1: Economic Indicators used in Figure 2 & 3

	Meaning
$RGDP_{ppp}$	Real gross domestic product purchasing-power-parity is gross domestic product adjusted for inflation or deflation and converted to international dollars using the purchasing-power-parity rate.
$T\%GDP$	Trade as a percentage of gross domestic product is the total sum of exports and imports of goods and services measured as a share of the gross domestic product.
ATE	Access to electricity is the percentage of the population with access to power in a region. But ATE does not imply a steady or constant supply of the service.
TSE	Tertiary school enrollment is the gross enrollment ratio of the nation's total enrollment ($TSE, SSE, and\ PSE$) of students into a tertiary institution, regardless of age, to the population of the age group that officially corresponds to the level of education.
SSE	Secondary school enrollment is the gross enrollment ratio of the nation's total enrollment ($TSE, SSE, and\ PSE$) of students into a secondary institution, regardless of age, to the population of the age group that officially corresponds to the level of education.
PSE	Primary school enrollment is the gross enrollment ratio of the nation's total enrollment ($TSE, SSE, and\ PSE$) of students into a primary institution, regardless of age, to the population of the age group that officially corresponds to the level of education.

Source: (World Development Index (WDI), 2019)

of the fundamental socio-economic challenges—beginning with but not limited to the lack of high-quality human capital. The potential of youths in LACs is immeasurable, and youths' are defined as people between the ages 15–29 years, which account for more than 163 Million (Mn.) persons in the LACs region as of 2017 (OECD et al. 2016). In the LACs, 18% of the youth population is in the labor force, while the remaining 82% are not in the working class and Not Engaged in Education or Training (NEET), an acronym coined by (OECD et al. 2016). The statistic is most prevalent among the disadvantaged group, meaning those who are classified as NEET. Low-skilled human capital makes productivity growth difficult in any economy; hence, an inclusive human capital and entrepreneurship approach

26

with sustainable and applicable instruments to the specific needs of a country will increase productivity and equity in the region.

Figure 2: Gross Domestic Product per capita purchasing-power-parity (*GDP*%23 45%675888) (constant 2011 international $) of SLACs (1990 – 2017)

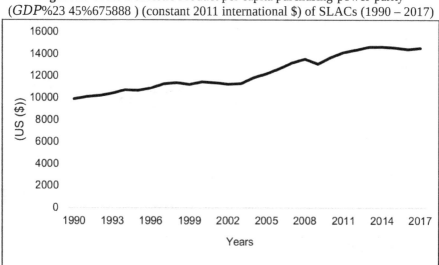

Source: (WDI, 2019)
Author's creation

If the SLACs are to compete effectively with the rest of the world, the region must urgently remedy itself by raising its human capital or Human Development Index (*HDI*). Figure 2 shows that our SLACs $GDP_{per\ capita\ ppp}$ has risen since the 1990s. Although the $GDP_{per\ capita\ ppp}$ in these nations has been increasing, human capital has not. One primary reason Latin American workers lack the right skills is the lack of access to quality education: less than half of the youth population in the region graduate from a tertiary institution, while the rest are in the NEET group.

Figure 3 shows that our SLACs have *ATE* with a mean of 92% of the population and a range of 12%. The enrollment rate in these countries varied from *TSE*, *SSE*, and *PSE* schools, where *TSE* has a mean of 30%, *SSE* 85%,

Figure 3: Economic Indicators of our SLACs

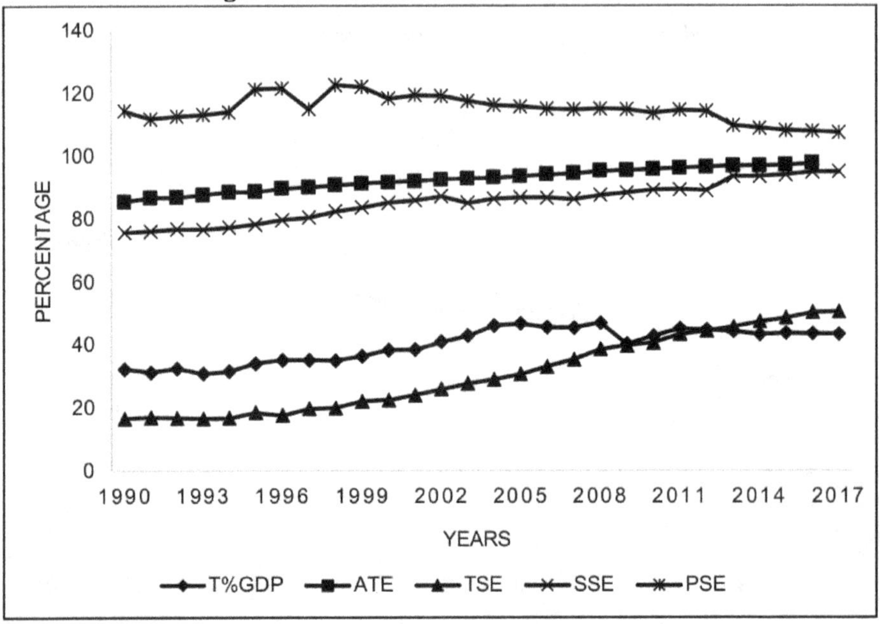

Source: (WDI, 2019)
Author's creation

and *PSE* 115%, with a range of 33%, 19%, and 15%, respectively. The result implies a vast disparity between *TSS*, *SSE*, and *PSE*. Meanwhile, *T%GDP* in Latin America has had an upward trend since the '90s, which means that the region is becoming more open and business-friendly in the international market despite the slow growth in the *TSE* rate. Figure 3 shows some line graphs above the 100% threshold. This implies that *PSE* enrollment rates are above the school capacity; i.e., if a classroom was built to accommodate only 50 students, the class may have 60+ students in it; this is also a result of free mandatory primary education for all in most of our SLACs. Our 14 SLACs were selected due to the availability of macroeconomic development indicators, a common problem when studying economic growth policies from emerging nations.

Based on existing literature and our descriptive statistic (Figures 3 & 6), one can infer that our SLACs require a more integrated system to reinforce the roles that promote higher education from an enrollment count to an attainment count.

EDUCATIONAL HISTORY, SIMILARITIES, AND DIFFERENCES OF THE SLACs

Most of the SLACs got their independence in the 1820s. The SLAC embraced the trinity of equality of John Locke (life, liberty, and property) and Thomas Hobbes' social contractarianism theory. These two theorems are known to be the foundation for most democratic political systems. The revolutionary troops didn't adopt Western neocolonialism, which collided with the SLACs' culture, experiences, and history of the indigenous people (Verges, 1999). The neocolonialism era came with notable educational reforms that established indigenous universities in Bolivia, Ecuador, and Mexico, intending to reconquer and modify their native language and traditional systems (Aman, 2014). Some LACs like Bolivia, Cuba, and Venezuela have adopted Karl Mark's and Friedrich Engels' (abolition of private property) as their nation's new contractarianism following Hobbes's government-monarchism and disregarding Locke's government by and for the people.

According to (Aman, 2015), the neoliberal ideology and the emergence of a new global commerce divide from merchandise to human cargo imposed on Latin America date back to when the region was part of the European map in the 20th century. The World Bank (WB) and International Monetary Fund (IMF) exposed the area to harsh and unjust conditions.

Several communities have countered these efforts by the IMF and WB within the region, from the indigenous social movement in Bolivia to Venezuela's Chavistas, to the Zapatistas in the Chiapas region of Mexico, to the landless movement in Brazil (Aman and Ireland, 2015). These resistance movements, backed by the Roman Catholic Church, have created its brand of education as an expression of anti-hegemonic resilience.

These anti-hegemonic events brought about Marxism philosophy, substantive democracy, and a post-liberalized era. As a result, the newly inducted manifesto, the educational system in some parts of the region, assimilated its proposed ideology. Bolivia, Ecuador, and Mexico are good examples of countries that challenged the dominant Western paradigm and scientific theories (Aman, 2014). President Juan Evo Morales declared the decolonization of education from Western influences, and in the '80s, such concepts and practices found their way into the Nicaraguan educational policies (Aman and Ireland, 2015). The SLAC consists of one North American country (Mexico), five Central American countries (Costa Rica, Honduras, Nicaragua, Panama, and El Salvador), and eight South American countries (Argentina, Bolivia, Brazil, Chile, Colombia, Peru, Uruguay, and Venezuela).

Figure 4 shows the expenditure side of the Real Gross Domestic Product (*RGDPppp*) at a chained (in Mn. 2011 USD) of the SLACs from 1950–2014 based on their moving average. Figure 4 depicts a steady upward trend of *RGDPppp* from 1950–2014. Figure 5 shows the Human Development Index (*HDI*) of the SLACs from 1950–2014. And like *RGDPppp*, it also depicts an upward trend from 1950–2014. The increasing social and economic development over the past decades has led to progress in well-being. These countries have adjusted their social policies in response to the needs of their residents, which has resulted in a steady increase in the

Figure 4: *RGDP*ppp of the SLACs (1950 – 2014)

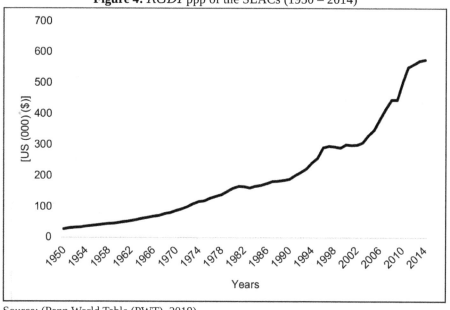

Source: (Penn World Table (PWT), 2019)
Author's creation

nation's human capital productivity and *HDI*. Most of these nations' signs of progress have been widely recognized, reaching essential milestones like becoming members of the OECD, creating budgets as a percentage of the *GDP* specifically for education, and deregulating their nations' education system to benefit local institutions in the country's rural regions.

Our SLAC education systems are grouped into a centralized and decentralized educational system. In this study, the centralized will be defined as a condition where a single government agency, usually the Ministry of Education (ME), governs the nation's educational system (federal, state, and local). While the decentralized educational system, for this study, is defined as when governance power is shared among the federal, state, and local governments. In most cases, the responsibilities of distributing resources across all levels of the education sector and governments will come from the ME. In contrast with first-world nations like the US, the responsibility for formulating and implementing educational policies does not lie solely with the Department of Education but with other autonomous public education administrative departments; this analogy is similar to that of the OECD member nations.

Figure 5: *HDI* of the SLACs (1950 – 2014)

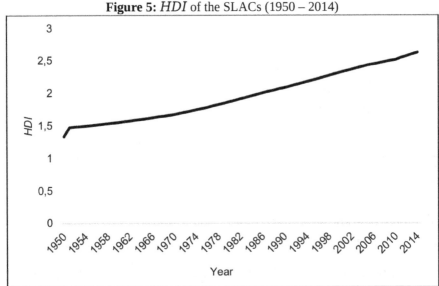

Source: (PWT, 2019)
Author's creation

The 14 countries in the study have achieved universal access to primary education for their residents; however, some have gained access to preschool, and others are still in the works. In light of these successes, the education attainment rate in the lower and upper high school and university levels remains unsatisfactory, and the dropout rate is relatively high. Beyond using the education budget as a political propaganda tool to win votes from grade-school parents, Latin American politicians are well known for using education resources as political patronage (Plank, 1996) (Brown & Hunter, 2004).

According to (Brown & Hunter, 2004), the construction of schools and employment of principals, teachers, and staff are used as a wheel of clientelism and nepotism. The authors' presented some theoretical assertions that democratically run governments favored public spending on primary education versus authoritarian governments, which did not. Elected leaders like Alberto Fujimori of Peru (1990–2000), Vicente Fox of Mexico (2000–2006), and Fernando Henrique of Brazil (1995–2002) made use of this political strategy to reap some political capital and electoral dividends (Brown & Hunter, 2004). Education economists like (Birdsall et al., 1998), (Paul & Wolff, 1996), and (Gonzalez Rozada, 2002) have criticized governments for implementing politicalized education budgeting (Brown & Hunter, 2004). But a substantial body of literature has suggested the centrality of human capital formation for economic growth, economic development, and poverty alleviation (Brown & Hunter, 2004). The allocation of significant grants to improve a nation's educational system can enhance the prospects of the nation's human capital in that region. For emerging economies, it is essential to devote a larger share of the education budget to the primary school sector, for which the public returns are high relative to spending on other areas of the educational system (Brown & Hunter, 2004). Because people in poverty are a significant slice of the population in most SLACs, the low-income earner benefits more from the investment in primary education.

Generally, it is common knowledge that the labor-market return to education is higher at the primary level and then decreases at subsequent levels (Colclough et al., 2010). Most developing countries prioritize investment in their educational system. Still, the social return (positive social externalities) is lower than the private return due to government financing policies for free education (public investment in education) (Colclough et al., 2010). In the developing world, the evidence of wage returns to education continues to grow, showing a 10% increase in a person's wage for one additional year of schooling (Colclough et al., 2010). Until recent studies, it was generally accepted that wage returns in developing countries are usually higher at the primary level than subsequent levels ((Porta et al., 2006), (Psacharopoulos & Patrinos, 2004), (Jamal et al., 2003), (Patrinos & Sakellariou, 2006), (Pastore & Verashchagina, 2006), and (Colclough et al., 2010)). According to (Psacharopoulos & Patrinos, 2002), the return to schooling declines over time, but other studies suggest that primary education is insufficient. However, ((Nguyen's, 2002), (Lassibille and Tan's, 2005), (Kijima's, 2006), (Ali's, 2006), (Laguna and Porta's, 2004), (Tansel's, 2008), (Bellony and Reilly's, 2009), (Van Leeuwen's, 2005), and (Fiszbein et al., 2007)) disagree with their assertions and results, while (Reilly and Bellony, 2009), had conclusions that were for both primary and higher education.

SIMILARITIES AND DIFFERENCES BETWEEN THE 14 SELECTED LATIN AMERICAN COUNTRIES' POLICY ORIENTATIONS

Figure 6 shows how the 14 SLACs relate and differ from one another in terms of policy orientation. Few countries in the Americas and the Caribbean have experienced drastic changes in their educational system, governance, and policies as our SLACs. The social, ideological, and political approaches used by their governments to improve the academic standards of their countries have been successful in so many ways, like increasing the literacy level of their nations by providing primary education for everyone and increasing the nations' aggregate human capital index (OECD et al., 2016).

Figure 6: The Educational Orientation Matrix table of the SLAC.

	Argentina	Bolivia	Brazil	Chile	Colombia	Costa Rica	Honduras	Mexico	Nicaragua	Panama	Peru	El Salvador	Uruguay	Venezuela
Spanish as the official language of instruction	*	*		*	*	*	*	*	*	*	*	*	*	*
Portuguese as the official language of instruction			*											
English as a bilingual language of instruction				*	*	*		*		*				
National Education Institution and Policy (compulsory & free basic education)	*	*	*	*	*	*	*	*	*	*	*	*	*	*
Free Tertiary Education													*	*
Specified budget for Education (spending as a % of GDP or a Mandated Education Financing Law)	*	*	*	*	*	*					*			*
Decentralized the educational system			*	*			*	*						
Reformed the education practices			*	*			*	*			*			*

Author's creation

From Figure 6, one can infer that all 14 nations' have a national educational institution for regulating and creating educational policies, compulsory free primary education for all residents, except Uruguay and Venezuela, which have free but not mandatory education up to the university level; and speak Spanish as its official language for learning, except Brazil, which speaks Portuguese. Chile, Colombia, Costa Rica, Mexico, and Panama have reasonably tried to promote the English language in their educational system. Argentina, Bolivia, Brazil, Chile, Costa Rica, Panama, and Venezuela all have a specified educational budget as a percentage of their nation's *GDP* and a mandated education financing law.

Bolivia, Chile, Honduras, Mexico, Peru, and Venezuela have all passed educational reform bills in their countries and decentralized (excluding Peru and Venezuela) their education system to make it more flexible for regional, state, and local official educational policymakers. There has been good progress in all 14 countries' educational systems. Despite the significant policy efforts in these nations, academic quality and equity concerns remain at the forefront of their educational orientations (OECD et al., 2016). These recognitions and willingness to work on the stated problems are invaluable to improving human capital in these countries and considering the individual countries' analysis of their educational orientations.

DISCUSSION AND CONCLUSION

The educational governance is overly centralized rather than decentralized: the school system in the 14 SLACs (see Figure 6), especially those in the rural areas, have little and, in most cases, zero autonomy over their departmental or school educational policies to fit their unique situation, compared to nations that practice a decentralized education system like most OECD countries, except for Bolivia, Chile, Honduras, and Mexico. Little or zero local school autonomy hinders the effective use of educational resources, as school authorities cannot match their available resources and policies to their specific needs. Also, the responses from the central governing authority to the local schools are usually slow (OECD et al.,

2016). The education system is centered on the quantity of student enrollment rather than education quality and attainment. All 14 countries in the study have mandatory and free primary education as education policy for all nation residents. This resulted in a high level of educational coverage between 85% and 99% of the country. Although a good policy, the focus should shift from student enrollment to attainment and from the number of schools to the quality of the schools with state-of-the-art equipment (OECD et al., 2016). This shift from quantity to quality will create a culture of excellence throughout their respective countries' education systems, improving human capital.

In recent decades, all 14 nations have been known for their considerable efforts in spreading the coverage of school supplies on a broader range to reach every region in their countries. Although expansion has been considerably slow in most countries on our list, the operation of the extensive—more supportive schooling network is becoming more available in these nations to ensure children have easy access to educational learning materials, especially children in the rural areas, while enforcing the mandatory and free public education policy. To achieve this, improving the supplies and the range of educational services will be a step in the right direction.

The accreditation standards and the General Law on Education (GLE) that are required in developed countries like the US can be adopted in the SLACs. Such as the Elementary and Secondary Education Act of 1965 (ESEA); the Every Student Succeeds Act (ESSA); the Individuals with Disabilities Education Act (IDEA); Title II of the Americans with Disabilities Act; Title IX of the Amendments of 1972; Title VI of the Civil Rights Act of 1964; the Workforce Innovation and Opportunities Act (WIOA); the Rehabilitation Act of 1973, as amended through PL 114 – 95; the Higher

Education Act (HEA); and the Family Education Rights and Privacy Act (FERPA). These are all good governing policies to ensure students get the support they need and reduce the dropout rate. Considering these [suggested new educational policies, new financing programs such as peer loans and private and government grant initiatives should be introduced to help low-income students further their education up to the tertiary level. Also, except for Argentina, Bolivia, Brazil, Chile, Colombia, Costa Rica, Panama, and Venezuela—who also have some form of specified education spending as a percentage of the nation's *GDP* or a mandated national education financing law—it is recommended that the remaining countries emulate this policy. Although notable efforts have been made to increase the influx of students into these nations' educational systems in the past few years, there is still a long way to go to achieve a reformed curriculum for teaching that will better equip their students for global competition. Considering the new curriculum system, an improved, modernized professional teacher-training process and standard should be introduced.

A highly relevant department to be established in the education governance system is the Institute for Education Accountability (IEA) (OECD et al., 2016). The IEA department will bring a democratic and independent voice to each country's educational system, and the department's jurisdiction will also cover principal officers, policymakers, and elected government officials. For example, the execution of public expenditure on the educational system, recruitment, deployment, and promotion of teachers. Among the many accountability responsibilities assigned to the IEA, the department will also identify the sources of inefficiencies in the educational system (OECD et al., 2016).

Within the 14 SLACs, there has been a lack of high-quality educational research and development, low investment in the research and development departments, and weak links between research findings and educational policies in the systems. The ME in each country should strengthen the research and development sector by increasing its investment in the department. Creating a public center for educational research and development is a way to solve this issue while alleging it is the department's finding with new educational policies. In many developed nations, the schools' leadership has become a priority for educational policy and strategic planning because the governing bodies are responsible for implementing educational reforms and thus central to improving the educational system.

It is safe to conclude that education in SLACs has evolved over the years deviating from the foundational colonial orientations. From our investigation, countries were more concerned with enrollment numbers (see Figure 3) exceeding full capacity at the primary level and almost at full capacity at the secondary level than the student learning and advancement in their educational career. The disparity between education attainment at all levels of the education system and the great divide between enrollment rates in the primary, secondary, and tertiary levels have brought about a learning crisis. A learning crisis is a situation where students are enrolled in a formal academic institution but fail to learn, and these numbers are much higher within rural communities. It is a blurred line between a child in the NEET group and one enrolled and failing to learn.

Figure 6 shows that 57% of our case study has some form of a specified budget as a percent of the nation's *GDP* is mandated into their law for education spending. This bold movement led people to question the government if other socio-economic issues like (roads, running water, and power supply) are less important than human capital investment. I'll argue that the most critical resource among the factors of production is a highly trained individual. As a socio-economic investment, the human mind is the most essential because it can give a community a comparative and absolute advantage over its competitors. Understandably, the results and dividends from the expensive investment in education are a long-run case study. Still, nations like Singapore have spent similar amounts on primary education as a percentage of their nations' *GDP* and achieved a high return on their investment. Today with a population of 5.6 Mn people, Singapore is ranked 16th among other countries and ranks 2nd in the Program for International Student Assessment (PISA). The study advises policymakers and economists to create, advocate, and implement a systematic learning assessment at all levels of the educational system, including the administrative staff and academics. Because just pouring money into an already broken system will only be funding inefficiency in the educational systems, which leads to the devaluation of human capital investment.

REFERENCES

Abbas, Q., & Foreman-Peck, J. (2008). Human capital and economic growth: Pakistan, 1960-2003. *The Lahore Journal of Economics*, 13(1), 1-27. https://doi.org/10.35536/lje.2008.v13.i1.a1

Abdullah, A., Doucouliagos, H., & Manning, E. (2015). Does education reduce income inequality? A meta-regression analysis. *Journal of Economic Surveys*, 29(2), 301-316. https://doi.org/10.1111/joes.12056

Abmann, C. (2008). Assessing the effect of current account and currency crises on economic growth. *SSRN Electronic Journal (working paper)*. https://doi.org/10.2139/ssrn.1081402

Abramovitz, M. (1986). Catching up, forging ahead, and falling behind. *The Economic History Association*, 46(2), 385-406. https://doi.org/10.1017/S0022050700046209

Adelakun, O. J. (2011). Human capital development and economic growth in Nigeria. *European Journal of Business and Management*, 3(9), 29-38.

Aghion, P., & Howitt, P. (1992). A model of growth through creative destruction. *Econometrica*, 60, 323-51. https://doi.org/10.2307/2951599

Akpolate, A. G. (2014). The long-term impact of human capital investment on GDP: A panel cointegrated regression analysis. *Economic Research International*, 10. https://doi.org/10.1155/2014/646518

Alexiou, C. (2009). Government spending and economic growth: Econometric evidence from south-eastern Europe (SEE). *Journal of Economic and Social Research*, 11(1), 1-16.

Ali, A. (2006). On Human Capital in Post-Conflict Sudan: Some Exploratory Results. Working Papers Series 0602. Khartoum: Arab Planning Institute.

Ali, M., Egbetokun, A., & Memon, M. H. (2018). Human capital, social capabilities, and economic growth. *Economies*, 6(2). https://doi.org/10.3390/economies6010002

Amaghionyeodiwe, L. A. (2009). Government health care spending and the poor: evidence from Nigeria. *International Journal of Social Economics*, 36(3), 220-236. https://doi.org/10.1108/03068290910932729

Aman, R. (2014). Impossible Interculturality? Education and the colonial difference in a multicultural world. Linkoping: Linkoping University Press. https://doi.org/10.3384/diss.diva-106245

Aman, R. (2015). Why interculturalidad is not interculturality: Colonial remains and paradoxes in translation between supranational bodies and indigenous social movement. Cultural Studies, 205-228. https://doi.org/10.1080/09502386.2014.899379

Aman, R., & Ireland, T. (2015). Education and other modes of thinking in Latin America. International Journal of Lifelong Education, 34(1), 1-8. https://doi.org/10.1080/02601370.2015.1007719

Anyanwu, J. C. (2014). Factors affecting economic growth in Africa: Are there any lessons from China? African Development Review, 26(3). https://doi.org/10.1111/1467-8268.12105.

Arrow, K., Dasgupta, P., Goulder, L., Daily, G., Ehrlich, P., Heal, G., Walker, B. (2004). Are we consuming too much? Journal of Economic Perspective, 18(3), 147-172. https://doi.org/10.1257/0895330042162377

Barro, R. J., & Lee, J.-W. (1993). International comparisons of educational attainment. Journal of Monetary Economics The Economic Fluctuation and Growth Program: NBER Working Paper No. 4349, 32(3), 363-394. https://doi.org/10.1016/0304-3932(93)90023-9

Becker, G. S. (1962). Investment in human capital: A theoretical analysis. Journal of Political Economy, 9-49. https://doi.org/10.1086/258724

Becker, G. S. (1975). Human capital: A theoretical and empirical analysis, with special reference to education. NBER.

Bellony, A., & Reilly, B. (2009). An Analysis of Labor Market Earning in St. Lucia. Social and Economic Studies, 58(3 & 4), 111-147.

Benhabib, J., & Spiegel, M. M. (1994). The role of human capital in economic development evidence from aggregate cross-country data. Journal of Monetary Economics, 34(2). 143-173. https://doi.org/10.1016/0304-3932(94)90047-7

Bils, M., & Klenow, J. P. (2000). Does schooling cause growth? American Economic Review, 90(5), 1160-1183. https://doi.org/10.1257/aer.90.5.1160

Birdsall, N., Londono, J. L., & O'Donnell, L. (1998). Education in Latin America: Demand and distribution are factors that matter. CEPAL Review, 66, 39 - 52. https://doi.org/10.18356/b3c64b3b-es

Blankenau, W. F., Simpson, N. B., & Tomljanovich, M. (2007). Public education expenditures, taxation, and growth: Linking data to theory. American Economic Review, 97(2), 393-397. https://doi.org/10.1257/aer.97.2.393

Bloom, S., Leveno, K., Spong, C., Gilbert, S., Hauth, J., Landon, M., . . . NICHD-MFMU. (2006). Decision-to-incision times and maternal and infant outcomes. NCBI, 108(1), 6-11. https://doi.org/10.1097/01.ogx.0000243899.37632.68

Boyce, L. A., Zaccaro, S. J., & Wisecarver, M. Z. (2010). Propensity for self-development of leadership attributes: Understanding, predicting, and supporting performance of leaders self-development. Elsevier, 21(1), 159-178. https://doi.org/10.1016/j.leaqua.2009.10.012

Brown, S. D., & Hunter, W. (2004). Democracy and Human Capital Formation: Education Spending in Latin America 1980 - 1997. Comparative Political Studies, 37(7), 842 – 864. https://doi.org/10.1177/0010414004266870

Chaudhry, S. I., & Rahman, U. S. (2009). The impact of gender inequality in education on rural poverty in Pakistan: An empirical analysis. European Journal of Economics, Finance and Administrative Sciences, 15.

Colclough, C., Kingdon, G., & Patrino, H. (2010). The Changing Pattern of Wage Return to Education and its Implication. Development Policy Review, 28(6), 733-747. https://doi.org/10.1111/j.1467-7679.2010.00507.x

Dahal, G. (2016). The contribution of education to economic growth: Evidence from Nepal. Journal of Applied Economic Sciences, V(2), 22-41. https://doi.org/10.20472/IAC.2016.023.032

De Gregorio, J., & Lee, J.W. (2003). Growth and adjustment in East Asia and Latin America. Central Bank of Chile Working Paper.

Dessus, S. (1999). Human capital and growth: The recovered role of education system. World Bank Policy Research Working Paper No. 2632. https://doi.org/10.1596/1813-9450-2632

Devarajan, S., Swaroop, V., & Zou, H.F. (1996). The composition of public expenditure and economic growth. Journal of Monetary Economics, 37(2), 313-344. https://doi.org/10.1016/S0304-3932(96)90039-2

Diaz, A. M. (2013). The employment advantage of skilled urban municipalities in Colombia. Ens. Polit. Econ., 31, 70.

Dimand, R. W., & Spencer, J. B. (2011). Trevor Swan and the neoclassical growth model. History of Political Economy, 41(5), 107-126.

https://doi.org/10.1215/00182702-2009-019

Drucker, J., & Goldstein, H. (2007). Assessing the regional economic development impacts of universities: A review of current approaches. International Regional Science, 30(1), 20-46. https://doi.org/10.1177/0160017606296731

Easterly, W., & Levine, R. (2001). It's not factor accumulation: Stylized facts and growth models. The World Bank Economic Review, 15(2), 177-219. https://doi.org/10.1093/wber/15.2.177

Edrees, A. (2016). Human capital, infrastructure, and economic growth in Arab world: A panel granger causality analysis. Business and Economics Journal.

Engelbrecht, H.J. (1997). International R&D spillover, human capital, and productivity in OECD economies: An empirical investigation. European Economic Review, 41(8), 1479-1488. https://doi.org/10.1016/S0014-2921(96)00046-3

Fiszbein, A., Patrinos, H., & Giovagnoli, P. (2007). Estimating the Return to Education in Argentina using quantile regression analysis 1992-2002. Economica, 53(1-2), 53-72.

Gittleman, M., & Wolff, E. N. (1993). International comparisons of inter-industry wage differentials. Review of Income and Wealth, 39(3). https://doi.org/10.1111/j.1475-4991.1993.tb00461.x

Goode, R. B. (1959). Adding to the stock of physical and human capital. The American Economic Review, 49(2), 147-155.

Google Earth. (2019, 3 5). Google Earth. (Google) Retrieved 3 5, 2019, from https://www.google.com/eart

Hall, E. R., & Jone, I. C. (1997). Levels of economic activity across countries. The American Economic Review, 87(2), 173-177.

Haunshek, A. E., & Woessmann, L. (2008). The role of cognitive skill in economic development. Journal of Economic Literature, 46(3), 607-68. https://doi.org/10.1257/jel.46.3.607

Hawkes, D., & Ugur, M. (2012). Evidence on the relationship between education, skills, and economic growth in low-income countries [PDF file]. London: Evidence for Policy and Practice Information and Co-ordinating Centre.

Heckman, J. J. (2000). Policies to foster human capital. Research in Economics, 54(1), 3-56. https://doi.org/10.1006/reec.1999.0225

Hicks, N. L. (1980). Is there a tradeoff between growth and basic needs? Finance and Development; Washington, D.C., 17(2), 17-20.

Holden, L., & Biddle, J. (2017). The introduction of human capital theory into education policy in the United States. History of Political Economy, 49(4), 537-574. https://doi.org/10.1215/00182702-4296305

Hobbes, T. (1651). Leviathan.

Holden, L., & Biddle, J. (2017). The Introduction of Human Capital Theory into Education Policy in the United States. History of Political Economy, 49(4), 537-574. https://doi.org/10.1215/00182702-4296305

Jamal, H., Toor, F., Ashraf, I., & Khan, F. S. (2003). Private Return to Education: Evidence for Pakistan Research. Report 50.

Kanayo, O. (2013). The impact of human capital formation on economic growth in Nigeria. Journal of Economics, 4(2), 121-132. https://doi.org/10.1080/09765239.2013.11884972

Khembo, F., & Tchereni, H. M. (2013). The impact of human capital on economic growth in the SADC region. Developing Country Studies, 3(4).

Kijima, Y. (2006). Why did wage inequality increase? Evidence from Urban India 1983-1999. Journal of Development Economics, 81(1), 97-117. https://doi.org/10.1016/j.jdeveco.2005.04.008

Kiran, B. (2014). Testing the impact of educational expenditures on economic growth: new evidence from Latin American countries. Quality & Quantity: International Journal of Methodology, 48(3), 1181-1190. https://doi.org/10.1007/s11135-013-9828-2

Klenow, J. P., & Rodriguez-Clare, A. (1997). The neoclassical revival in growth economics: Has gone too far? NBER Macroeconomics Annual, 12, 73-114. https://doi.org/10.2307/3585220

Laguna, J., & Porta, E. (2004). Analisis de la Rentabilidad de la Educacion en Nicaragua. Ministerio de Educacion, Cultura y Deportes, Gobierno de Nicaragua.

Lassibille, G., & Tan, J. (2005). The Returns to Education in Rwanda. Journal of African Economies, 14(1), 92-116. https://doi.org/10.1093/jae/ejh035

Levine, R., & Renelt, D. (1992). A sensitivity analysis of cross-country growth regressions. The American Economic Review, 82(4), 942-963.

Liao, L., Du, M., Bing, W., & Yu, Y. (2019). The impact of educational investment on sustainable economic growth in Guangdong, China: A cointegration and causality analysis. Sustainability, 11(3). https://doi.org/10.3390/su11030766

Liew, V. K.S. (2004). Which lag length selection criteria should we employ. Economic Bulletin, 3(3), 1-9.

Locke, J. (1689). Two Treatises of Government.

Lucas, J. R. (1988). On the mechanics of economic development. Journal of Monetary Economics, 22, 3-42. https://doi.org/10.1016/0304-3932(88)90168-7

Macham, D. A. (2015). Economic growth and development in Sub-Saharan Africa, Asia, and Latin America: The impact of human capital. Master of Art Thesis.

Mankiw, N. G., Romer, D., & Weil, N. D. (1992). A contribution to the empirics of economic growth. The Quarterly Journal of Economics, 107(2), 407-437. https://doi.org/10.2307/2118477

Mark, K., & Engels, F. (1848). Manifesto of the Communist Party.

Mehara, M. (2013). The causality between human capital and economic growth in oil-exporting countries: Panel cointegration and causality. Journal of Business Management and Social Sciences Research, 2(6).

Mehrara, M., & Musai, M. (2013). The relationship between economic growth and human capital in developing countries. International Letters of Social and Humanistic Sciences, 5, 55-62. https://doi.org/10.18052/www.scipress.com/ILSHS.5.55

Mincer, J. (1958). Investment in human capital and personal income distribution. Journal of Political Economy, 66(4), 281-302. https://doi.org/10.1086/258055

Nelson, R. R., & Phelps, S. E. (1966). Investment in humans, technological diffusion, and economic growth. The American Economic Review, 56(1/2), 69-75.

Nguyen, N. N. (2002). Trends in the Education Sector from 1993-1998. Education Studies, 28(1). https://doi.org/10.1596/1813-9450-2891

Njong, A. M. (2010). The effects of educational attainment on poverty reduction in Cameroon. Journal of Education Administration and Policy Studies, 2(1), 001-008.

OECD. (2017). Argentina Multi-dimensional Economic Survey. OECD.

OECD/ECLAC/CAF. (2016). Latin American Economic Outlook 2017: Youth, Skills, and Entrepreneurship. Paris: OECD Publishing. Https://doi.org/10.1787/leo-2017-en

Osiobe, E. U. (2020). Human Capital, Capital Stock Formation, and Economic Growth: A Panel Granger Causality Analysis. Journal of Economics and Business, 3(2), 567-580. https://doi.org/10.31014/aior.1992.03.02.221

Osiobe, E. U. (2019). A Literature Review of Human Capital and Economic Growth. Business and Economic Research, 9(4), 179-196. https://doi.org/10.529/ber.v9i4.15624

Pastore, F., & Verashchagina, A. (2006). Private Return to Human Capital Over Transition: A Case Study of Belarus. Economic of Education Review, 25(1), 91-107. https://doi.org/10.1016/j.econedurev.2004.11.003

Patrinos, H., & Sakellariou, C. (2006). Economic Volatility and Return to Education in Venezuela: 1992 – 2002. Applied Economics, 38(17), 1991-2005. https://doi.org/10.1080/00036840500427338

Paul, J. J., & Wolff, L. (1996). The economics of higher education.

Pedroni, P. (2002). Critical value for cointegration test in heterogeneous panels with multiple regressors — Oxford Bulletin of Economics and Statistics, 61(S1). https://doi.org/10.1111/1468-0084.0610s1653

Penn World Tables. (2019). Retrieved 1 25, 2019, from http://datacentre2.chass.utoronto.ca/pwt/alphacountries.html

Pelinescu, E. (2015). The impact of human capital on economic growth. Procedia Economics and Finance, 22, 184-190. https://doi.org/10.1016/S2212-5671(15)00258-0

Plank, D. (1996). The means of our salvation: Public education in Brazil 1930 - 1995.

Porta, E., Laguna, J., & Morales, S. (2006). Tasas de Rentabilidad de la Education en Guatemala. USAID.

Psacharopoulos, G., & Partinos, H. A. (2002). Returns to Investment in Education: A Further Update. Policy Research Working Paper, WPS: 2881.

Psacharopoulos, G., & Patrinos, H. A. (2004). Returns to investment in education: A further update. Education Economics, 12(2), 111-34. https://doi.org/10.1080/0964529042000239140

Quiggin, J. (1999). Human capital theory and education policy in Australia. Australian Economic Review, 32(2), 130-44. https://doi.org/10.1111/1467-8462.00100

Quiggin, J. (2002). Human capital theory and education policy in Australia. Australian Economic Review, 32(2). https://doi.org/10.1111/1467-8462.00100

Rahman, M. (2011). Causal relationship among education expenditure, health expenditure, and GDP: A case study for Bangladesh. International Journal of Economics and Finance, 3(3). https://doi.org/10.5539/ijef.v3n3p149

Rehmana, H. U., Kamrana, M., Basra, S. M., Afzala, I., & Farooq, M. (2015). Influence of seed priming on performance and water productivity of direct-seeded rice in alternating wetting and drying. Rice Science, 22(4), 189-196. https://doi.org/10.1016/j.rsci.2015.03.001

Reilly, B., & Bellony, A. (2009). The Determinants of Labor Market Earnings in a Small Caribbean Island: The Case of Dominica. The Journal of Developing Areas, 43(1), 65-85. https://doi.org/10.1353/jda.0.0046

Riihelaninen, J. M. (2013). Government Education Expenditure in the European Union during the Economic Crisis (2008-2011). Europe: European Union.

Romer, D. (1996). Advanced Macroeconomics. New York, NY: Mc Graw Hill Education.

Romer, P. (1989). Human capital and growth: Theory and evidence. NBER Working Paper No. 3173. https://doi.org/10.3386/w3173

Romer, P. (1990). Endogenous technological change. Journal of Political Economy, 98(5), 71-102. https://doi.org/10.1086/261725

Romer, P. (1994). The origins of endogenous growth. The Journal of Economic Perspective, 8(1), 3-22. https://doi.org/10.1257/jep.8.1.3

Rostow, W. W. (1960). The Process of Economic Growth.

Rozada, G. M., & Menedez, A. (2002). Public university in Argentina: Subsidizing the rich? Economic of Education Review, 21(4), 341-351. https://doi.org/10.1016/S0272-7757(01)00030-9

Sanguinetti, P. (2016, December 20). Skilling up: human capital and Latin America. (World Economic Forum) Retrieved March 17, 2019, from https://www.weforum.org/agenda/2016/12/skilling-up-human-capital-and-latin-america

Schultz. (2009). Occupational adaptation theory. In E. C. Crepeau, Willard's & Spackman's Occupational Therapy. 11th Edition.

Schultz, T. (1961). Investment in Human Capital. American Economic Review, 51(1), 1-17.

Schultz, T. W. (1963). The economic value of education. New York: Columbia University Press.

Sen, A. (1999). Development as freedom.

Sharma, P., & Sahni, P. (2015). Human capital and economic growth in India: A co-integration and causality analysis. Ushus J B Mgt, 14(2), 1-18. https://doi.org/10.12725/ujbm.31.1

Singh, R. J., Haacker, M., & Lee, K.W. (2009). Determinants and macroeconomic impact of remittances in Sub-Saharan Africa. IMF Working Paper, WP/09/216. https://doi.org/10.5089/9781451873634.001

Smith, A. (1776). An Inquiry into the Nature and Causes of the Wealth of Nations. https://doi.org/10.1093/oseo/instance.00043218

Solow, N. R. (1956). A contribution to the theory of economic growth. The Quarterly Journal of Economics, 70(1), 65-95. https://doi.org/10.2307/1884513

Soumare, I. (2015). Does FDI improve economic development in North African countries? Applied Economics, 47(51), 5510-5533. https://doi.org/10.1080/00036846.2015.1051655

Stonier, A. W., & Hague, D. (1972). A Textbook of Economic Theory, 4th Edition. Prentice-Hall Press.

Tansel, A., & Labor, I. f. (2008). Changing Return to Education for Men and Women in a Developing Country: Turkey, 1994, 2002-2005. Paper Presented at the ESPE 2008 conference.

Temple, J. (1999). A positive effect of human capital on growth. Economic Letter, 65(1), 131-134. https://doi.org/10.1016/S0165-1765(99)00120-2

Terada-Hagiwara, A., & Kim, Y. J. (Dec 2010). A survey on the relationship between education and growth with implications for developing Asia. ADB Economics Working paper series, WPS112904, No. 236.

Tilak, J. B. (1997). The dilemma of reforms in financing higher education in India. Higher Education Policy, 10(1), 7-21. https://doi.org/10.1016/S0952-8733(96)00031-1

UNESCO. (1997). 50 Years for Education.

United Nations. (2015). Sustainable Development Goals for a sustained economic development path. (United Nations). [Online] Available: https://sustainabledevelopment.un.org/index.php?page=view&type=9502&menu=1565&nr=7

United Nations (2009). Millennium Development Goals Report. New York, NY: United Nations. Department of Public Information.

U.S.News. (2020, 1 26). Retrieved from https://www.usnews.com/

Uzawa, H. (1965). Optimum technical change in an aggregative model of economic growth. International Economic Review, 6(1), 18-31. https://doi.org/10.2307/2525621

Van Leeuwen, B. (2005). Estimating the Return to Education in Indonesia 1890-2002. Amsterdam: International Institute of Social History (mimeo).

Verges, F. (1999). Monsters and Revolutionaries: Colonial Family Romance and Message. Durham: Duke University Press. https://doi.org/10.1215/9780822379096

Vijayakumar, S. (2013). An empirical study on the nexus of poverty, GDP growth, dependency ratio, and employment in developing countries. Journal of Competitiveness, 5(2), 67-82. https://doi.org/10.7441/joc.2013.02.05

Wedgwood, R. (2007). Education and poverty reduction in Tanzania. International Journal of Educational, 27(4), 383-396. https://doi.org/10.1016/j.ijedudev.2006.10.005

Weiss, A. (1995). Human capital vs. signaling explanations of wage. Journal of Economic Perspectives, 9(4), 133-154. https://doi.org/10.1257/jep.9.4.133

World Development Index Group. (2019, June 11). The World Bank. (World Development Indicators) Retrieved 3 18, 2019, from https://data.worldbank.org/region/latin-america-and-caribbean

THE UNITED STATES OF MEXICO

INTRODUCTION

The Estados Unidos Mexicanos, or the United States of Mexico, also called Mexico, is a republic located between the Caribbean Sea and the Gulf of Mexico to the east and the Pacific Ocean to the west. It shares maritime borders with the nations of Cuba and Honduras. Mexico is the 13th largest country globally, the 3rd largest country in North America, and the 3rd largest nation in Latin America (Google Earth (G.E.), 2019). According to the Global Corruption Index (GCI), Mexico is ranked 46th out of 140 countries (Schwab, 2018). The nation has a population of 126.2 million people as of 2018, making it the 11th most populous country in the world (World Development Index (WDI), 2019), the 2nd most populous nation in Latin America, and the most populous Spanish-speaking nation in the world

Figure 1:
Mexico on the continental map of Latin America

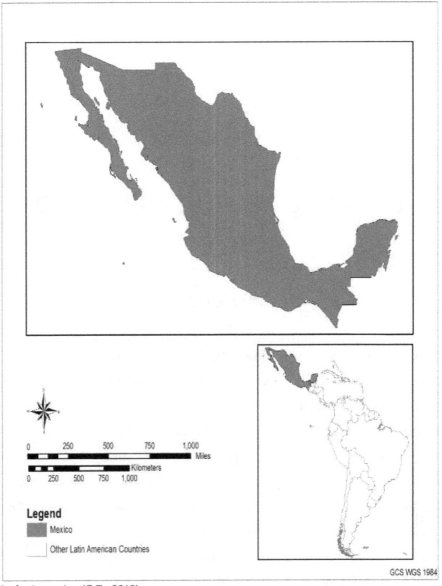

Author's creation (G.E., 2019).
*Gray - specific country of interest

(WDI, 2019). In the 2018 Environmental Performance Index (EPI), Mexico is ranked 72nd in the world and 8th in Latin America (Yale Center for Environmental Law & Policy (YCELP), 2018).

In 1994, the nation became the first Latin American country to join the Organisation for Economic Cooperation and Development (OECD). In the same year, the peso's devaluation threw Mexico into economic turmoil, which triggered the worst recession in the nation in over half a century. Today, the country continues to make economic progress, but[1] the ongoing social-economic concern(s) include but are not

limited to low Gross Domestic Product per capita *(GDP per capita)*, the high underemployment rate, political-and-social-economic inequality in the distribution of resources, including (*less than equal opportunities for the Amerindian population*).

Mexico City © Alejandro Islas

But, to foster economic growth, development, and stability in Mexico as an active member of the United States-Mexico-Canada Agreement (USMCA), the OECD, and the United Nations (U.N.), the nation is governed in a decentralized manner by the federal republic of Mexico, which shares its sovereignty with the 31 Mexican states. In the study, the Selected Latin America and the Caribbean (SLAC) countries that will be studied as a comparison benchmark are Argentina, Bolivia, Brazil, Chile, Colombia, Costa Rica, Honduras, Mexico (excluded), Nicaragua, Panama, Peru, El Salvador, Uruguay, and Venezuela.

Figure 2 shows Mexico's Real Gross Domestic Product purchasing power parity *(RGDPppp)* 1981 = 100 index from 1950–2014 compared to

Figure 2:

A comparison of our SLAC $RGDP_{ppp}{}^1$ at chained (in Mil.[2] 2011 USD[3] (average)) with that of Mexico (1950 – 2014) 1981 = 100

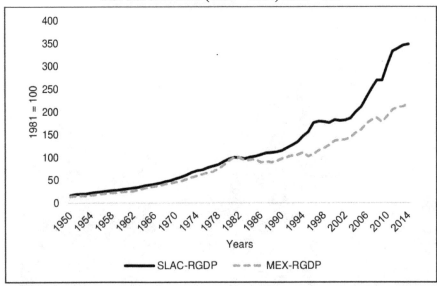

[3] United States Dollar
Source: (Penn World Tables (PWT), 2019).
Author's creation

54

our SLAC moving average. Figure 2 shows Mexico marginally under-performing the benchmark moving average from 1950–2014, implying that when the numbers in Figure 3 are converted into the index 1981 = 100 to measure the changes in the value of Mexico's *(RGDPppp)*, to see the direction of production in the economy, Mexico underperformed the SLAC by a significant margin from 1983–2014.

It is unique to see an inverse relationship between the index 1981 =100 (Figure 2) and the actual figures (Figure 3). Figure 3 shows Mexico's *RGDPppp* real numbers compared to the SLAC moving average from 1950–2014. Figure 3 depicts Mexico outperforming the benchmark moving average from 1950–2014.

Figure 3:
A comparison of our SLAC *RGDPppp* at chained (in Mil. 2011 USD (Average)) with that of Mexico (1950 – 2014)

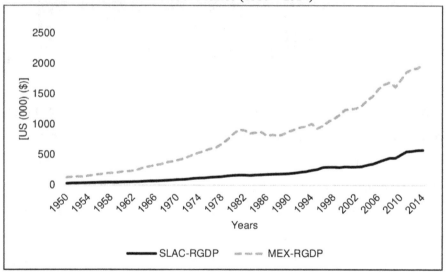

Source: (PWT, 2019).
Author's creation

The country faces an enormous disparity between the rich and the poor. According to the Mexican government, 9% of its population lives in extreme poverty and 33% in moderate poverty. Hence, approximately 42% of its population lives in poverty or below the first-world living standard. The country's main exporting product is petroleum, and in 2005, Mexico

© Ashstar01

produced 3.8 million barrels a day, making it the 5th largest producer in the world. Today, the nation ranks below the top 10 oil-producing countries globally, producing less than half of its production during its prime. However, American carmakers have built many of their cars in Mexico. It is estimated that 89 of the world's 100 auto-part makers have a production facility in Mexico. A newspaper report by CNN (Gillespie, 2018) estimated that remittances from the United States to Mexico were about $26 billion in 2017, ranking it the second largest receiver of remittances in the world behind India.

Figure 4 shows how volatile Mexico's economy is compared to the SLAC moving average. Figure 4 depicts the two economies at par from

1950–2014, which implies that Mexico's responsiveness to economic shocks is somewhat similar to our SLAC. Mexico's economy is strong despite the forging of ties with the U.S. and Canada through the USMCA. Over the years, the educational system in the country has been highly influenced by the Roman Catholic church. The church established the first university in North America in Mexico City in 1551.

Figure 4:
A comparison of our SLAC % change of *RGDPppp* at chained (in Mil. 2011 USD (Average)) with that of Mexico (1951 – 2014)

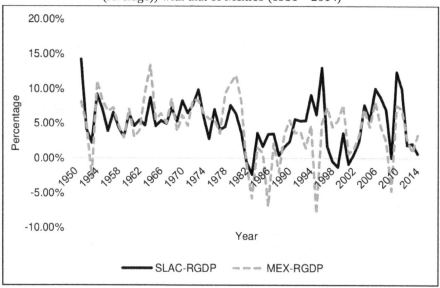

Source: (PWT, 2019).
Author's creation

In the 19th century, mandatory primary education for children between the ages of 7 and 15 was introduced in Mexico, and the educational system in the nation increased its standards and regulations. After the 1910–1920 revolution, the Mexican government focused on eradicating illiteracy, promoting rural education, and the inclusion of American Indian indigenous peoples. Figure 5 shows Mexico's Human Development Index *(HDI)* compared to the SLAC moving average from 1950–2014. Figure 5 depicts Mexico marginally outperforming the benchmark moving average from 1950–2014. This implies that Mexico's *HDI* rate is slightly higher than our SLAC's. However, over the years, it has been a significant challenge for the government of Mexico to build a national identity by fostering education due to the diversity of languages in the nation. Compared with other major SLAC like Argentina and Brazil, the education participation rates in Mexico are low despite education in the country expanding so rapidly.

Figure 5:

A comparison of our SLAC *HDI* (average) with that of Mexico (1950 – 2014)

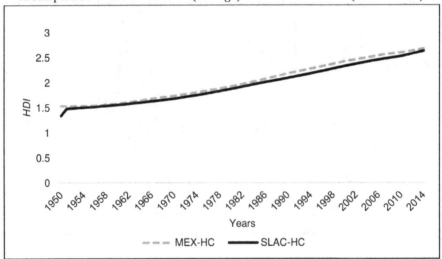

Source: (PWT, 2019).
Author's creation

As a result of the mandatory basic education policy in the nation, the illiteracy rates between the ages of 7–15 have decreased from 82% at the end of the 19th century to less than 5% today. Because of the declining illiteracy rate, education enrollments have increased at all levels of the educational system, resulting in more than 12-fold of students (36.4 million). In Mexico, the educational system administration has a shared responsibility with the national Secretaria de Educación Pública (SEP), the Ministry of Education (M.E.), and the 32 state-level jurisdictions in the nation. Since 1992, Mexico has decentralized its educational system and limited the federal government's role in its educational system.

San Luis Pampanga Arch Roads School

Medical school building, UNAM campus, Mexico City. © Daniel Case

SUMMARY

Education Policy Orientation Main Findings:

- Spanish is the predominant language used in the educational system.
- The Mexican education system has a longer compulsory education timeline than any other country in our case study up to upper secondary education.
- The government expanded access to Early Childhood Education and Care (ECEC).
- In 2013, the education system introduced a dual training system that combines school and work-based learning.

Policies That Moved the Country Forward:

- The Mexican education system passed a constitutional reform bill in 2012 and an amendment bill for the general educational system Ley General de Educación in 2013.
- A bill for program inclusion and equal education called the Programa para la Inclusion y la Equidad Educative was passed in 2014.
- A national scholarship program called Programa Nacional de Becas was created in 2014.
- The country created the Movimiento Contra el Abandono Escolar programs to reduce the school dropout rate in 2013 – 2014.
- In 2017, the national education ministry introduced the Nuevo Modelo Educativo, a new educational model.

Policies Implication and Recommendation:

As remarkable as these stated educational system policies are, they all come with unanticipated sets of problems both in the short- and long-run.

- To reduce the learning gaps between the rural and urban areas, and improve the education system's overall quality, the Mexican education system should adopt the Massive Open Online Course (MOOC) system.

- It is encouraged that the Mexican ministry of education expands Vocational Education and Training (VET).

- Although the federal government has expanded access to ECEC, it is recommended that the expansion of the ECEC should be implemented at the state and municipal levels.

- The free primary education policy is a great idea, but it should also be backed by raising the performance of all students and making it more inclusive, basically expanding the Programa para la Inclusion y la Equidad Educativa in the rural areas and preparing students for the future by encouraging completion of secondary education and improving the quality and relevant skills of students.

- It is recommended that the Mexican educational system create an education mechanism of financial and human resource allocation(s) aligned with the needs of the mainstream economy.

- It is recommended that more financial capital be used to support the physical capital of the education system, such as construction, maintenance, and improvement of buildings and roads.

Contribution to Mexico's Literature on Human Capital and Economic Growth:

Although an aggregate model was used in the study, the chapter contributes to the literature on Human Capita *(HC)*, economic growth, and development by highlighting the essential educational policies passed by the Mexican government. Studies delving into Mexico's economy include (Lustig, 1998; OECD, 2018; Young, 2006; Ibarra et al., 2000; Coatsworth, 1979; Coleman, 2005; Niederberger, 1979). The theoretical formulation of the relationship between *HC* and economic growth in Mexico has been studied by (Garcia-Verdu, 2007; Aschauer, 1998; Lee & Mason, 2010; Mincer, 1958; Diaz-Bautista, 2000 & 2017; Gyimah-Brempong & Wilson, 2004; Kottaridi & Stengos, 2010; Rodriguez-Oreggia, 2005; Levin & Raut, 1997; Brock & German-Soto, 2013; Auty, 2001a & 2001b; Psacharopoulos et al., 2006; Taylor & Martin, 2001; Fuller et al., 1986; Becker, 1975). However, this relationship was not true in all studies; for example, (Quiggin, 1999 & 2002; Devarajan et al., 1996).

REFERENCE

Aschauer, D. A. (1998). The Role of Public Infrastructure Capital in Mexican Economic Growth. Economia Mexicana. Nueva Epoca, 7(1), 47-78.

Auty, R. M. (2001). Resource Abundance and Economic Development. New York: Oxford University Press.

Auty, R. M. (2001). The Political economy of resource-driven growth. European Economic Review, 45(4-6), 839-846.
https://doi.org/10.1016/S0014-2921(01)00126-X

Becker, G. S. (1975). Human Capital: A Theoretical and Empirical Analysis, with Special Reference to Education. NBER.

Brock, G., & German-Soto, V. (2013). Regional industrial growth in Mexico: Do human capital and infrastructure matter? Journal of Policy Modeling, 35(2), 228-242.
https://doi.org/10.1016/j.jpolmod.2012.10.003

Coatsworth, J. H. (1979). Indispensable Railroad in a Backward Economy: The Case of Mexico. The Journal of Economic History, 39(4), 939-960.
https://doi.org/10.1017/S0022050700098685

Coleman, M. (2005). U.S. statecraft and the U.S.-Mexico border as security/economy nexus. Political Geography, 24(2), 185-209.
https://doi.org/10.1016/j.polgeo.2004.09.016

Devarajan, S., Swaroop, V., & Zou, H.-f. (1996). The Composition of Public Expenditure and Economic Growth. Journal of Monetary Economics, 37(2), 313-344. https://doi.org/10.1016/S0304-3932(96)90039-2

Diaz-Bautista, A. (2000). Convergence and economic growth in Mexico. Frontera Norte, 12(24).

Diaz-Bautista, A. (2017). Agglomeration economies, growth, and the new economic geography in Mexico. EconoQuantum, 14(1).

Fuller, B., Edwards, J. H., & Gorman, K. (1986). When does education boost economic growth? School expansion and school quality in Mexico. Sociology of Education, 59(3), 167-181. https://doi.org/10.2307/2112341

Garcia-Verdu, R. (2007). Demographics, Human Capital and Economic Growth in Mexico: 1950-2005. Poverty Reduction and Economic Management unit Latin America and Caribbean region The World Bank.

Gillespie, P. (2018, 1 3). CNN Business. (CNN) Retrieved 11 18, 2019, from https://money.cnn.com/2018/01/02/news/economy/mexico-remittances/index.html

Google Earth. (2019, 3 5). Google Earth. (Google) Retrieved 3 5, 2019, from https://www.google.com/earth/

Gyimah-Brempong, K., & Wilson, M. (2004). Health human capital and economic growth in Sub-Saharan African and OECD countries. The Quarterly Review of Economics and Finance, 44(2), 296-320. https://doi.org/10.1016/j.qref.2003.07.002

Ibarra, A. A., Reid, C., & Thorpe, A. (2000). The Political Economy of Marine Fisheries Development in Peru, Chile, and Mexico. Journal of Latin American Studies, 32(2), 503-527. https://doi.org/10.1017/S0022216X00005824

Kottaridi, C., & Stengos, T. (2010). Foreign direct investment, human capital, and non-linearities in economic growth. Journal of Macroeconomics, 32(3), 858-871. https://doi.org/10.1016/j.jmacro.2010.01.004

Lee, R., & Mason, A. (2010). Fertility, Human Capital, and Economic Growth over the Demographic Transition. European Journal of Population/Revue europeenne de Demographie, 26(2), 159-182. https://doi.org/10.1007/s10680-009-9186-x

Levin, A., & Raut, L. K. (1997). Complementarities between export and human capital in economic growth: Evidence from the semi-industrialized countries. Economic Development and Cultural Change, 46(1), 155-174. https://doi.org/10.1086/452325

Lustig, N. C. (1998). Mexico the remaking of an economy. Washington, DC: The Brookings Institution.

Mincer, J. (1958). Investment in Human Capital and Personal Income Distribution. Journal of Political Economy, 66(4), 281-302. https://doi.org/10.1086/258055

Niederberger, C. (1979). Early Sedentary Economy in the Basin of Mexico. Science, 203(4376), 131-142. https://doi.org/10.1126/science.203.4376.131

OECD. (2018). Education Policy Outlook Mexico. OECD.

Osiobe, E. U. (2019). A Literature Review of Human Capital and Economic Growth. Business and Economic Research, 9(4), 179-196. https://doi.org/10.5296/ber.v9i4.15624

Osiobe, E. U. (2020). Human Capital and Economic Growth in Latin America: A Cointegration and Causality Analysis. The Economics and Finance Letters, 218-235. https://doi.org/10.18488/journal.29.2020.72.218.235

Osiobe, E. U. (2020). Human Capital, Capital Stock Formation, and Economic Growth: A Panel Granger Causality Analysis. Journal of Economics and Business, 569-580. https://doi.org/10.31014/aior.1992.03.02.221

Osiobe, E. U. (2020). Understanding Latin America's Educational Orientations: Evidence from 14 Nations. Education Quarterly Review, 249-260. https://doi.org/10.31014/aior.1993.03.02.137

Osiobe, Ejiro U. (2021). An Overview of the United Mexican States' Educational Policies. Economic Development Educational Research, Abuja: The Ane Osiobe International Foundation.

Psacharopoulos, G., Velez, E., Panagides, A., & Yang, H. (2006). Return to education during economic boom and recession: Mexico 1984, 1989, and 1992. Education Economics, 4(3), 219-230. https://doi.org/10.1080/09645299600000022

Quiggin, J. (1999). Human capital Theory and Education Policy in Australia. Australian Economic Review, 32(2), 130-44. https://doi.org/10.1111/1467-8462.00100

Quiggin, J. (2002). Human Capital Theory and Education Policy in Australia. Australian Economic Review, Volume 32, Issue 2. https://doi.org/10.1111/1467-8462.00100

Rodriguez-Oreggia, E. (2005). Regional disparities and determinants of growth in Mexico. The Annals of Regional Science, 39(2), 207-220. https://doi.org/10.1007/s00168-004-0218-5

Schwab, K. (2018). The Global Competitiveness Report. Geneva: World Economic Forum.

Taylor, J. E., & Martin, P. L. (2001). Chapter 9 Human Capital: Migration and rural population change. Handbook of Agricultural Economics, 1(Part A), 457-511. https://doi.org/10.1016/S1574-0072(01)10012-5

World Development Index Group, (2019, June 11). The World Bank. (World Development Indicators) Retrieved 3 18, 2019, from https://data.worldbank.org/region/latin-america-and-caribbean

Yale Center for Environmental Law & Policy; Center for International Earth Science Information Network; World Economic Forum. (2018). The 2018 Environmental Performance Index. Environmental Performance Index.

Young, E. V. (2006). Hacienda and Market in Eighteenth-Century Mexico: The Rural Economy of the Guadalajara Region, 1675-1820. Maryland: Rowman & Littlefield Publishers, Inc.

EL SALVADOR

INTRODUCTION

El Salvador, also known as the land of volcanoes, is located in the center of Central America. The nation is the 148th largest country globally and the 10th largest country in Central America (Google Earth (GE), 2019). With a population size of 6.4 million in 2018, the nation ranks 111th worldwide by population (World Development Index (WDI), 2019). In terms of the Global Competitive Index (GCI), El Salvador ranks 98th out of 140 (Schwab, 2018), and it ranks 106th in the world and 17th in Latin America in the 2018 Environmental Performance Index (EPI) (Yale Center for Environmental Law & Policy (YCELP), 2018).

Although one of the smallest landmass nations in Central America, El Salvador is the most densely populated of the other seven Central

Figure 1:
El Salvador on the continental map of Latin America

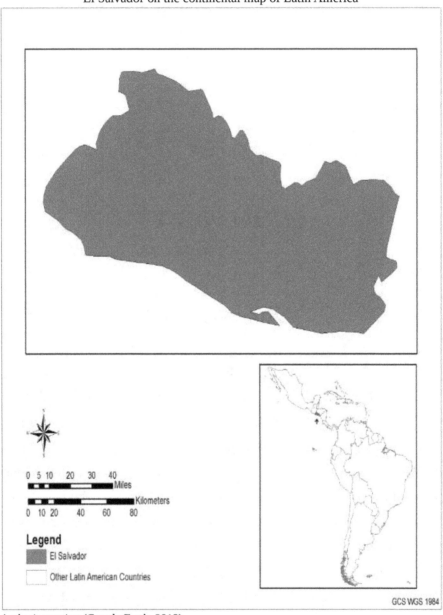

Author's creation (Google Earth, 2019)
*Gray specific country of interest

American countries. El Salvador is known for its agricultural sector, and today, the country is heavily dependent on the exportation of coffee beans in the international market. In the 20th century, the service industry dominated El Salvador's economy. El Salvador was in a civil war from the late 1970s through the early 1990s, which made it the focus of international attention. In 1992, the UN mediated a peace accord(s), which was the bedrock that led to El Salvador becoming a democratic nation.

Street vendors in San Salvador © Diego Tirira

In the study, the Selected Latin America and the Caribbean (SLAC) countries that will be studied as a comparison benchmark are Argentina, Bolivia, Brazil, Chile, Colombia, Costa Rica, Honduras, Mexico, Nicaragua, Panama, Peru, El Salvador (excluded), Uruguay, and Venezuela.

Figure 2 shows El Salvador's Real Gross Domestic Product purchasing power parity *(RGDPppp)* 1981 = 100 from 1950–2014 compared

Figure 2:
A comparison of our SLAC *RGDPppp* at chained (in Mil. 2011 USD (average))
with that of El Salvador (1950 – 2014) 1981 = 100

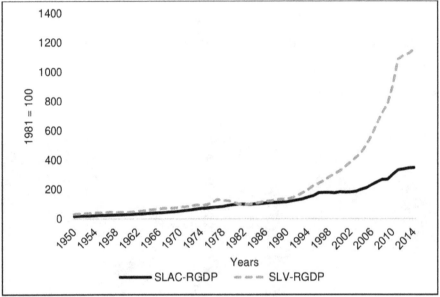

Source: Penn World Table (PWT, 2019).
Author's creation

to that of the SLAC moving average. Figure 2 depicts El Salvador outperforming the benchmark moving average from 1950–2014, which is different from the depiction in Figure 3. This implies when the numbers in Figure 3 are converted to an index of 1981 = 100 to measure the changes in the value of *RGDPppp* To see the direction of production in the economy. The nation suffers from persistently low levels of growth. Still, the country has accomplished noteworthy progress regarding political developments, including ending the civil war in 1992, transitioning into a democratic state, and holding six consecutive democratic presidential elections. The government has continued to progress in advancing human development outcomes mainly through increasing and improving access to public services, including but not limited to increased access to healthcare facilities and feeding programs.

Figure 3:
A comparison of our SLAC *RGDPppp* at chained (in Mil. 2011 USD (Average)) with that of El Salvador (1950 – 2014)

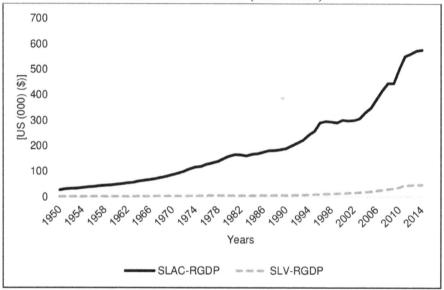

Source: (PWT, 2019).
Author's creation

Figure 3 shows El Salvador's *RGDPppp* number compared to the SLAC moving average from 1950–2014. Figure 3 depicts El Salvador underperforming that of our benchmarked moving average, with a slope that can be somewhat flat. In El Salvador, publicly and privately run institutions are under the Ministry of Education's (ME) jurisdiction. Since 1968, El Salvador's educational system has been composed of preschool to university-level education.

Figure 4 shows El Salvador to be more volatile than the SLAC. The volatility on the chart implies that the nation of El Salvador is easily impacted by economic shocks (positive and negative). In 1995, the El Salvador legislative assembly passed an education bill that sanctioned the creation of new institutions under the departmental supervision system and improved higher education institutional quality. Public education was and is still a top priority in the nation, even more than health care for the El Salvadoran government. As a result, school enrollment and the general literacy level also increased.

Figure 4:
A comparison of our SLAC % change of *RGDP$_{ppp}$* at chained (in Mil. 2011 USD (Average)) with that of El Salvador (1951 – 2014)

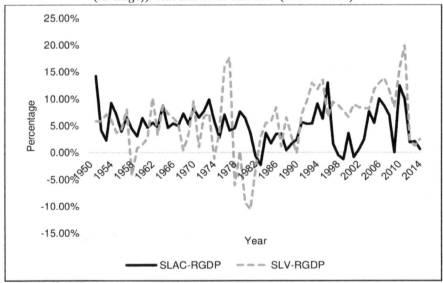

Source: (PWT, 2019).
Author's creation

Figure 5 shows El Salvador's Human Development Index *(HDI)* as it compares to that of the LAC (see Figure – 5) moving average from 1950–2014. Figure 67 depicts El Salvador underperforming the benchmark moving average from 1950–2014. El Salvador's *HDI* growth path is much lower than our SLAC's.

Figure 5:

A comparison of our SLAC *HDI* (average) with that of El Salvador (1950 – 2014)

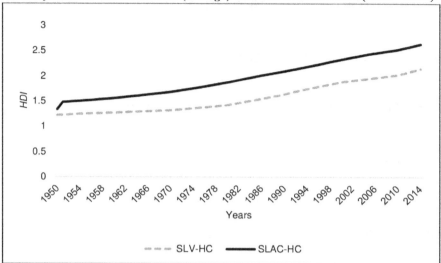

Source: (PWT, 2019).
Author's creation

Students studying specimens during a festival.

SUMMARY

Education Policy Orientation Main Findings:

- Primary education is free and mandatory through the ninth grade (up to 14). Above 14 years, schooling is self-paid.
- Spanish is the predominant language used in El Salvador's school system.

Policies Implication and Recommendation:

While education has slowly become more accessible to El Salvadorians after the end of the country's civil war in 1992, the nation's poverty rate continues to prevent children from low-income families from learning in the classrooms. Even the few educational policies set in place by the ME have some setbacks that need improvement.

- The education infrastructure is mainly located in the cities, leaving out residents in rural areas. It is recommended that the Ministry of Education in El Salvador sign and approve contracts to build more schools and libraries in rural areas.
- In El Salvador, only primary education is free and mandatory for El Salvadorians, resulting in low enrollment rates at the other level of the education system. It is recommended that educational programs be introduced in their education system to encourage students to further their education.

Contribution to El Salvador Literature on Human Capital and Economic Growth:

Although an aggregate model was used for the benchmark comparison, this study contributes to the literature on the role of *HC* in economic growth and development by highlighting the essential educational policies passed by the El Salvador government and how these policies affected the *HDI* and the level of the El Salvador economy. Studies delving into El Salvador's economy include but are not limited to (Chopra, 1999; Boyce, 1996; Quispe-Agnoli & Whisler, 2006; Sanchez-Ancochea, 2008; Colburn, 2009). The theoretical formulation of the relationship between Human Capital (*HC)* and economic growth in El Salvador has been studied by (Edwards et al. 2015; Petras, 1987; Pugh et al., 2008; Panitch & Konings, 2008; CPRU-WB, 2003). However, this relationship didn't hold true in all studies (Levin & Renelt, 1992; Temple, 1999).

REFERENCE

Boyce, J. K. (1996). Economic Policy for Building Peace: The Lessons of El Salvador. Lynne Rienner.

Chopra, J. (1999). Peace-Maintenance: The evolution of international political authority. London and New York: Routledge.

Colburn, F. D. (2009). The Turnover in El Salvador. Journal of Democracy, 20(3), 143-152. https://doi.org/10.1353/jod.0.0106

Conflict Prevention and Reconstruction Unit (2003). The Economic and Social Cost of Armed Conflict in El Salvador. New York: The World Bank Group.

Edwards Jr., D. B., Libreros, J. A., & Martin, P. (2015). The geometry of policy implementation: Lessons from the political economy of three education reform in El Salvador during 1990-2005. International Journal of Educational Development, 44, 28-41. https://doi.org/10.1016/j.ijedudev.2015.05.001

Google Earth. (2019, 3 5). Google Earth. (Google) Retrieved 3 5, 2019, from https://www.google.com/earth/

Levine, R., & Renelt, D. (1992). A Sensitivity Analysis of Cross-Country Growth Regressions. The American Economic Review, 82(4), 942-963.

Osiobe, E. U. (2019). A Literature Review of Human Capital and Economic Growth. Business and Economic Research, 9(4), 179-196. https://doi.org/10.5296/ber.v9i4.15624

Osiobe, E. U. (2020). Human Capital and Economic Growth in Latin America: A Cointegration and Causality Analysis. The Economics and Finance Letters, 218-235. https://doi.org/10.18488/journal.29.2020.72.218.235

Osiobe, E. U. (2020). Human Capital, Capital Stock Formation, and Economic Growth: A Panel Granger Causality Analysis. Journal of Economics and Business, 569-580. https://doi.org/10.31014/aior.1992.03.02.221

Osiobe, E. U. (2020). Understanding Latin America's Educational Orientations: Evidence from 14 Nations. Education Quarterly Review, 249-260. https://doi.org/10.31014/aior.1993.03.02.137

Osiobe, Ejiro U. (2021). An Overview of El Salvador's Educational Policies. Economic Development Educational Research, Abuja: The Ane Osiobe International Foundation.

Panitch, L., & Konings, M. (2008). American Empire and the Political Economy of Global Finance. New York: Palgrave Macmillan. https://doi.org/10.1057/9780230227675

Petras, J. (1987). Political Economy of State Terror: Chile, El Salvador, and Brazil. Crime and Social Justice(27-28), 88-109.

Pugh, M., Cooper, N., & Turner, M. (2008). Whose Peace? Critical Perspectives on the Political Economy of Peacebuilding. New York: Palgrave Macmillan. https://doi.org/10.1057/9780230228740

Quispe-Agnoli, M., & Whisler, E. (2006). Official Dollarization and the Banking System in Ecuador and El Salvador. Economic Review-Federal Reserve Bank of Atlanta, 91(3), 55-111.

Sanchez-Ancochea, D. (2008). Chapter 7: The Political Economy of DR-CAFTA in Costa Rica, the Dominican Republic, and El Salvador. In The Political Economy of Hemispheric Integration (pp. 171-200). New York: Palgrave Macmillan. https://doi.org/10.1057/9780230612945_7

Schwab, K. (2018). The Global Competitiveness Report. Geneva: World Economic Forum.

Temple, J. (1999). A Positive Effect of Human Capital on Growth. Economic Letter, 65(1), 131-134. https://doi.org/10.1016/S0165-1765(99)00120-2

World Development Index Group, (2019, June 11). The World Bank. (World Development Indicators) Retrieved 3 18, 2019, from https://data.worldbank.org/region/latin-america-and-caribbean

Yale Center for Environmental Law & Policy; Center for International Earth Science Information Network; World Economic Forum. (2018). The 2018 Environmental Performance Index. Environmental Performance Index.

Ejiro U. Osiobe

HONDURAS

INTRODUCTION

Honduras is the second-largest country in Central America. The nation is officially the Republic of Honduras (República de Honduras). From its inland area, it is the 101st largest country in the world and the 2nd largest country in Central America (Google Earth (GE), 2019). With a population of 9.6 million people as of 2018, the country ranks 93rd in the world by population (World Development Index (WDI), 2019). Out of 195 nations in the world, in the 2018 Environmental Performance Index (EPI), Honduras is ranked 114th, and it is 19th in Latin America (Yale Center for Environmental Law & Policy (YCELP), 2018).

The capital of Honduras is Tegucigalpa, but unlike most other Central American countries, another city (Comayaguela) in the nation is equally essential, industrious, and commercially stable. Honduras is an

Ejiro U. Osiobe

Figure 1:
Honduras on the continental map of Latin America

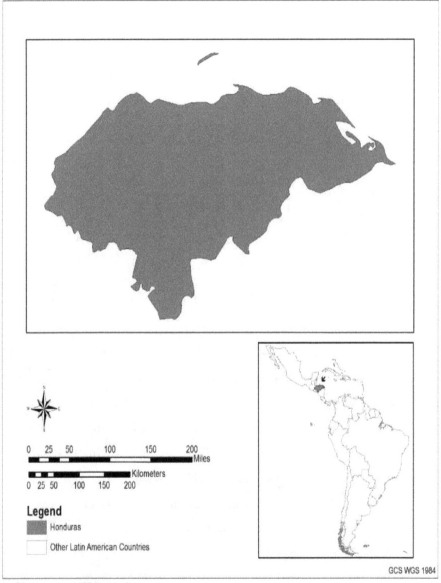

Author's creation (GE, 2019)
*Gray - specific country of interest

emerging nation, with most of its workers functioning under challenging conditions. The nation's natural resources include silver, lead, zinc, low-grade iron ore, extensive pine forests, and agricultural lands along the northern coast and interior river valleys. The workers' landmass is divided between the highlands and the lowlands. The highlands are where mining takes place and agricultural practices such as farming and livestock. These practices have dominated this area, while the valleys are where plantation agriculture is concentrated. Regarding the Global Competitive Index (GCI), Honduras is ranked 101st out of 140 analyzed countries (Schwab, 2018).

Painted stairway in Cantarranas © Luis Alfredo Romero

The nation's economy is primarily agriculture, which accounts for 14% of its Gross Domestic Product *(GDP)*, and coffee accounts for 22% of its export revenues. Before "Hurricane Mitch" in 1998, bananas were the nation's second-largest export, and as of 2012, the country has recovered over

72% of its banana exports (WDI, 2019). Honduras has extensive forests, mineral, and marine renewable and non-renewable resources. In 1999, the country signed the Enhanced Structural Adjustment Facility (ESAF), later called the Poverty Reduction and Growth Facility (PRGF), which the International Monetary Fund (IMF) endorsed. In the study, the Selected Latin America and the Caribbean (SLAC) countries that will be studied as a comparison benchmark are Argentina, Bolivia, Brazil, Chile, Colombia, Costa Rica, Honduras (excluded), Mexico, Nicaragua, Panama, Peru, El Salvador, Uruguay, and Venezuela.

Honduran bananas

Figure 2 shows Honduras's Real Gross Domestic Product purchasing power parity *(GDP)* 1981 = 100 index from 1950–2014 compared to the SLAC moving average. Figure 2 depicts Honduras at par with the benchmark moving average from 1950–2014, except from 1982–1998 and 2000-2010, where Honduras marginally outperformed our SLAC moving average, and 2011– 2014 when Honduras underperformed it.

Figure 2:
A comparison of our SLAC *RGDPppp* at chained (in Mil. 2011 USD (average)) with that of Honduras (1950 – 2014) 1981 = 100

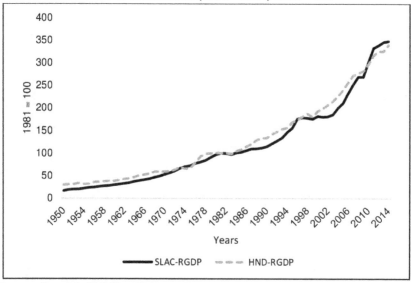

Source: (Penn World Tables (PWT, 2019).
Author's creation

Figure 3 shows Honduras's *RGDPppp* actual numbers. Compared to the SLAC moving average from 1950–2014, Figure 3 depicts Honduras underperforming from 1950–2014, showing a relatively flat trend. The educational system in Honduras may be relevant to this finding. The Honduran educational system, centrally governed by the Ministry of Education (ME), gets its blueprint from the European educational system. According to Honduran law, primary education is accessible and free to all citizens and mandatory. In recent years, significant efforts have been initiated to combat illiteracy, especially for children under 15. This illiteracy can affect higher education in the nation. In 1847, the National Autonomous

Figure 3:
A comparison of our SLAC *RGDPppp* at chained (in Mil. 2011 USD (average)) with that of Honduras (1950 – 2014)

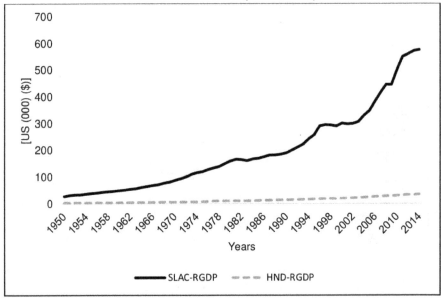

Source: (PWT, 2019).
Author's creation

University of Honduras (NAUH) or Universidad Nacional Autonoma de Honduras (UNAH) was founded. In 1987, the academic policies augmented the higher education law(s), establishing the Council of Higher Education (CHE). This action reduced the participation of Honduras' ME. Article 160 of the Honduran Constitution "declares that UNAH is a decentralized body autonomous from the State responsible for authorizing, organizing, directing, and developing the nation's professional and higher education." Hence, the country's higher education system is officially centered, though nominally independent of the government.

The CHE is presided over by the president of UNAH and is staffed by six appointed UNAH academic professionals, six top nationwide administrators from public and private national universities, and the head of the CHE's Executive Directorship. The CHE's responsibilities include but are not limited to, the creation and enforcement of higher education policy and approving the establishment of new public and private universities.

Figure 4:
A comparison of our SLAC % change of $RGDP_{ppp}$ at chained (in Mil. 2011 USD (Average)) with that of Honduras (1951 – 2014)

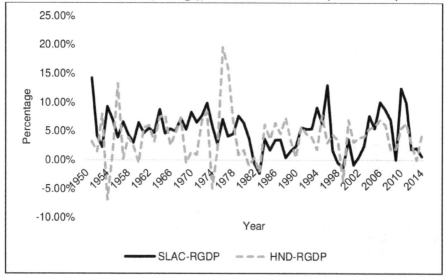

Source: (PWT, 2019).
Author's creation

Figure 4 shows the $RGDP_{ppp}$ volatility of Honduras and our SLAC, with Honduras being more volatile than the SLAC moving average from 1950–2014. The council established two separate bodies for the CHE to accomplish its goals and objectives. The first body founded was the Council of Technical Consultants (CTC), made up of academic professionals nationwide responsible for writing reports to the CHE on matters about the status quo and recommending improvement strategies for the higher education system around Honduras. The second body established by the CHE is the Executive Directorship (ED), whose goals are, but are not limited to, the authorization of new university departments and the setting of the academic benchmarks required to earn an academic degree.

Figure 5:
A comparison of our SLAC *HDI* (average) with that of Honduras (1950 – 2014)

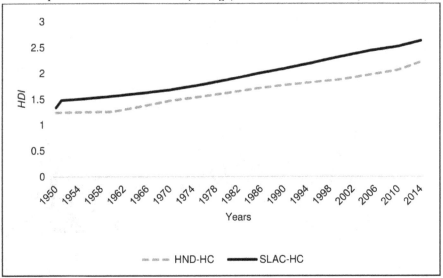

Source: (PWT, 2019).
Author's creation

Figure 5 shows Honduras's Human Development Index *(HDI)* compared to the SLAC moving average from 1950–2014. Figure 5 depicts Honduras underperforming its selected peer group. Through the UNAH, the CHE dictates and formulates academic standards for the higher education system in the nation, with the aim and objectives of regulating the development of universities in the country.

New universities and their branch campuses are required by UNAH regulation to follow these standards and institutions set by the CHE.

Students lined up outside their new school in San Ramón, Choluteca, Honduras

SUMMARY

Education Policy Orientation Main Findings:

- Article 160 of the Honduran Constitution declares that the UNAH is a decentralized body autonomous from the State to authorize, organize, direct, and develop the nation's professional and higher education system.
- The government provides free schooling up to the sixth grade.
- The Good Works Scholarship Fund (GWSF) offers 275 USD per student toward supporting the purchase of back-to-school supplies.

Policies that Moved the Country Forward:

- The 2012 Education Law amended the fundamental free education law to extend its free primary education from Grade 6 to Grade 9. It also changed teachers' hiring and supervision process and made preschooling mandatory, accessible, and free nationwide.
- Honduras's new 2017–2030 educational plan will partner with the Global Partnership for Education (GPE) and the World Bank (WB) delegations to promote educational advancement in the country.

Policies Implications and Recommendations:

These different education growth policies provide enormous lessons that other economies can learn. These lessons reveal their own sets of challenges as to how economic growth, development, and stability policies can affect Human Capital *(HC)* and Capital Strock *(CS)* formation enhancement in an economy.

- The mandatory and free education up to the sixth grade in Honduras is commendable, but most students stop their education upon graduating from the ninth grade. It is recommended that the government introduce more education programs to ensure that students reach the highest level of academic achievement.

- The GWSF is not a fixed fund for every student. Children who live close to a school receive less, while those who live far from a school receive more, as transportation costs are the highest in achieving their educational goals. It is recommended that every student receive a fixed amount of funds, and extra funds must be given per mile of distance from the home to school to cover transportation costs. Also, more schools should be constructed in rural areas to reduce students' travel time.

- The GWSF fails to cover the entire cost of a student's schooling. It is recommended that the GWSF be expanded to 100% funding for every student.

- In Honduras, impoverished families have almost no access to education beyond the 9th grade. It is recommended that the government create programs that foster enrollment into schooling beyond the 9th grade.

Contribution to Honduran Literature on Human Capital and Economic Growth:

Although an aggregate model was used in the study, this study contributes to the literature on the role of *HC* in economic growth and development by highlighting the critical educational policies passed by the Honduran government and how these policies affected the *HDI* level of the Honduran economy. Other studies delved into the Honduran economy include but are not limited to (Bedi & Marshall, 2002; Noe, 1989; Johnston & Lefebvre, 2013; Carter et al., 2006; Godoy et al., 1997). The theoretical formulation of the relationship between *HC* and economic growth in Honduras has been studied by (Abrams, 1987; Agiomigianakis et al. 2002; Auty, 2001; Cameron & Thorpe, 2000; Bedi & Born, 1995; Almendarez, 2016). However, this relationship was not demonstrated in all studies, for example, (Levin & Renelt, 1992; Temple, 1999).

REFERENCE

Abrams, E. M. (1987). Economic Specialization and Construction Personnel in Classic Period Copan, Honduras. American Antiquity, 52(3), 485-499. https://doi.org/10.2307/281595

Agiomirgianakis, G., Asteriou, D., & Monastiriotis, V. (2002). Human Capital and Economic Growth Revisited: A Dynamic Panel Data Study. International Advances in Economic Research, 8(3), 177-187. https://doi.org/10.1007/BF02297955

Almendarez, L. (2016). Human Capital Theory: Implications for Educational Development in Belize and the Caribbean. Caribbean Quarterly, 59(3-4), 23-33. https://doi.org/10.1080/00086495.2013.11672495

Auty, R. M. (2001). The Political economy of resource-driven growth. European Economic Review, 45(4-6), 839-846. https://doi.org/10.1016/S0014-2921(01)00126-X

Bedi, A. S., & Born, J. (1995). Wage determinants in Honduras credentials versus human capital. Social and Economic Studies, 44(1), 145-163.

Bedi, A. S., & Marshall, J. H. (2002). Primary school attendance in Honduras. Journal of Development Economics, 69(1), 129-153. https://doi.org/10.1016/S0304-3878(02)00056-1

Cameron, S., & Thorpe, A. (2000). Human capital investment in agricultural communities: lessons from Honduras. Applied Economics Letters, 7(9), 585-589. https://doi.org/10.1080/13504850050059050

Carter, M. R., Little, P. D., Mogues, T., & Negatu, W. (2006). Shocks, sensitivity and resilience: tracking the economic impacts of environmental disaster on assets in Ethiopia and Honduras. Working or Discussion Paper, 32, 1-45.

Godoy, R., O'Neill, K., Groff, S., Kostishack, P., Cubas, A., Demmer, J., … Martinez, M. (1997). Household determinants of deforestation by Amerindians in Honduras. World Development, 25(6), 977-987. https://doi.org/10.1016/S0305-750X(97)00007-7

Google Earth. (2019, 3 5). Google Earth. (Google) Retrieved 3 5, 2019, from https://www.google.com/earth/

Johnston, J., & Lefebvre, S. (2013). Honduras Since the Coup: Economic and Social Outcomes. Washington, DC: Center for Economic and Policy Research.

Levine, R., & Renelt, D. (1992). A Sensitivity Analysis of Cross-Country Growth Regressions. The American Economic Review, 82(4), 942-963.

Noe, P. H. (1989). The Structural Roots of Crisis: Economics Growth and Decline in Honduras 1950 - 1984.

Osiobe, E. U. (2019). A Literature Review of Human Capital and Economic Growth. Business and Economic Research, 9(4), 179-196. https://doi.org/10.5296/ber.v9i4.15624

Osiobe, E. U. (2020). Human Capital and Economic Growth in Latin America: A Cointegration and Causality Analysis. The Economics and Finance Letters, 218-235. https://doi.org/10.18488/journal.29.2020.72.218.235

Osiobe, E. U. (2020). Human Capital, Capital Stock Formation, and Economic Growth: A Panel Granger Causality Analysis. Journal of Economics and Business, 569-580. https://doi.org/10.31014/aior.1992.03.02.221

Osiobe, E. U. (2020). Understanding Latin America's Educational Orientations: Evidence from 14 Nations. Education Quarterly Review, 249-260. https://doi.org/10.31014/aior.1993.03.02.137

Osiobe, Ejiro U. (2021). An Overview of Honduras' Educational Policies. Economic DevelopmentEducational Research, Abuja: The Ane Osiobe International Foundation.

Penn World Table Equation: Human Capital in PWT 9.0. (2019). PWT 9.0. (Penn World Table) Retrieved 10 6, 2019, from https://www.rug.nl/ggdc/docs/human_capital_in_pwt_90.pdf

Schwab, K. (2018). The Global Competitiveness Report. Geneva: World Economic Forum.

Temple, J. (1999). A Positive Effect of Human Capital on Growth. Economic Letter, 65(1), 131-134. https://doi.org/10.1016/S0165-1765(99)00120-2

World Development Index Group, (2019, June 11). The World Bank. (World Development Indicators) Retrieved 3 18, 2019, from https://data.worldbank.org/region/latin-america-and-caribbean

Yale Center for Environmental Law & Policy; Center for International Earth Science Information Network; World Economic Forum. (2018). The 2018 Environmental Performance Index. Environmental Performance Index.

Ejiro U. Osiobe

NICARAGUA

INTRODUCTION

Nicaragua's name comes from Nicarao, the chief of an Indigenous tribe in the country that lived around Lake Nicaragua during the 15th and 16th centuries. The country is located in the center of Central America. Nicaragua is the 96th largest nation globally by landmass, the largest country in Central America, and the 9th largest Latin American country (Google (GE), 2019). With a population of 6.4 million, it is the 110th largest country in the world (World Development Index (WDI), 2019). Nicaragua is ranked 97th in the world and 14th in the Latin Americas in the 2018 Environmental Performance Index (EPI) (Yale Center for Environmental Law & Policy (YCELP), 2018). Regarding the Global Competitive Index (GCI), the country is ranked 104th out of 140 (Schwab, 2018).

Figure 1:
Nicaragua on the continental map of Latin America

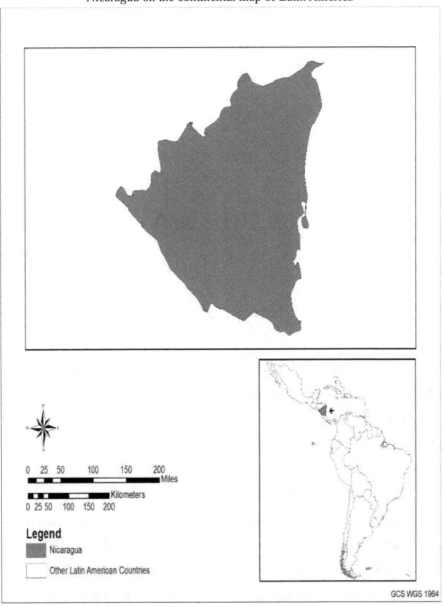

Author's creation (GE, 2019).
*Gray - specific country of interest

Nicaragua is the most impoverished nation in Central America and has widespread underemployment, poverty, and external debt. The agriculture sector is the nation's most productive sector, and its main products are bananas, sugarcane, cotton, corn, rice, coffee, and sesame. The country falls short of having an absolute or comparative advantage on any products in the international market. Today, Nicaragua is characterized by its agricultural economy. Still, the history of the nation's autocratic government and unstable regional Growth and development has led to almost all population settlement and economic activity to move to the western region of the country. In the international market, remittances from family members abroad and foreign assistance from Non-Governmental Organizations (NGOs) are the nation's primary sources of foreign income. Still, in recent times, the revenue from

Figure 2:

A comparison of our SLAC side $RGDP_{ppp}$ at chained (in Mil. 2011 USD (Average)) with that of Nicaragua (1950 – 2014) 1981 = 100

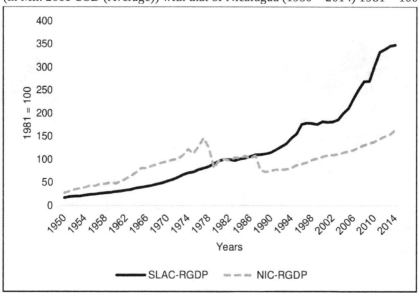

Source: (Penn World Table (PWT, 2019).
Author's creation

the tourism sector has increased. In the study, the Selected Latin America and the Caribbean (SLAC) countries that will be studied as a comparison benchmark are Argentina, Bolivia, Brazil, Chile, Colombia, Costa Rica, Honduras, Mexico, Nicaragua (excluded), Panama, Peru, El Salvador, Uruguay, and Venezuela.

Figure 2 shows Nicaragua's Real Gross Domestic Product purchasing power parity (*RGDPppp*) 1981 = 100 index from 1950–2014 compared to the SLAC moving average. Figure 2 depicts Nicaragua outperforming the benchmark moving average from 1950–1979, which is at par with the moving average from 1980–1987, and underperforming the benchmark moving average from 1988–2014. This implies when the numbers in Figure 3 are converted to an index of 1981 = 100 to measure the changes in the value of their *RGDPppp*, to see the direction of production in the economy, Nicaragua showed a dramatic decrease in the nation's progress from 1950–2014.

Managua street scene © Susan Ruggles

The main potential for economic growth lies in the agricultural sector. However, energy, tourism, manufacturing, construction, mining, and consumer goods and services also have the growth potential to support and foster economic development. At one point, Nicaragua's economy was ranked as one of the fastest-growing economies, with Foreign Direct Investment (FDI) flowing into the country. The 1972 earthquake disaster led to many of the nation's economic problems as it tried to boost its commercial and industrial activities.

Figure 3:
A comparison of our SLAC *RGDPppp* at chained
(in Mil. 2011 USD (Average)) with that of Nicaragua (1950 – 2014)

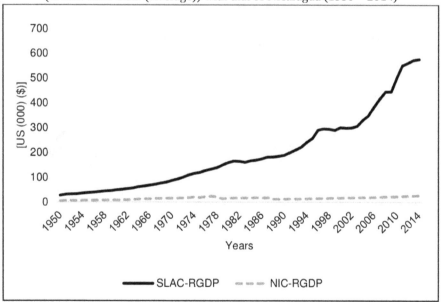

Source: (PWT, 2019).
Author's creation

Figure 3 shows Nicaragua's *RGDPppp* actual numbers compared to our SLAC moving average from 1950–2014. Figure 3 depicts Nicaragua's *RGDPppp* actual values, relatively flat, compared to that of the SLAC from

1950–2014, hence the primary reason for creating the 1981 = 100 index for the study. In the 20th century, the renewed US assistance and aid from international lending agencies brought the country's inflation rate under control, leading to minor economic growth in some parts of the country. However, the government's austerity and structural adjustment programs reduced or eliminated most government welfare, further impoverishing the country's poorest citizens. In 1990, to combat illiteracy in the country, the government passed Law 89.

Figure 4 shows Nicaragua to be on par with our SLAC regarding positive and negative reactions to economic shocks from 1950–2014,

Figure 4:
A comparison of our SLAC % change of *RGDPppp* at chained
(in Mil. 2011 USD (Average)) with that of Nicaragua (1951 – 2014)

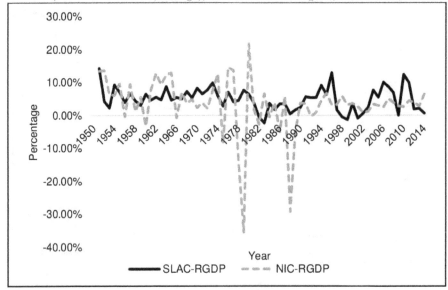

Source: (PWT, 2019).
Author's creation

excluding 1978–1980 and 1987–1991. Nicaragua's constitutional law grants the nation's institutions of higher education academic, financial, and administrative autonomy. Because of this regulation, the National University Council (CNU) was established to be the official consulting and coordinating body for all colleges and universities in the nation, while the Nicaraguan Ministry of Education (ME) is in charge of the higher policy, enacting national educational policies, disseminating state educational funds, and approving new colleges and universities in the nation. But, the CNU's quality assurance functions are with the licensing of new private universities. Therefore, universities in the nation function under almost complete independence, operating with zero federal quality assurance agency regulation.

Figure 5:
A comparison of our SLAC *HDI* (average) with that of Nicaragua (1950 – 2014)

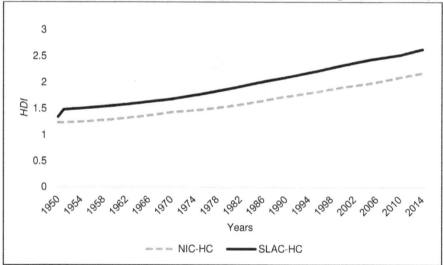

Source: (PWT, 2019).
Author's creation

Figure 5 shows Nicaragua's *HDI* compared to that of the SLAC moving average from 1950–2014. Figure 5 depicts Nicaragua underperforming the benchmark moving average from 1950–2014.

Nicaragua's Human Development Index (*HDI*) showed a steady upward trend on the actual *HDI*, and the growth rate trend was like that of the real human capital index. This implies that Nicaragua's *national literacy HDI* rate is below our SLAC moving average.

One Laptop per Child, Fuente de Vida, Juigalpa, Nicaragua. © Daniel Drake

SUMMARY

Education Policy Orientation Main Findings:

- Primary education is free and compulsory (not enforced) to all residents.
- Communities on the Atlantic Coast can learn in their native language or Spanish.
- According to the nation's constitution, the education system can create and implement its policies.
- Spanish is the predominant language used in the school system.

Policies that Moved the Country Forward:

- Free and compulsory primary education for all families in the region.
- The nation has a centralized institution, ME, governing all levels of its education system.

Policies Implication and Recommendation:

Despite significant progress made in Nicaragua's educational system, such as but not limited to:
- The reduction in the adult illiteracy population to 5%.
- Net increase in the nation's primary and secondary school enrollment rate. The nation's education sector is faced with various challenges.
- Although the enrollment rate has increased, the dropout rate has also increased, especially for schools in the country's rural areas. It is recommended that the Nicaraguan government create after-school programs and in-school programs to reduce the dropout rate while encouraging students to stay in school.

- The difference between attending a class and learning can be seen in the Nicaraguan school system, with low student learning outcomes in the nation's regional assessment exams.

- There is a low quality of preschool education, particularly among the rural community in the nation. It is recommended that the government increase its funding opportunities in those areas to foster learning in those regions.

Contribution to Nicaragua's Literature on Human Capital and Economic Growth:

This study contributes to the literature on the role of Human Capital (HD) in economic growth and development by highlighting the critical educational policies passed by the Nicaraguan government and how these policies affected the HDI level of the Nicaraguan economy. Studies delving into Nicaragua's economy include (Anderson et al. 2003; Leogrande, 2010; Hartlyn & Morely, 1986; Dore, 1986; Pisani & pagan, 2003; Wilson, 2013). The theoretical formulation of the relationship between HC and economic growth in Nicaragua has been studied by (Winters, 1964; Abdulai & Eberlin, 2001; Lane, 2000; Zapata et al., 2010; Van den Berg, 2017; Dijkstra, 1999; Behrman et al., 1985; Rosati & Rossi, 2001; Vanegas et al., 2010 & 2015; Bradshaw & Lineker, 2003; Maluccio, 2010; Blau, 1986). The theoretical formulation of the relationship between HC and economic growth consistently predicts that knowledge embodied in humans is essential for innovation, productivity, and economic development. However, this relationship doesn't occur in all scenarios (Levin & Renelt, 1992; Benhabib & Spiegel, 1994; Temple, 1999).

REFERENCE

Abdulai, A., & Eberlin, R. (2001). Technical efficiency during economic reform in Nicaragua: evidence from farm household survey data. Economic System, 25(2), 113-125. https://doi.org/10.1016/S0939-3625(01)00010-3

Anderson, L., Lewis-Beck, M. S., & Stegmaier, M. (2003). Post-socialist democratization: a comparative political economy model of the vote for Hungary and Nicaragua. Electoral Studies, 22(3), 469-484. https://doi.org/10.1016/S0261-3794(02)00009-4

Behrman, J. R., Wolfe, B. L., & Blau, D. M. (1985). Human Capital and Earning Distribution in a Developing Country: The Case of Prerevolutionary Nicaragua. Economic Development and Cultural Change, 34(1), 1-29. https://doi.org/10.1086/451507

Benhabib, J., & Spiegel, M. M. (1994). The role of human capital in economic development evidence from aggregate cross-country data. Journal of Monetary Economics, Elsevier, vol. 34(2), pages 143-173. https://doi.org/10.1016/0304-3932(94)90047-7

Blau, D. M. (1986). Fertility, Child Nutrition, and Child Mortality in Nicaragua: An Economic Analysis of Interrelationships. The Journal of Developing Areas, 20(2), 185-202.

Bradshaw, S., & Linneker, B. (2003). Civil society responses to poverty reduction strategies in Nicaragua. Progress in Development Studies, 3(2), 147-158. https://doi.org/10.1191/1464993403ps058ra

Dijkstra, A. G. (1999). Technocracy Questioned: Assessing Economic Stabilisation in Nicaragua. Bull. Latin Am. Res., 18(3), 295-310. https://doi.org/10.1111/j.1470-9856.1999.tb00136.x

Dore, E. (1986). Nicaragua: The Experience of the Mixed Economy. In Latin American Political Economy: Financial Crisis and Political Change (pp. 319-350). New York: Routledge.

Google Earth. (2019, 3 5). Google Earth. (Google) Retrieved 3 5, 2019, from https://www.google.com/earth/

Hartlyn, J., & Morley, S. A. (1986). Latin American Political Economy: Financial Crisis and Political Change. New York: Routledge.

Lane, H. (2000). Sustainable Development Versus Economic Growth: A Case Study on Natural Disaster in Nicaragua. The Journal of Environment and Development, 9(2). https://doi.org/10.1177/107049650000900205

Leogrande, W. M. (2010). Making the economy scream: Us economic sanctions against Sandinista Nicaragua. Third World Quarterly, 17(2), 329-348. https://doi.org/10.1080/01436599650035716

Levine, R., & Renelt, D. (1992). A Sensitivity Analysis of Cross-Country Growth Regressions. The American Economic Review, 82(4), 942-963.

Maluccio, J. A. (2010). The Impact of Conditional Cash Transfers on Consumption and Investment in Nicaragua. The Journal of Development Studies, 46(1), 14-38. https://doi.org/10.1080/00220380903197952

Osiobe, E. U. (2019). A Literature Review of Human Capital and Economic Growth. Business and Economic Research, 9(4), 179-196. https://doi.org/10.5296/ber.v9i4.15624

Osiobe, E. U. (2020). Human Capital and Economic Growth in Latin America: A Cointegration and Causality Analysis. The Economics and Finance Letters, 218-235. https://doi.org/10.18488/journal.29.2020.72.218.235

Osiobe, E. U. (2020). Human Capital, Capital Stock Formation, and Economic Growth: A Panel Granger Causality Analysis. Journal of Economics and Business, 569-580. https://doi.org/10.31014/aior.1992.03.02.221

Osiobe, E. U. (2020). Understanding Latin America's Educational Orientations: Evidence from 14 Nations. Education Quarterly Review, 249-260. https://doi.org/10.31014/aior.1993.03.02.137

Osiobe, Ejiro U. (2021). An Overview of Nicaragua's Educational Policies. Economic Development Educational Research, Abuja: The Ane Osiobe International Foundation.

Penn World Table Equation: Human Capital in PWT 9.0. (2019). PWT 9.0. (Penn

World Table) Retrieved 10 6, 2019, from
https://www.rug.nl/ggdc/docs/human_capital_in_pwt_90.pdf

Pisani, A. J., & Pagan, A. J. (2003). Sectional Queuing in a Transitional Economy: The Case of Nicaragua in the 1990s. Labor, 571-597. https://doi.org/10.1111/j.1121-7081.2003.00253.x

Rosati, F. C., & Rossi, M. (2001). Children's working hours, school enrolment and human capital accumulation: evidence from Pakistan and Nicaragua. Working Paper. https://doi.org/10.1920/wp.ifs.2001.0113

Schwab, K. (2018). The Global Competitiveness Report. Geneva: World Economic Forum.

Temple, J. (1999). A Positive Effect of Human Capital on Growth. Economic Letter, 65(1), 131-134. https://doi.org/10.1016/S0165-1765(99)00120-2

Van den Berg, H. (2017). Economic Growth and development. Hackensack: World Scientific Publishing Co. https://doi.org/10.1142/9058

Van den Berg, H. (2017). Economic Growth and Development 3rd edition. Singapore: World Scientific Publishing Co. Pte. L.td.

Van den Berg, M. (2010). Household income strategies and natural disaster: Dynamic livelihoods in rural Nicaragua. Ecological Economics, 69(3), 592-602. https://doi.org/10.1016/j.ecolecon.2009.09.006

Vanegas, S. M., Gartner, W., & Senauer, B. (2015). Tourism and Poverty Reduction: An Economic Sector Analysis for Costa Rica and Nicaragua. Tourism Economics, 21(1), 159-182. https://doi.org/10.5367/te.2014.0442

Wilson, B. R. (2013). Delivering the Goods: Fair Trade, Solidarity, and the Moral Economy of the Coffee Contract in Nicaragua. Human Organization, 72(3), 177-187. https://doi.org/10.17730/humo.72.3.f678404745007011

Winters, D. H. (1964). The Agricultural Economy of Nicaragua. Latin American Politics and Society, 6(4), 501-519. https://doi.org/10.2307/165000

Yale Center for Environmental Law & Policy; Center for International Earth Science Information Network; World Economic Forum. (2018). The 2018 Environmental Performance Index. Environmental Performance Index.

Zapata, M. J., Hall, M. C., Lindo, P., & Vanderschaeghe, M. (2010). Can community-based tourism contribute to development and poverty alleviation? Lessons from Nicaragua. Current Issues in Tourism, 14(8), 725-749. https://doi.org/10.1080/13683500.2011.559200

COSTA RICA

INTRODUCTION

The Central American nation of Costa Rica is one of the few countries in the region that enjoys two coastlines, one at the Pacific Ocean and one at the Caribbean Sea. It is the world's 126th largest country, the 6th largest country in Central America, the 11th largest country in the South Americas (Google Earth (GE), 2019), the 120th most populous in the world with a population of 4.9 million people as of 2018 (World Development Index (WDI), 2019), and on the Global Competitive Index (GCI), Costa Rica is ranked 55th out of 140 countries (Schwab, 2018).

In a region often racked by violence and disruption, Costa Rica is one of the most peaceful countries in Central America. Since the late 19th century, Costa Rica has had only two brief periods of violence that have

Ejiro U. Osiobe

Figure 1:
Costa Rica on the continental map of Latin America

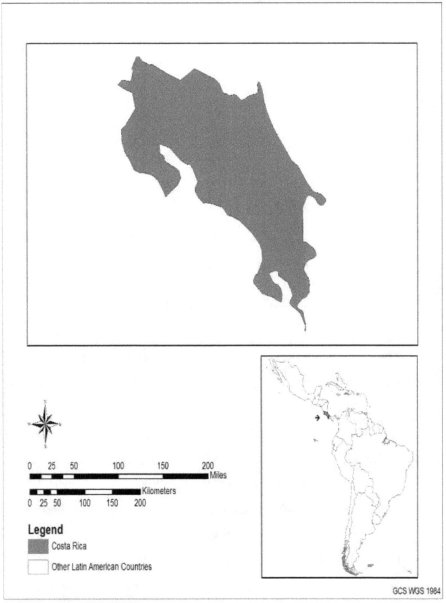

Author's creation (GE, 2019)
*Gray - specific country of interest

110

marred its development. Its economy is mainly agricultural, and its agrarian economy has created a high standard of living for its citizens. In the 19th century, agriculture and land ownership were the economic mainstays. Currently, however, the tourism industry is rapidly expanding and transforming Costa Rica's economy, primarily through ecotourism, a new aspect of the tourism industry led by progressive environmental policies.

The country has also diversified its economy to include different sectors such as finance, corporate services for foreign companies, and pharmaceuticals. Today, Costa Rica is the only country on the planet with pharmaceuticals. Today, Costa Rica is the only country that has met all five United Nations Development Program (UNDP) criteria established to measure environmental sustainability. In the study, the Selected Latin

Figure 2:
A comparison of our SLAC *RGDPppp* at chained (in Mil. 2011 (Average)) with that of Costa Rica (1950 – 2014) 1981 = 100

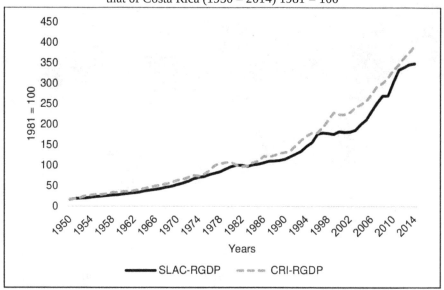

Source: (Penn World Table (PWT), 2019)
Author's creation

111

America and the Caribbean (SLAC) countries that will be studied as a comparison benchmark are Argentina, Bolivia, Brazil, Chile, Colombia, Costa Rica (excluded), Honduras, Mexico, Nicaragua, Panama, Peru, El Salvador, Uruguay, and Venezuela.

Figure 2 shows Costa Rica's Real Gross Domestic Product purchasing power parity *(RGDPppp)* 1981 = 100 index from 1950–2014 compared to our SLAC moving average. Figure 2 depicts Costa Rica marginally outperforming the benchmark moving average from 1950 to 2014. This implies that when the numbers in Figure 3 are converted to an index of 1981 = 100 to measure the changes in the value of *RGDPppp* to see

© Jorge Cancela

the economy's direction, Costa Rica marginally outperformed the SLAC. In all of Central America, Costa Rica is regarded as the most stable democratic state, and it has the most highly educated workforce, most of whom speak

English and Spanish. The country is a presidential democratic republic. On average, Costa Rica spends roughly 6.9% of its budget on education than the 4.4% global average spent on education. In the 2018 Environmental Performance Index (EPI), Costa Rica is ranked 30th (Yale Center for Environmental Law & Policy (YCELP), 2018) in the world and 1ˢᵗ in Latin America, and it was rated the best-performing country twice by the new economics foundation.

Figure 3:
A comparison of our SLAC *RGDPppp* at chained (in Mil. 2011 USD (Average)) with that of Costa Rica (1950 – 2014)

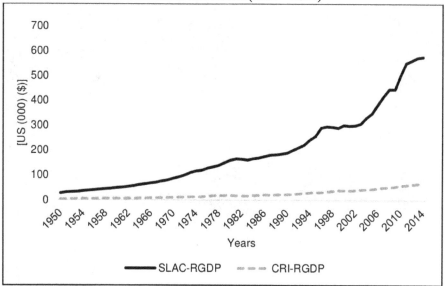

Source: (PWT, 2019)
Author's creation

Figure 3 shows Costa Rica's *RGDPppp* actual numbers compared to our SLAC's moving average from 1950–2014. Figure 3 depicts Costa Rica below the benchmark moving average from 1950–2014. Today, Costa Rica's main product is coffee, first planted in the nation in 1808; by the 1820s, coffee surpassed sugar, cacao, and tobacco as the nation's primary export product to the rest of the world. Coffee production remained the country's principal source of wealth and helped create a middle class in the 20th century. In line with the nation's growing economy, Costa Rica will become a carbon-free country by 2021. In 2016, 98.1% of the country's electricity was generated from green sources: solar, geothermal, biomass, and, mainly, hydro. Costa Rica has been economically stable, although the country has seen moderate inflation between 2.0% and 2.6%, high Gross Domestic Product (*GDP)* growth rates, and increased *GDP per capita.*

Costa Rican coffee beans

Figure 4 shows Costa Rica to be more economically volatile than the average of the SLAC. The volatility implies that the nation was impacted more by economic shocks (positive and negative) than the benchmarked moving average. Today in the country, quality healthcare is provided by the government at a low cost to users, housing is very affordable, and in Latin America, the nation is known for the quality of its educational system.

Figure 4:
A comparison of our SLAC % change of *RGDPppp* at chained (in Mil. 2011 USD (average)) with that of Costa Rica (1951 – 2014)

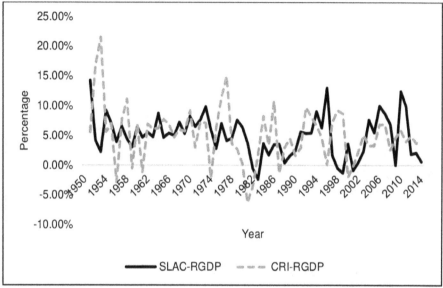

Source: (PWT, 2019)
Author's creation

Because of Costa Rica's quality educational system, the country has one of the highest literacy rates in Latin America, about 97% of the total population. This may be because Costa Rica has invested nearly 30% of its national budget into its primary and secondary educational system for the last three decades.

Figure 5 shows Costa Rica's Human Development Index *(HDI)* compared to that of the SLAC moving average from 1950–2014. Figure 5 depicts Costa Rica marginally outperforming the benchmark moving average from 1950–2014. Costa Rica's *HDI* showed a steady upward trend, implying that Costa Rica's *HDI* growth pattern is slightly higher than that of our SLAC. In Costa Rica, education promises an excellent academic experience and a sound financial investment for one's future. It is perhaps notable that tuition in Costa Rica averages about 50% less than in-state rates for most US colleges.

Figure 5:
A comparison of our SLAC *HDI* (average) with that of Costa Rica (1950 – 2014)

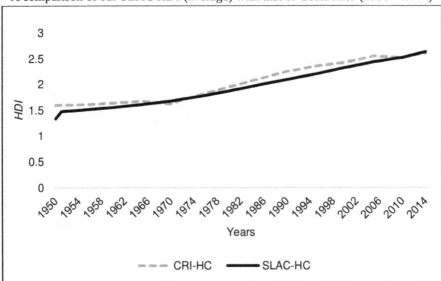

Source: (PWT, 2019)
Author's creation

SUMMARY

Education Policy Orientation Main Findings:

- According to the Costa Rica News, the nation ranks 4th out of 94 countries in accessibility.
- Preschool and general primary education are compulsory and free.
- In 1990, the country pledged to work toward the targets set out by the Education for All (EFA) under the direction of the United Nations Educational, Scientific, and Cultural Organization (UNESCO).
- The nation has special programs to compensate for the lack of teachers in rural area schools, and the country has a 93.6% rate of access to education.

Policies that Moved the Country Forward:

- In 1869, the nation made basic education free and mandatory for all citizens.
- Article 79 of the Costa Rican constitution guarantees freedom of education.
- Article 80 of the Costa Rican constitution states that the government should stimulate the private educational sector.
- Article 82 of the Costa Rican constitution ordered the government to provide food and clothing to students in poverty.
- As of the 1990s, English and computer science are mandatory school courses.

- The country invests over 30% of its national budget in primary and secondary schools.
- Secondary education isn't mandatory, but it is free.
- The nation has a unified governing body for its educational system called the Costa Rican Ministry of Education (ME).
- The government pays education professionals more to attract young, bright, highly skilled workders into the education system.

Policies Implication and Recommendation:

These education growth policies provide enormous lessons that other economies can learn from. These lessons come with their challenges as to how economic growth, development, and stability policies can affect Human Capital *(HC)* and Capital Stock *(CS)* formation in enhancing an economy.

- Although the free primary education policy has successfully increased enrollments, one major challenge the policy has faced is increased class repeating rates and high school dropout rates. It is recommended that student per capita learning rates should be the focus rather than enrollment rates.
- Although the nation invests more than 30% of its national budget in primary and secondary school education, in recent years, the public Costa Rican education system has suffered from budget cuts and is experiencing a lack of funding. It is recommended that these budget cuts be stopped, and loan programs should be provided for low-income households.

Kids receive free backpacks with school supplies.

Contribution to Costa Rican Literature on Human Capital and Economic Growth:

Although an aggregate model was used for all 14 countries in the study, this study contributes to the literature on the role of education and *HC* in economic growth and development by highlighting the essential educational policies passed by the Costa Rican government and how these policies affected the *HCI* level in the nation.

Studies delving into Costa Rica's economy include (Sanchez-Ancochea, 2008; Levin & Raut, 1997; Vanegas et al., 2015; Lee & Mason, 2010; Mayer, 2001; Barro, 1991). The theoretical formulation of the relationship between *HC* and economic growth in Costa Rica has been studied by (Agiomigianakis et al., 2002; McDonald & Roberts, 2002). These studies consistently predict that knowledge embodied in humans is essential

119

for innovation, productivity, and economic growth. However, this relationship was not true in all studies; see, for example, (Levin & Renelt, 1997; Devarajan et al., 1996).

REFERENCE

Agiomirgianakis, G., Asteriou, D., & Monastiriotis, V. (2002). Human Capital and Economic Growth Revisited: A Dynamic Panel Data Study. International Advances in Economic Research, 8(3), 177-187. https://doi.org/10.1007/BF02297955

Barro, J. R. (1991). Human Capital and Growth in Cross-Country Regressions. The Quarterly Journal of Economics, 407-443. https://doi.org/10.2307/2937943

Devarajan, S., Swaroop, V., & Zou, H.-f. (1996). The Composition of Public Expenditure and Economic Growth. Journal of Monetary Economics, 37(2), 313-344. https://doi.org/10.1016/S0304-3932(96)90039-2

Google Earth. (2019, 3 5). Google Earth. (Google) Retrieved 3 5, 2019, from https://www.google.com/earth/

Lee, R., & Mason, A. (2010). Fertility, Human Capital, and Economic Growth over the Demographic Transition. European Journal of Population/Revue europeenne de Demographie, 26(2), 159-182. https://doi.org/10.1007/s10680-009-9186-x

Levin, A., & Raut, L. K. (1997). Complementarities between export and human capital in economic growth: Evidence from the semi-industrialized countries. Economic Development and Cultural Change, 46(1), 155-174. https://doi.org/10.1086/452325

Mayer, J. (2001). Technology Diffusion, Human Capital and Economic Growth in Developing Countries. UNCTAD Discussion Paper.

McDonald, S., & Robert, J. (2002). Growth and multiple forms of human capital in an augmented Solow model: a panel data investigation. Economic Letters, 74(2), 271-276. https://doi.org/10.1016/S0165-1765(01)00539-0

Osiobe, E. U. (2019). A Literature Review of Human Capital and Economic Growth. Business and Economic Research, 9(4), 179-196. https://doi.org/10.5296/ber.v9i4.15624

Osiobe, E. U. (2020). Human Capital and Economic Growth in Latin America: A Cointegration and Causality Analysis. The Economics and Finance Letters, 218-235. https://doi.org/10.18488/journal.29.2020.72.218.235

Osiobe, E. U. (2020). Human Capital, Capital Stock Formation, and Economic Growth: A Panel Granger Causality Analysis. Journal of Economics and Business, 569-580. https://doi.org/10.31014/aior.1992.03.02.221

Osiobe, E. U. (2020). Understanding Latin America's Educational Orientations: Evidence from 14 Nations. Education Quarterly Review, 249-260. https://doi.org/10.31014/aior.1993.03.02.137

Osiobe, Ejiro U. (2021). An Overview of Costa Rica's Educational Policies. Economic Development Educational Research, Abuja: The Ane Osiobe International Foundation.

Sanchez-Ancochea, D. (2008). Chapter 7: The Political Economy of DR-CAFTA in Costa Rica, the Dominican Republic, and El Salvador. In The Political Economy of Hemispheric Integration (pp. 171-200). New York: Palgrave Macmillan. https://doi.org/10.1057/9780230612945_7

Schwab, K. (2018). The Global Competitiveness Report. Geneva: World Economic Forum.

Vanegas, S. M., Gartner, W., & Senauer, B. (2015). Tourism and Poverty Reduction: An Economic Sector Analysis for Costa Rica and Nicaragua. Tourism Economics, 21(1), 159-182. https://doi.org/10.5367/te.2014.0442

World Development Index Group, (2019, June 11). The World Bank. (World Development Indicators) Retrieved 3 18, 2019, from https://data.worldbank.org/region/latin-america-and-caribbean

PANAMA

INTRODUCTION

The nation of Panama is located in Central America on the Isthmus of Panama, the land bridge between the Caribbean Sea and the Pacific Ocean. It is the 116th largest country in the world and 5th largest country in Central America (Google (GE), 2019). The country's capital is Panama City, and the nation had a population of 4.1 million people in 2018, ranking it 128 in the world in population size (World Development Index (WDI), 2019). Panama is known for its strategic transportation hub across the globe. Until the 19th century, the shipment of gold and silver was moved to Spain. In terms of the GCI, Panama ranks 64th out of 140 countries (Schwab, 2018). In the 2018 Environmental Performance Index (EPI), Panama is ranked 56th in the world and 5th in Latin America (Yale Center for Environmental Law & Policy (YCELP), 2018).

Figure 1:
Panama on the continental map of Latin America

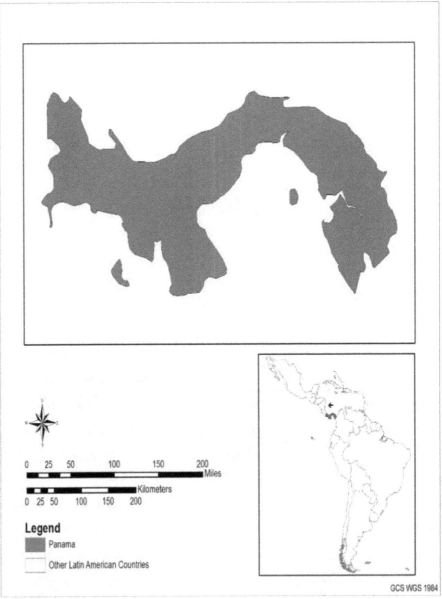

Author's creation (GE, 2019)
*Gray - specific country of interest

The Panama Canal significantly impacts the nation's economic security, as the canal secures the country's role in global socioeconomic affairs and commerce. In December 1999, the US relinquished its jurisdiction over the financial and economic matters of the Panama Canal, giving the nation full sovereignty over the canal. This sovereignty led to an

Locomotives Tow Container Ship through Miraflores Locks - Panama Canal © Adam Jones

unprecedented rightward shift in the production possibility frontier of Panamanian society. In that sense, Panama became an independent nation both economically and politically hence, totally controlling the entirety of its national territory. In the study, the Selected Latin America and the Caribbean (SLAC) countries that will be studied as a comparison benchmark are Argentina, Bolivia, Brazil, Chile, Colombia, Costa Rica, Honduras, Mexico, Nicaragua, Panama (excluded), Peru, El Salvador, Uruguay, and Venezuela.

Ejiro U. Osiobe

Figure 2:
A comparison of our SLAC *RGDPppp* at chained
(in Mil. 2011 USD (average)) with that of Panama (1950 – 2014) 1981 = 100

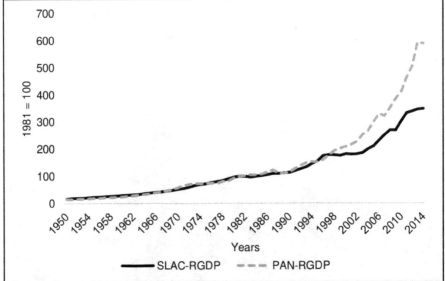

Source: (Penn World Table (PWT), 2019).
Author's creation

Figure 2 shows Panama's Real Gross Domestic Product purchasing power parity (*RGDPppp*) compared to that of the SLAC moving average from 1950–2014. Figure 52 depicts Panama's *RGDPppp* 1981 = 100 index at per with our selected Latin American countries from 1950–1999 and outperforming our benchmark moving average from 2000–2014. This implies when the numbers in Figure 53 are converted to an index 1981 = 100 to measure the changes in the value of their *RGDPppp* to see the direction of production in the economy, Panama outperformed the SLAC by a significant margin.

Figure 3 shows Panama's *RGDPppp* actual numbers as they compare to that of our SLAC moving average from 1950–2014. Figure 3 depicts Panama underperforming the benchmark moving average from 1950–2014

126

Figure 3:
A comparison of our SLAC *RGDP*$_{ppp}$ at chained
(in Mil. 2011 USD(Average)) with that of Panama (1950 – 2014)

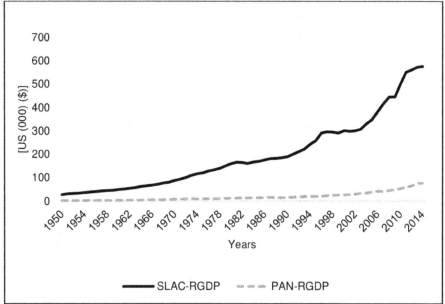

and relatively flat at an increasing rate. The services industry has grown in Panama because of the international (offshore) banking industry and the canal's traffic. The public administration and other services sectors are also essential as they help support the growth and development of the nation.

Figure 4 shows Panama's *RGDPppp* to be more negatively volatile to economic shocks and at par with positive and zero economic shocks to our SLAC. In Panama, elementary education is mandatory and free for children ages 6–15. Two opposing statistics hold separate views regarding Panama's population literacy ratio data.

Figure 5 shows Panama's Human Development Index *(HDI)* compared to the SLAC moving average from 1950–2014. Figure 5 depicts Panama outperforming the benchmark moving average from 1950–2014. The education system in Panama suffers substantially from inequality around geographical areas. Although public education is free for the states' compulsory years of schooling, state-of-the-art institutions are limited to the big cities, while the countryside schools are underfunded. But, compared to

Figure 4:
A comparison of our SLAC % change of *RGDPppp* at chained
(in Mil. 2011 USD (average)) with that of Panama (1951 – 2014)

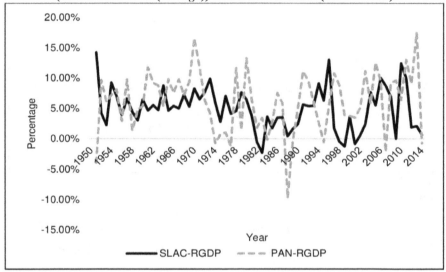

Source: (PWT, 2019).
Author's creation

the other Latin American countries, the education standard in Panama is relatively high because of its government investment in the nation's educational system and research. The literacy rate in Panama is about 93% due to the free and mandatory education policy for children between 6–15. Although private schools can manage their institutions, the Ministry of Education (ME) regulates the Panamanian education system.

Figure 5:
A comparison of our SLAC *HDI* (average) with that of Panama (1950 – 2014)

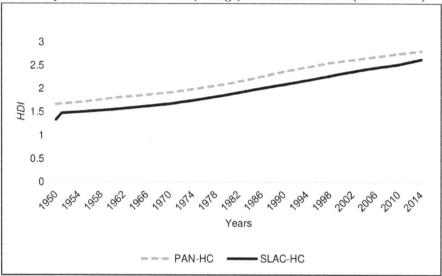

Source: (PWT, 2019).
Author's creation

Balboa High School, Panama

Ejiro U. Osiobe

SUMMARY

Education Policy Orientation Main Findings:

- Free and mandatory preschool and basic education were indicated in the nation's 1941 constitution.
- Spanish is the predominant language used in their education system.
- 20% of the government expenditure budget is spent on education.

Policies that Moved the Country Forward:

- In recent years, Panama has been increasing its education spending and expanding its international ties to strengthen its educational system while improving its capacity and education quality.
- Panama aims to train its teachers to use English as part of its education quality effort.

Policies Implication and Recommendation:

The Panamanian education system has strong policies that have helped improve and grow the nation's Human Capital *(HC)*. These educational policies still have room for improvement, especially in expanding rural per and primary education coverages and improving the quality of teachers.

- The mandatory free basic education has been a success in the big cities; hence the Panamanian education system suffers from substantial inequalities between the rural and the urban schools.

130

More funding is recommended to go into rural areas to reduce these inequalities.

- With free education and the right educational incentives, enrollment levels increase. It is recommended that the government improve the structure of the school buildings' quality of the school curriculum, ensuring that students stay in school and reducing the dropout rate in the country.

Contribution to Panama Literature on Human Capital and Economic Growth:

This study contributes to the literature on the role of *HC* in economic growth and development by highlighting the essential educational policies passed by the Panamanian government and how these policies affected the *HCI* level of the Panamanian economy. Studies delved into Panama's economy (Wali, 1993; Moreno-Villalaz, 1999; Goldfajn et al., 2001; Millett, 1990). The theoretical formulation of the relationship between *HC* and economic growth in Panama has been studied by (Bakari & Mabrouki, 2017; Klytchnikova & Dorosh, 2012; Pagano et al., 2012; Dettenhofer & Hampl 2009; Hanushek, 2013; Stein et al., 2008; Heckman & Hotz, 1986; Runk, 2012; Zimbalist & Weeks, 1991; Knight et al., 1993). The theoretical formulation of the relationship between *HC* and economic growth consistently predicts that knowledge embodied in humans is essential for innovation, productivity, and economic growth. However, this relationship was not true in all studies (Levine & Renelt, 1992; Quiggin, 1999 & 2002; Temple, 1999).

REFERENCE

Bakari, S., & Mabrouki, M. (2017). Impact of Exports and Imports on Economic Growth: New Evidence from Panama. Journal of Smart Economic Growth, 2(1), 67-79.

Dettenhofer, M., & Hampl, N. (2009). Development of a Biomedical Innovation Economy Panama. Journal of Technology Management and Innovation, 4(2). https://doi.org/10.4067/S0718-27242009000200002

Goldfajin, I., Olivares, G., Frankel, J., & Milesi-Ferretti, G. M. (2001). Full Dollarization: The Case of Panama. Economia, 1(2), 101-155. https://doi.org/10.1353/eco.2001.0003

Google Earth. (2019, 3 5). Google Earth. (Google) Retrieved 3 5, 2019, from https://www.google.com/earth/

Hanushek, E. A. (2013). Economic growth in developing countries: The role of human capital. Economic of Education Review, 37, 204-212. https://doi.org/10.1016/j.econedurev.2013.04.005

Heckman, J. J., & Hotz, J. V. (1986). An Investigation of the Labor Market Earnings of Panamanian Males Evaluating the Sources of Inequality. The Journal of Human Resources, 21(4), 507-542. https://doi.org/10.2307/145765

Klytchnikova, I., & Dorosh, P. (2012). Tourism Sector in Panama: Regional Economic Impacts and the Potential to Benefit the Poor. New York: The World Bank Group. https://doi.org/10.1596/1813-9450-6183

Knight, M., Loayza, N., & Villanueva, D. (1993). Testing the Neoclassical Theory of Economic Growth: A Panel Data Approach. IMF Staff Papers, 40(3), 512-541. https://doi.org/10.2307/3867446

Levine, R., & Renelt, D. (1992). A Sensitivity Analysis of Cross-Country Growth Regressions. The American Economic Review, 82(4), 942-963.

Millett, R. L. (1990). The Aftermath of Intervention: Panama 1990. Journal of Interamerican Studies and World Affairs, 32(1), 1-16. https://doi.org/10.2307/166127

Moreno-Villalaz, J. L. (1999). Lesson from the Monetary Experience of Panama: A Dollar Economy with Financial Integration. Cato Journal, 18(3).

Osiobe, E. U. (2019). A Literature Review of Human Capital and Economic Growth. Business and Economic Research, 9(4), 179-196. https://doi.org/10.5296/ber.v9i4.15624

Osiobe, E. U. (2020). Human Capital and Economic Growth in Latin America: A Cointegration and Causality Analysis. The Economics and Finance Letters, 218-235. https://doi.org/10.18488/journal.29.2020.72.218.235

Osiobe, E. U. (2020). Human Capital, Capital Stock Formation, and Economic Growth: A Panel Granger Causality Analysis. Journal of Economics and Business, 569-580. https://doi.org/10.31014/aior.1992.03.02.221

Osiobe, E. U. (2020). Understanding Latin America's Educational Orientations: Evidence from 14 Nations. Education Quarterly Review, 249-260. https://doi.org/10.31014/aior.1993.03.02.137

Osiobe, Ejiro U. (2021). An Overview of Panama's Educational Policies. Economic Development Educational Research, Abuja: The Ane Osiobe International Foundation.

Pagano, A. M., Light, M. K., Sanchez, O. V., Ungo, R., & Tapiero, E. (2012). Impact of the Panama Canal expansion on the Panamanian economy. Maritime Policy and Management, 39(7), 705-722. https://doi.org/10.1080/03088839.2012.729273

Penn World Table Equation: Human Capital in PWT 9.0. (2019). PWT 9.0. (Penn World Table) Retrieved 10 6, 2019, from https://www.rug.nl/ggdc/docs/human_capital_in_pwt_90.pdf

Quiggin, J. (1999). Human capital Theory and Education Policy in Australia. Australian Economic Review, 32(2), 130-44. https://doi.org/10.1111/1467-8462.00100

Quiggin, J. (2002). Human Capital Theory and Education Policy in Australia. Australian Economic Review, Volume 32, Issue 2. https://doi.org/10.1111/1467-8462.00100

Runk, J. V. (2012). Indigenous Land and Environmental Conflicts in Panama: Neoliberal Multiculturalism, Changing Legislation, and Human Rights. Journal of Latin American Geography, 11(2), 21-47. https://doi.org/10.1353/lag.2012.0036

Schwab, K. (2018). The Global Competitiveness Report. Geneva: World Economic Forum.

Stein, A. D., Melgar, P., Hoddinott, J., & Martorell, R. (2008). Cohort Profile: The Institute of Nutrition of Central America and Panama (INCAP) Nutrition Trial Cohort Study. International Journal of Epidemiology, 37(4), 716-720. https://doi.org/10.1093/ije/dyn028

Temple, J. (1999). A Positive Effect of Human Capital on Growth. Economic Letter, 65(1), 131-134. https://doi.org/10.1016/S0165-1765(99)00120-2

Wali, A. (1993). The Transformation of a Frontier: State and Regional Relationship in Panama, 1972-1990. Human Organization, 52(2), 115-129. https://doi.org/10.17730/humo.52.2.t7266ng1131820t2

World Development Index Group, (2019, June 11). The World Bank. (World Development Indicators) Retrieved 3 18, 2019, from https://data.worldbank.org/region/latin-america-and-caribbean

Yale Center for Environmental Law & Policy; Center for International Earth Science Information Network; World Economic Forum. (2018). The 2018 Environmental Performance Index. Environmental Performance Index.

Zimbalist, A., & Weeks, J. (1991). Panama at the Crossroads. Las Angeles: University of California Press. https://doi.org/10.1525/9780520325180

COLOMBIA

INTRODUCTION

Colombia is located in the northwestern part of South America. It is the 26th largest country globally and the 4th largest country in South America (Google Earth (GE), 2019). With a population of 49.6 million people as of 2018, the nation is the 3rd most populous nation in Latin America and ranks 29th in terms of the global population (World Development Index (WDI), 2019).

In the 2018 Environmental Performance Index (EPI)--(Yale Center for Environmental Law & Policy (YCELP) 2018), Colombia is ranked 42nd in the world and 2nd in Latin America. Colombia's economy was based entirely on gold mining in the colonial period. Today, the economy is based on agriculture, exploiting hydrocarbon fuels and several precious metals,

Figure 1:
Colombia on the continental map of Latin America

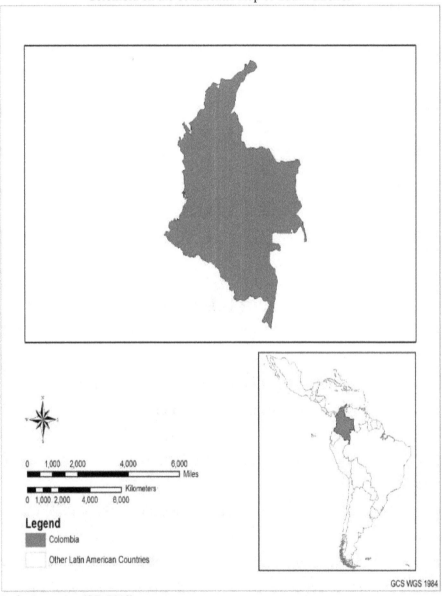

Author's creation (GE, 2019)
*Gray - specific country of interest

and manufacturing of goods and services for consumption internally and abroad. In the past, the nation's political instability has led to an unequal distribution of the nation's wealth and the illegal drug trade (mainly cocaine), which remains a major disruptive factor in Colombian life. Regardless of these setbacks, the country ranks 60th out of 140 countries in the Global Competitiveness Index Report (GCIR) (Schwab, 2018).

In the study, the Selected Latin America and the Caribbean (SLAC) countries that will be studied as a comparison benchmark are Argentina, Bolivia, Brazil, Chile, Colombia (excluded), Costa Rica, Honduras, Mexico,

Figure 2

A comparison of our SLAC $RGDP_{ppp}$ at chained (in Mil. 2011 USD (average)) with that of Colombia (1950 – 2014) 1981 = 100

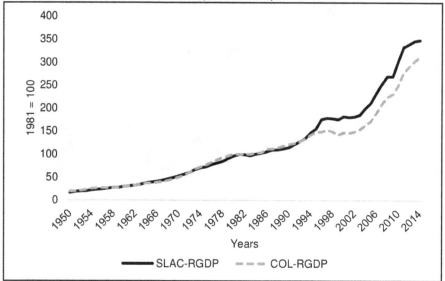

Source: (Penn World Table (PWT), 2019).
Author's creation

Nicaragua, Panama, Peru, El Salvador, Uruguay, and Venezuela. Figure 2 shows Colombia's Real Gross Domestic Product purchasing power parity

(*RGDPppp*) 1981 = 100 compared to the SLACs moving average from 1950–2014. Figure 2 depicts Colombia at par with the benchmark moving average from 1950–1997, but from 1998–2014, Colombia underperformed that SLAC moving average. This implies when the number in Figure 3 is converted to an index 1981 = 100 to measure the changes in the value of their *RGDPppp* and to see the direction of production in the economy, Colombia underperforms our SLAC.

A person from the Arhuaca community selling wares in Cartagena © landrescamilo

The economic system of Colombia is dominated by primarily private enterprises, where direct government participation is limited, especially in the communication, railways, and petroleum sectors. The government tries to foster economic growth, development, and stability to encourage private enterprise through indirect measures, including but not limited to favorable tax policies, government subsidies, and the availability and extension of business credits. In Colombia, regional economic development organizations, such as the Cauca Valley Corporation1, have been established to promote economic growth, development, and stability, emphasizing hydroelectric power development and flood control. Nevertheless, Colombia was one of the few SLAC not to suffer a debt crisis in the '80s, and from 1980–1990, the nation had the healthiest economy in South America.

Figure 3 shows Colombia's actual *RGDPppp* number compared to the SLAC moving average from 1950–2014. Figure 3 depicts Colombia at par with the benchmark moving average for most years, except from 1970–1994, when it outperformed our stated average, and 1995–2009 when the nation marginally underperformed that of our SLAC moving average. Today, agriculture remains a primary component of the Colombian economy, although the industrial development in the country since the 1940s is

Figure 3
A comparison of our SLAC *RGDPppp* at chained (in Mil. 2011 USD (Average))
with that of Colombia (1950 – 2014)

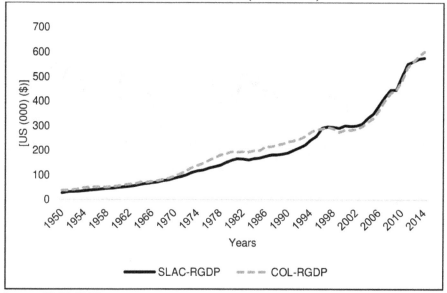

Source: (PWT, 2019).
Author's creation

remarkable. A reasonable portion of the nation's landmass is uncultivated due to the country's poor soils and unfavorable climate conditions. However, the country is blessed with abundant renewable and non-renewable resources.

Their non-renewable resources include gold reserves, petroleum, and coal, while the renewable resources include land for agriculture and its river belts, which are used to generate hydroelectric power. Excluding Brazil, Colombia's potential for hydroelectric power stations is of higher significance than any other nation on the continent. Colombia produces about three-fourths of the nation's electricity; however, the 1992–1993 drought interrupted service, and supplemental thermoelectric plants have been built to substitute the hydroelectric power stations.

Figure 4:
A comparison of our SLAC % change of *RGDPppp* at chained (in Mil. 2011 USD (Average)) with that of Colombia (1951 – 2014)

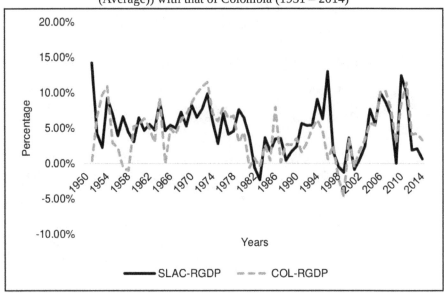

Source: (PWT, 2019).
Author's creation

education system has grown exponentially since the 1960s, and education funding has increased five-fold. As a result of the increase in funds, Colombia's primary school enrollment rate more than doubled, resulting in a six-fold rise in secondary school enrollment and an increase in university enrollment. Despite this funding progress, there is a gap in equal access, opportunities, and quality of education in Colombia between the rural and urban areas. An example of this gap is the location of most of the nation's universities established in big cities.

Columbian students in their respective uniforms.

In light of these disparities, the Colombian government introduced a new initiative within the last two decades to address the inequalities in the educational system. In 2002, Colombia's government launched a comprehensive academic improvement program called the *revolución educativa.*

The *revolución educativa* reform is a complete transformation of the nation's educational system, aimed at improving the educational system's quality and increasing access across the country, especially in rural areas. Colombia's Ministry of Education (ME), the Ministerio de Educación Nacional, regulates all levels of the educational system in all 32 states/departments of the nation. In Colombia, the ME also administers academic accordance and accreditation within the ministry's regulations and guidelines.

The state's authority of education is called the Secretariat of Education/Secretaría de Educación. The Federal ME outlines each grade level's educational learning objectives and subject areas. Still, schools can organize their specific study plans at the lower levels per region, state, and community. Per the 2010 constitutional mandate, the basic education cycle in Colombia became free and compulsory for all citizens between the ages of 5–15. At the university level, fees are based on the individual's socioeconomic background.

The Columbia ME offers two options for the school calendar, known as the "A" and "B" calendars, to its residents. Most states/departments use calendar A, which consists of two semesters from February to November. The second calendar is the B-calendar, divided into two semesters but runs from September to June. In addition to the reform, efforts were made in the 2010 Colombian mandate (passed by the Colombian Constitutional Court) that all public primary schools should be accessible to all its citizens. In 2012, the constitutional commission was extended to public secondary schools.

As a result of these policies, Colombia's educational budget increased by 5.75% in 2015. This policy aims to make Colombia the most civilized and developed country in the Latin Americas by 2025. Recent data shows increasing access to the educational system translate's into an

142

increased rate in educational attainment levels, especially in students from low-income populations. This implies that students from all economic backgrounds in Colombia benefit from increased educational spending and opportunities.

Figure 5
A comparison of our SLAC *HDI* (average) with that of Colombia (1950 – 2014)

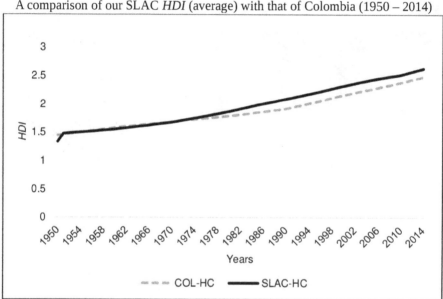

Source: (PWT, 2019).
Author's creation

Figure 5 shows Colombia's Human Development Index *(HDI)* compared to the SLAC moving average from 1950–2014. Figure 5 depicts Colombia at par with the benchmark moving average from 1950–1978 and underperforming the average from 1979–2014. This implies that Colombia's *HDI* growth pattern shows that the national literacy rate in the country is at par with that of our SLAC from 1950–1978 and underperformed our benchmark moving average from 1979–2014 on residents' years of schooling and return to education (PWT, 2019).

National University of Colombia, School of Engineering

SUMMARY

Education Policy Orientation Main Findings:

- Spanish is the instructional language in the country, but some private schools operate using English, German, or French as their instructional language.
- Basic education is free and mandatory.
- Textbooks are loaned out to low-income households.
- At the university level, fees are set according to each student's socioeconomic status and background.
- English was added as a foreign language to the overall education plan after the launch of the 2004 National Bilingual Program by the ME.

Policies that Moved the Country Forward:

- In 1886, a law was passed into the constitution that the ME regulates the education system.
- 10% of the government's budget must be spent on the country's education system.
- Bill 1064 of 2006 and the 2888 decree of 2007 provide integrated technical degrees and university degrees that link education for employment and human development.
- Columbia commits 4.5% of its *GDP* to education.
- English is part of the nation's curriculum, but bilingualism is the nation's standard.

Policies Implication and Recommendation:

These different sets of education growth policies provide enormous lessons that other economies can learn. These lessons come with their own sets of challenges as to how economic growth, development, and stability strategies can affect Human Capital *(HC)* and Capital Structure *(CS)* formation enhancement in an economy.

- According to the Institute of International Education, Colombia is ranked 22nd in the world and 3rd in South America in education spending. Still, with 55% of children attending rural schools dropping out before concluding their studies, it is recommended that more programs be introduced that ensure the national student graduate rate increases.

- Easy access to educational services is still a significant problem in rural areas. It is estimated that about 2 in 10 children living in rural areas don't attend school. Although 4.6% of the nation's Gross Domestic Product *(GDP)* is invested in the country's education system, only 0.5% of the budget is spent in rural communities; on the other hand, rural education represents 80% of the educational offer, with many isolated schools and some of them lacking electricity. It is recommended that more resources be channeled to these areas, and a decentralized budgeting system will help promote the educational needs of the rural communities.

- The education records in Colombia show that the enrollment rate in early childhood and tertiary education has more than doubled, and students spend two additional years at school than 20 years ago. It is recommended that the ME in Colombia also pay attention to the quality of the education system and not just the enrollment rate, although the nation is among the top countries to show a significant improvement in reading in the 2012 Organisation for Economic Cooperation and Development (OECD) Program for International Student Assessment (PISA).

Contribution to Colombia's Literature on Human Capital and Economic Growth:

Although an aggregate model was used to compare Colombia with the SLAC, this study contributes to the literature on the role of *HC* in economic growth and development by highlighting the essential educational policies passed by the Colombian government and how these policies affected the *HDI* level of the Colombian economy. Studies that have delved into Colombia's economy include (Barro, 1991 & 1993; Birchenall, 20001; Florez et al., 2003; Rubio, 1997; Cardenas & Ponton, 1995 & 2001; Riascos & Vargas, 2011; Marotta et al., 2007; and Cardenas, 2001).

The theoretical formulation of the relationship between *HC* and economic growth in Colombia has been studied by (Agiomigianakis et al., 2002; Gillis et al., 1992; Osiobe, 2019, 2020a, 2020b, & 2020c). The theoretical formulation of the relationship between *HC* and economic growth consistently predicts that knowledge embodied in humans is essential for innovation, productivity, and economic growth. However, this relationship was not consistent in all studies; for example, (Devarajan et al., 1996; Temple, 1999; Quiggin, 1999 & 2002).

REFERENCE

Agiomirgianakis, G., Asteriou, D., & Monastiriotis, V. (2002). Human Capital and Economic Growth Revisited: A Dynamic Panel Data Study. International Advances in Economic Research, 8(3), 177-187. https://doi.org/10.1007/BF02297955

Barro, J. R. (1991). Human Capital and Growth in Cross-Country Regressions. The Quarterly Journal of Economics, 407-443. https://doi.org/10.2307/2937943

Barro, R. J., & Lee, J.-W. (1993). International Comparisons of Educational Attainment. Journal of Monetary Economics The Economic Fluctuation and Growth Program: NBER Working Paper No. 4349, 32(3), 363-394. https://doi.org/10.3386/w4349

Birchenall, J. A. (2001). Income distribution, human capital, and economic growth in Colombia. Journal of Development Economics, 66(1), 271-287. https://doi.org/10.1016/S0304-3878(01)00162-6

Cardenas, M. (2001). Economic growth in Colombia: A Reversal of 'Fortune'? CID Working Paper No. 83.

Cardenas, M., & Ponton, A. (1995). Growth and convergence in Colombia: 1950-1990. Journal of Development Economics, 47(1), 5-37. https://doi.org/10.1016/0304-3878(95)00003-8

Devarajan, S., Swaroop, V., & Zou, H.-f. (1996). The Composition of Public Expenditure and Economic Growth. Journal of Monetary Economics, 37(2), 313-344. https://doi.org/10.1016/S0304-3932(96)90039-2

Florez, C. E., Ribero, R., & Samper, B. (2003). Health, Nutrition, Human Capital and Economic Growth in Colombia 1995-2000. Documento CEDE ISSN 1657-7191.

Gillis, M., Perkins, D. H., Roemer, M., & Snodgrass, D. R. (1992). Economics of Development. New York: W.W. Norton & Company, Inc.

Google Earth. (2019, 3 5). Google Earth. (Google) Retrieved 3 5, 2019, from https://www.google.com/earth/

Marotta, D., Mark, M., Blom, A., & Thorn, K. (2007). Human Capital and University-Industry Linkages' Role in Fostering Firm Innovation: An Empirical Study of Chile and Colombia. The World Bank Group Policy Research Working Papers. https://doi.org/10.1596/1813-9450-4443

Osiobe, E. U. (2019). A Literature Review of Human Capital and Economic Growth. Business and Economic Research, 9(4), 179-196. https://doi.org/10.5296/ber.v9i4.15624

Osiobe, E. U. (2020). Human Capital and Economic Growth in Latin America: A Cointegration and Causality Analysis. The Economics and Finance Letters, 218-235. https://doi.org/10.18488/journal.29.2020.72.218.235

Osiobe, E. U. (2020). Human Capital, Capital Stock Formation, and Economic Growth: A Panel Granger Causality Analysis. Journal of Economics and Business, 569-580. https://doi.org/10.31014/aior.1992.03.02.221

Osiobe, E. U. (2020). Understanding Latin America's Educational Orientations: Evidence from 14 Nations. Education Quarterly Review, 249-260. https://doi.org/10.31014/aior.1993.03.02.137

Osiobe, Ejiro U. (2021). An Overview of Colombia's Educational Policies. Economic Development Educational Research, Abuja: The Ane Osiobe International Foundation.

Penn World Table Equation: Human Capital in PWT 9.0. (2019). PWT 9.0. (Penn World Table) Retrieved 10 6, 2019, from https://www.rug.nl/ggdc/docs/human_capital_in_pwt_90.pdf

Quiggin, J. (1999). Human capital Theory and Education Policy in Australia. Australian Economic Review, 32(2), 130-44. https://doi.org/10.1111/1467-8462.00100

Quiggin, J. (2002). Human Capital Theory and Education Policy in Australia. Australian Economic Review, Volume 32, Issue 2. https://doi.org/10.1111/1467-8462.00100

Riascos, A. J., & Vargas, J. F. (2011). Violence and growth in Colombia: A review of the quantitative literature. The economics of peace and security journal, 6(2), 15-20. https://doi.org/10.15355/epsj.6.2.15

Rubio, M. (1997). Perverse Social Capital-Some Evidence from Colombia. Journal of Economic Issues, 31(3), 805-816. https://doi.org/10.1080/00213624.1997.11505966

Schwab, K. (2018). The Global Competitiveness Report. Geneva: World Economic Forum.

Temple, J. (1999). A Positive Effect of Human Capital on Growth. Economic Letter, 65(1), 131-134. https://doi.org/10.1016/S0165-1765(99)00120-2

World Development Index Group, (2019, June 11). The World Bank. (World Development Indicators) Retrieved 3 18, 2019, from https://data.worldbank.org/region/latin-america-and-caribbean

Yale Center for Environmental Law & Policy; Center for International Earth Science Information Network; World Economic Forum. (2018). The 2018 Environmental Performance Index. Environmental Performance Index.

VENEZUELA

INTRODUCTION

Officially known as the Bolivarian Republic of Venezuela, Venezuela is located at the top northern end of South America. The country is the 32nd largest globally and the 6th largest in South America (Google Earth (GE), 2019). With 28.9 million people in 2018, the nation ranks 50th in the world by population (World Development Index (WDI), 2019). Regarding the Global Competitive Index (GCI), Venezuela ranks 127th out of 140 countries. Venezuela is ranked 51st in the world and 4th in Latin America in the 2018 Environmental Performance Index (EPI) (Yale Center for Environmental Law & Policy (YCELP), 2018).

The nation has the world's largest oil reserves, and the oil industry accounts for a majority of all exports and accounts for more than half of state

Figure 1:
Venezuela on the continental map of Latin America

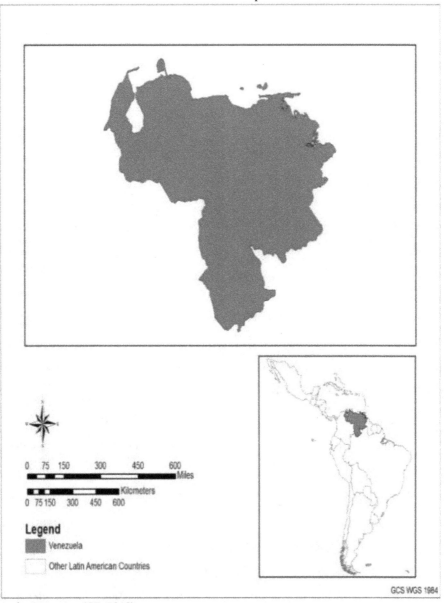

Author's creation (GE, 2019)
*Gray - specific country of interest

revenues. Today, production in the oil industry is down because the federal government mismanages the state-owned Petróleos de Venezuela, S.A. (PDVSA) oil company. In the study, the Selected Latin America and the Caribbean (SLAC) countries that will be studied as a comparison benchmark are Argentina, Bolivia, Brazil, Chile, Colombia, Costa Rica, Honduras, Mexico, Nicaragua, Panama, Peru, El Salvador, Uruguay, and Venezuela (excluded).

PDVSA oil Towers in Maracaibo

Venezuela's primary economic sectors are commerce, tourism, and education. In the 20th century, the nation of Venezuela grew from a relatively poor agricultural community to an urbanized one. This urbanization shift was possible by the country exploiting its petroleum reserves. However, these changes have led to an imbalance among the nation's socioeconomic regions and groups. Also, the big cities in Venezuela have seen massive uncontrolled migration from rural communities and mass international immigration from neighboring nations. Many SLAC, including Venezuela, have urban poverty, widespread governmental patronage, corruption, and massive foreign debt. The country's political and social ills have been met by natural disasters such as the great floods in 1999.

Figure 2 shows Venezuela's Real Gross Domestic Product purchasing power parity (*RGDPppp*) 1981 = 100 from 1950–2014 compared to the SLAC moving average. Figure 2 depicts Venezuela marginally at par with the

Figure 2:
A comparison of our SLAC *RGDPppp* at chained
(in Mil. 2011 USD (average)) with that of Venezuela (1950 – 2014) 1981 = 100

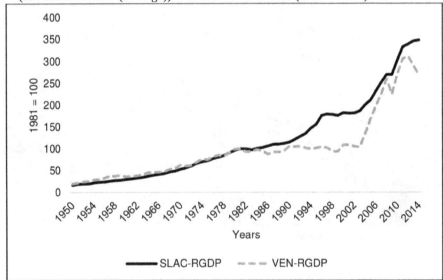

Source: (Penn World Tables (PWT), 2019).
Author's creation

SLAC moving average from 1950–1982 underperformed the benchmark moving average from 1983–2014, which trends are similar to that of Figure 3. This implies that, when the numbers in Figure 2 are converted to an index of 1981 = 100 to measure the change in the value of their *RGDPppp*, Venezuela under-performed the SLAC by a significant margin to see the direction of production in the economy.

Venezuela's economy is based primarily on producing, exploiting, and exporting petroleum. Between 1940 and 1970, the nation was the world's largest petroleum exporter. Today, the country remains one of the principal players in the oil export market and one of its primary partners in the United States (US). For many decades, the Venezuelan economy has relied on revenue from the petroleum industry to diversify and modernize other sectors of its economy. As a result of the slogan, "sembrando el petróleo" ("sowing the oil"), has been used in the country since the 1940s. The deposits of nickel, iron ore, coal, bauxite (the ore of aluminum), and hydroelectric power have also helped expand the nation's economy.

In the 1960s, the Venezuelan government implemented import-substitution economic policies that increased tariffs on international products to limit its importation of manufactured goods while subsidizing domestic products to grow its local manufacturing industry. In the 1970s, the Venezuelan government shifted its economic policies to socialism-oriented ones and went fully socialist in 2006 during the Hugo Chávez administration. The government nationalized the oil, gas, and iron ore industries.

Figure 3 shows the trends as Figure 2, with Venezuela's *RGDPppp* actual numbers being at par with our SLAC from 1950–1982 and underperforming from 1983–2014. By the 21st century, the nation's economy was pressured by massive foreign debt, high unemployment, rapid population growth, and illegal immigration. However, today, the economic situation has improved; around 2007, the nation had paid off some of its foreign debt. Primary and secondary education in Venezuela is free and compulsory between the ages of 6–15. This educational policy has led to more than nine-tenths of the Venezuelan population, age 15 and older, being literate. Recent economic urbanization and modernization that started in the 20th century significantly improved Venezuela's socioeconomic structure and educational system. The economic difficulties of the 1980s and 1990s governmental mismanagement still affect the system.

Figure 3:
A Comparison of our SLAC $RGDP_{ppp}$ at chained
(in Mil. 2011 USD (average)) with that of Venezuela (1950 – 2014)

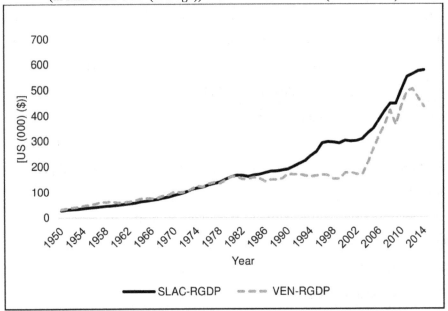

Source: (PWT, 2019).
Author's creation

Although Venezuela significantly increased the state's educational expenditure in the 20th century, almost half the money was spent on universities. In contrast, the primary and secondary educational levels suffered from low-quality equipment, unqualified teachers, and high student dropout rates. To solve this problem, the Venezuelan government began restructuring the educational system in the late 1990s. Today, the country faces many current socioeconomic concerns, including, but not limited to, violence on the streets, hyperinflation, an increasingly politicized military, and shortages of essential consumer goods and medical supplies. The overdependence on the petroleum industry and the mining industry's irresponsible mining operations has endangered the rainforest and indigenous peoples in the rural areas.

Figure 4:
A comparison of our SLAC % change of *RGDPppp* at chained (in Mil. 2011 USD (average)) with that of Venezuela (1951 – 2014)

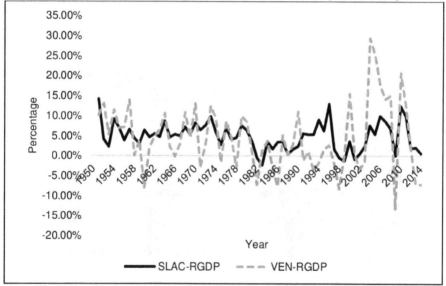

Source: (PWT, 2019).
Author's creation

Figure 4 shows Venezuela as more negative volatile than our SLAC from 1950–2014. This implies that the nation's economy experienced more negative economic shocks between 1950–2002 and a few positive ones between 2003–2010. According to the Wall Street Journal and Heritage Foundation, the nation has the weakest property rights laws in the world, scoring only 5.0 out of 100. Venezuela operates a command system economy, and its primary source of revenue is the petroleum sector, accounting for a third of the nation's *GDP*; the oil industry also accounts for 80% of the nation's net exports and more than half of the federal government revenues. Venezuela sells the least expensive petrol in the national market world due to the subsidization of the product to its consumer. Since the early 20th century, Venezuela has played a significant role in the trade of natural resources, and the nation is one of the founding members of The Organization of the Petroleum Exporting Countries (OPEC). Due to the 1980s oil glut, the nation's external debt and economic crisis increased, leading to a 100% peak in inflation rate in 1996 and a 66% rise in poverty rates.

Wayuu indigenous people learn to read and write. © Franklin Reyes.

Due to the Bolivarian Missions program, Venezuela made some socioeconomic progress in its communities in the 2000s, especially in education, health, and poverty alleviation issues. The government was jumpstarted by some of the United Nations Millennium Development Goals

(UN-MDG), agreed upon by 188 countries worldwide in September 2000. A new economic development plan launched in August 2018 proposed policies that will remove five zeroes and considerable devaluation of the nation's currency, an increase in the nation's minimum, massive state control of the economy, and blatant disregard for the rule of law.

Simón Bolívar University. © Joelazo

The current law governing the Venezuelan higher educational system dates back to the 1970s, and all stakeholders involved in the debate over higher education agree that the educational requirements of the nation need to be updated. In 2007, then-President Chavez introduced the new Bolivarian curriculum for privately and publicly run schools in the country. A new law was passed in 2009 granting more control over the country's communal councils over curriculum development. The universities operate independently of the government but are publicly funded by the government. However, the universities sovereign administrating rights ended in 2009 when a new amendment to the educational law was passed. Since the new educational law was passed in 2009, many university stakeholders in Venezuela have been fighting to avoid further erosion of their autonomy. However, with the establishment and expansion of new publicly run universities, the six state universities have been severely underfunded in line with new laws passed on federal funding policies.

Figure 5:
A Comparison of our SLAC *HDI* (average) with that of Venezuela (1950 – 2014)

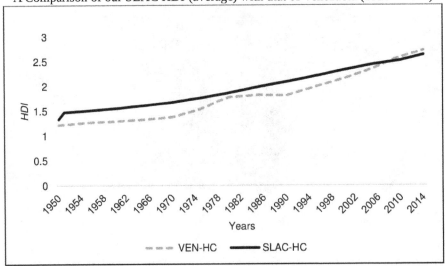

Source: (PWT, 2019).
Author's creation

The 21st-century educational reforms and outreach programs have improved the Venezuelan literacy rate, increased the number of children between the ages of 1–9 enrolled in primary school, and increased secondary school enrollments. These enrollment increases have led to a rise in the

160

enrollment rate at the tertiary level. However, the government administration made few policies to support this enrollment growth, leaving the universities and their students in a precarious position.

Figure 5 shows Venezuela's Human Development Index *(HDI)* compared to the SLAC moving average from 1950–2014. Figure 5 depicts Venezuela underperforming the benchmark moving average from 1950–2014.

Bolivarian University of Venezuela in Maturin

SUMMARY

Education Policy Orientation Main Findings:

- Primary and secondary education in Venezuela is free and compulsory between the ages of 6–15.
- Public education from preschool to university is free.
- The ME governs the nation's education system.
- In addition to the country's free basic and university education law, policies, and services guarantee continuing education are heavily promoted in Venezuela.

Policies that Moved the Country Forward:

- The country passed a 2009 education reform law.
- About 20% of the national budget is assigned to the education sector.
- As of 1995, the nation allocated about 5% of its *GDP* to public education.
- The 1980 law of organic education, *Ley Organica de Educacion,* was established in articles 14 (*Ley de Educacion 1940*), 15, 16, and 23 to promote and improve the nation's education standard.
- *In 1969 the government entered a revision process of the whole educational system called La Reforma educative.*

Policies Implication and Recommendation:

When the lights went out in the nation of Venezuela's schools, this was one of the hardest blows for the country's education systems, and schools were shut down for several days as it brought the system to darkness and desperation.

- The economic crisis and the nation's educational policies have made the Venezuelan government force public and private university professors, (non)academic workers, and students to search for new jobs outside the country or leave the country.

Most, if not all, of the Venezuelan education issues and policy implications, revolve around the nation's political stability. It is advised that a more economical scalable structure be adopted to move forward.

Contribution to Venezuela Literature on Human Capital and Economic Growth:

This study contributes to the literature on the role of Human Capital *(HC)* in economic growth and development by highlighting the critical educational policies passed by the Venezuelan government and how these policies affected the *HDI* level of the Venezuelan economy. Studies that have delved into Venezuela's economy include (Corrales & Penfold, 2011; Salas, 2005; Manzano & Monaldi, 2010; Purcell, 2013; Hassan, 1975; Nakatani & Herrera, 2008; Motta, 2010). The theoretical formulation of the relationship between *HC* and economic growth in Venezuela has been studied by (Bello et al. 2011; Hausmann, 2001; Zimmerman & Chu, 2013; Agnani & Iza, 2009; Brown & Lawson, 1989; Aitken et al., 1996). The theoretical formulation of the relationship between *HC* and economic growth consistently predicts that knowledge embodied in humans is essential for innovation, productivity, and economic growth. However, this relationship was inconsistent in some studies; for example (Benhabib & Spiegel, 1994 & 2005; Quiggin, 1999 & 2002).

REFERENCE

Agnani, B., & Iza, A. (2009). Growth in an Oil Abundant Economy: The Case of Venezuela. Journal of Applied Economics, 14(1), 61-79. https://doi.org/10.1016/S1514-0326(11)60005-6

Aitken, B., Harrison, A., & Lipsey, R. E. (1996). Wages and foreign ownership a comparative study of Mexico, Venezuela, and the United States. Journal of International Economics, 40(3-4), 345-371. https://doi.org/10.1016/0022-1996(95)01410-1

Bello, O. D., Blyde, J. S., & Restuccia, D. (2011). Venezuela's Growth Experience. Latin American Journal of Economics, 48(2), 199-226. https://doi.org/10.4067/S0719-04332011000200005

Benhabib, J., & Spiegel, M. M. (1994). The role of human capital in economic development evidence from aggregate cross-country data. Journal of Monetary Economics, Elsevier, vol. 34(2), pages 143-173. https://doi.org/10.1016/0304-3932(94)90047-7

Benhabib, J., & Spiegel, M. M. (2005). Chapter 13 Human Capital and Technology Diffusion. Handbook of Economic Growth, 1(A), 935-966. https://doi.org/10.1016/S1574-0684(05)01013-0

Brown, L. A., & Lawson, V. A. (1989). Polarization Reversal, Migration Related Shift in Human Resource Profiles, and Spatial Growth Policies: A Venezuelan Study. International Regional Science Review, 12(2), 165-188. https://doi.org/10.1177/016001768901200204

Corrales, J., & Penfold, M. (2011). Dragon in the Tropics: Hugo Chavez and the Political Economy of Revolution in Venezuela. Washington, DC: The Brooking Institution.

Google Earth. (2019, 3 5). Google Earth. (Google) Retrieved 3 5, 2019, from https://www.google.com/earth/

Hassan, M. F. (1975). Economic growth and employment problems in Venezuela: An analysis of an oil-based economy. Illinois: Web.

Hausmann, R. (2001). Venezuela's growth implosion: A neo-classical story? Kennedy School of Government: Harvard University Working Paper.

Manzano, O., & Monaldi, F. (2010). The Political Economy of Oil Contract Renegotiation in Venezuela. In The Natural Resources Trap: Private Investment without Public Commitment. London: The MIT Press. https://doi.org/10.7551/mitpress/9780262013796.003.0020

Motta, S. C. (2010). Populism's Achilles' Heel: Popular Democracy beyond the Liberal State and the Market Economy in Venezuela. Latin American Perspectives, 38(1), 28-46. https://doi.org/10.1177/0094582X10384208

Nakatani, P., & Herrera, R. (2008). Structural Change and Planning of the Economy in Revolutionary Venezuela. Review of Radical Political Economics, 40(3), 292-299. https://doi.org/10.1177/0486613408320019

Osiobe, E. U. (2019). A Literature Review of Human Capital and Economic Growth. Business and Economic Research, 9(4), 179-196. https://doi.org/10.5296/ber.v9i4.15624

Osiobe, E. U. (2020). Human Capital and Economic Growth in Latin America: A Cointegration and Causality Analysis. The Economics and Finance Letters, 218-235. https://doi.org/10.18488/journal.29.2020.72.218.235

Osiobe, E. U. (2020). Human Capital, Capital Stock Formation, and Economic Growth: A Panel Granger Causality Analysis. Journal of Economics and Business, 569-580. https://doi.org/10.31014/aior.1992.03.02.221

Osiobe, E. U. (2020). Understanding Latin America's Educational Orientations: Evidence from 14 Nations. Education Quarterly Review, 249-260. https://doi.org/10.31014/aior.1993.03.02.137

Osiobe, Ejiro U. (2021). An Overview of Venezuela's Educational Policies. Economic Development Educational Research, Abuja: The Ane Osiobe International Foundation.

Penn World Table Equation: Human Capital in PWT 9.0. (2019). PWT 9.0. (Penn World Table) Retrieved 10 6, 2019, from https://www.rug.nl/ggdc/docs/human_capital_in_pwt_90.pdf

Purcell, T. F. (2013). The Political economy of Social Production Companies in Venezuela. Latin American Perspective, 40(3), 146-168. https://doi.org/10.1177/0094582X13476007

Quiggin, J. (1999). Human capital Theory and Education Policy in Australia. Australian Economic Review, 32(2), 130-44. https://doi.org/10.1111/1467-8462.00100

Quiggin, J. (2002). Human Capital Theory and Education Policy in Australia. Australian Economic Review, Volume 32, Issue 2. https://doi.org/10.1111/1467-8462.00100

Salas, J. M. (2005). Ethnicity and Revolution: The Political Economy of Racism in Venezuela. Latin American Perspectives, 32(2), 72-91. https://doi.org/10.1177/0094582X04273869

World Development Index Group, (2019, June 11). The World Bank. (World Development Indicators) Retrieved 3 18, 2019, from https://data.worldbank.org/region/latin-america-and-caribbean

Yale Center for Environmental Law & Policy; Center for International Earth Science Information Network; World Economic Forum. (2018). The 2018 Environmental Performance Index. Environmental Performance Index.

Zimmerman, M. A., & Chu, H. M. (2013). Motivation, Success, and Problems of Entrepreneurs in Venezuela. Journal of Management Policy and Practice, 14(2), 76-90.

BRAZIL

INTRODUCTION

The nation of Brazil occupies about 50% of South America. It is the 5th biggest country by landmass globally and the largest country in South America (Google Earth (GE), 2019). With a population of about 209.5 million people as of 2018, the country ranks 6th globally by population (World Development Index (WDI), 2019). Brazil is ranked 69th in the world and 7th in the Latin Americas in the 2018 Environmental Performance Index (EPI)--(Yale Center for Environmental Law & Policy (YCELP) 2018).

In the 16th century, Brazil was known for its sugar trade in the international market, but in the 17th century, the nation's sugar industry saw a downturn due to the rise of the Caribbean sector. In the 18th century, there was a gold boom in the country after the discovery of Minas Gerais. In the

Figure 1:
Brazil on the continental map of Latin America

Author's creation (GE, 2019)
*Gray - specific country of interest

19th century, the Brazilian economy experienced a coffee boom that led to rapid growth, making Brazil the primary global producer of coffee, producing an equivalent of 75% of the total global coffee production (Loman, 2014).

It is estimated that Brazil's export of coffee in the international market was equal to 10% of its total Gross Domestic Product *(GDP)*. Due to the global recession, overproduction, and a fall in demand for the coffee price by 50% between 1929–1930, the Brazilian government found it hard to maintain the gold standard (Loman, 2014). In the study, the Selected Latin America and the Caribbean (SLAC) countries that will be studied as a comparison benchmark are Argentina, Bolivia, Brazil (excluded), Chile, Colombia, Costa Rica, Honduras, Mexico, Nicaragua, Panama, Peru, El Salvador, Uruguay, and Venezuela.

Figure 2:
Economic Century Highlight

16th Century rise of the sugar trade market

17th Century rise of the Caribbean sector

18th Gold boom (Minas Gerais)

19th Coffee economic boom

Author's creation

Figure 3 shows Brazil's Real Gross Domestic Product purchasing power parity (*RGDPppp*) 1981 = 100 index from 1950–2014 compared to the SLAC's moving average. Figure 3 depicts Brazil marginally underperforming the SLAC moving average between 1950–1970; from 1971-1974,

169

Figure 3:
A comparison of our SLAC *RGDPppp* at chained (in Mil. 2011 USD (average))
with that of Brazil (1950 – 2014) 1981 = 100

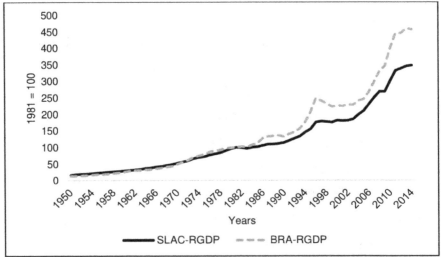

Source: (Penn World Tables (PWT), 2019).
Author's creation

Brazil was at equilibrium with the moving average, and from 1975–2014, Brazil outperformed the SLAC moving average. This implies when the numbers in Figure 4 are converted to an index of 1981 = 100 to measure the changes in the value of their *RGDPppp* to see the direction of production in the economy; Brazil outperformed the SLAC by a significant margin.

After World War II, as a member of the G – 15 (International Monetary Fund (IMF), 2019), Brazil implemented import-substituting industrialization as the country tried to become less dependent on commodity exports (Loman, 2019). In the 1970s, the nation experienced rapid economic growth and invested heavily in the manufacturing and infrastructure industry. This growth helped diversify the country and led to the Brazilian Miracle (Loman, 2019). The country's economy grew by 0.2% in 2018 (WDI,

© Passarinho/Pref.Olinda

2019), and as an emerging market, its economy has benefited from its abundant natural resources, literate population Human Development Index *(HDI)* 75% (PWT, 2019), trade opening, and a diversified industrial base. The nation has a Gross Domestic Product per capita *(GDPper capita)* of 8,920 current USD, and the country has a *GDP* of 1.869 Tril. current USD (WDI, 2019).

Figure 4 shows Brazil's *RGDPppp* actual numbers compared to the SLAC's moving average from 1950–2014. The Brazilian economy is bigger than the SLAC's moving average, as seen in Figure 18. Brazil outperforms the benchmark moving average from 1950–2014.

Figure 5 shows Brazil's similar pattern but is more volatile than the SLAC. Brazil's positive changes are usually more significant than the SLAC moving average, but the nation is at par with the negative changes in most cases. Due to the austerity program imposed by the IMF in late 1979, caused by adverse economic shocks, a 1985 bill was passed to foster growth

Figure 4:
A comparison of our SLAC *RGDPppp* at chained (in Mil. 2011 USD (average))
with that of Brazil (1950 – 2014)

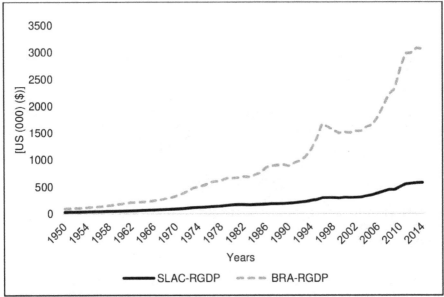

Source: (PWT, 2019).
Author's creation

in the country, and the economy rapidly grew in the '90s, which attracted billions of Foreign Direct Investments (FDIs) into the nation (Library of Congress – Federal Research Division (LoC—FRD), 2006). As of today, Brazil is ranked 72nd out of 140 countries in the Global Competitive Index (GCI) (Schwab, 2018). In Brazil, the state governments are responsible for administering and implementing elementary, primary, and secondary school education based on the national curricular guidelines set forth by the federal government and are complemented by the curricula set at the state and regional levels.

The nation's federal authorities regulate the higher-level educational system in Brazil through the Ministério da Educação (Ministry of Education, (ME)). The Brazilian education system is broadly divided into two systems.

The basic education, known as *educação básica*, includes early childhood education, which is called the *educação infantile*, and enrolls children aged 4–6 years old; elementary education, known as the *ensino fundamental*,

Figure 5:
A comparison of our LAC % change of *RGDPppp* at chained (in Mil. 2011 USD (average)) with that of Brazil (1951 – 2014)

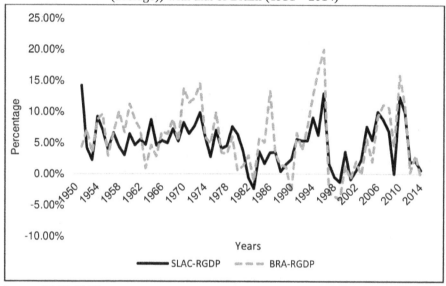

Source: (PWT, 2019).
Author's creation

enrolls children between the ages of 6–15 years; and secondary school, also known as the *ensino médio*, which enrolls children between the ages of 15–18 years. In Brazil, elementary through secondary level education is offered mainly by the public sector, although one can choose to take their child to a private school (WDI, 2017). The second system is higher education, which is known as *educação superior*.

Figure 6 shows Brazil's *HDI* compared to the SLAC's, moving average from 1950–2014. Figure 6 depicts Brazil marginally underperforming the benchmark moving average from 1950–2010 and slightly outperforming the set benchmark from 2011–2014. Brazil's *HDI* showed a steady upward trend, with a mean *HDI* of 1.73, a mean growth rate of 1.18%, and a range of 1.44. This implies that Brazil's *HDI* growth pattern

Figure 6:
A comparison of our LAC *HDI* (average) with that of Brazil (1950 – 2014)

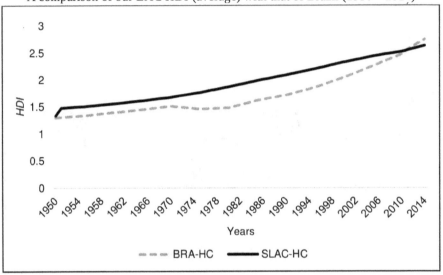

Source: (PWT, 2019).
Author's creation

underperformed that of our SLAC and then gradually started to outperform the SLAC moving average as the economic growth policies were implemented in the nation, leading to a higher return on education based on the schooling years (PWT, 2019).

SUMMARY

Education Policy Orientation Main Findings:

- The first nine years of the Brazilian education system (basic education) are compulsory and free.
- Portuguese is the predominant language used in the Brazilian educational system.
- In 2006, a constitutional amendment bill was passed, creating a fund for the development of basic education and appreciation of the teaching profession, allocating 18%–20% of the national tax revenue to the educational sector.

Policies That Moved the Country Forward:

- The Brazilian constitution of 1988 states that the federal government should spend 18% of its resources on education. At the state and local governments, it is 25%.
- A 2009 constitutional amendment was extended for 13 more years in 2016, and under that same constitutional amendment, 18%–20% of national revenue was allocated to the educational sector.
- Preschool education is optional, while primary and lower secondary education/basic education is compulsory and free.
- The ME was established to regulate the Brazilian education system.
- The ME rehabilitated some of the old National Institute for Education Research (NIER) as an office for education statistics and evaluation and established a National Fund for Basic Education (FUNDEF).

- The ME introduced the Plano Nacional de Educacao (PNE) program, aimed at increasing the number of free mandatory years of schooling in the country by 2024.

- In 2012, the Brazilian government directed 5.3% of the nation's *GDP* to the education sector and increased it to 10% by 2014.

Policy Implications and Recommendations:

The descriptive analysis offers a ground view of the Brazilian economy and the role of education. The 1990 Mercosur Free Trade Agreement (MFTA), a free trade market agreement created in the 1990s between six South American countries: Argentina, Bolivia, Brazil, Chile, Paraguay, and Uruguay, led to some economic implications that extended to the school systems since the agreement impacts political relations, technology, and globalization. The Ministerio de Educación y Cultura (The Ministry of Education and Culture (MEC)) is responsible for all levels of the nation's educational system (Relations Council on Foreign (RCF), 2019). The MFTA, the 2009 amended educational spending bill, and the free basic education policy in the country have played a significant role in economic growth and development. Nevertheless, these growth policies come with their own set of challenges as to how economic growth, development, and stability can affect Human Capital (HC) and Capital Stock Formation (CS).

- Legal laws, like the Brazilian constitution of 1988, state that the federal government should spend 18% of its resources on education, and at the state and local governments, that number should be 25%; in 2009, an amendment was made to the law, increasing the federal spending budget on education to 20%, which will come out of the country's national revenue account; in 2012, the Brazilian government passed a bill that allocated 5.3% of the nation's *GDP* to the education sector, and in 2014 it was increased to 10%. Although all these policies are good and positively impact the national economy, it is recommended that the nation consolidate the source of the educational funds while deregulating the control of spending once the funds have been distributed to state and local authorities. This deregulation will ensure the education district will promote agendas that best fit the needs of their students and ensure that sponsored programs have direct positive impacts on their local economies.

- Preschool education in the nation is optional; it is recommended that this section of the educational system be mandatory and free to ensure a smooth transition into the primary education system.

- The ME's rehabilitation of some old NIER has significantly impacted the Brazilian economy; it is recommended that this program be linked to colleges and universities, hence ensuring funding for the local tribes in the region and marginalized in the country.

- FUNDEF is one of the best policies in the Latin Americas, particularly in Brazil. Because of its success in the country, a similar program should be created to address the low enrollment rate in colleges and universities.

- The introduction of the PNE program that aims to increase the number of free mandatory years of schooling in the country by 2024 is an excellent idea; the only recommendation will be to expand the program to the secondary and tertiary educational levels.

Contribution to Brazil's Literature on Human Capital and Economic Growth:

Although an aggregate economic indicator model was used in the study (see Figure 3 – 6), this study contributes to the literature on the role of *HC* in economic growth and development by highlighting the essential educational policies passed by the Brazilian government and how these policies affected the *HDI* level of the Brazilian economy. Studies that have delved into Brazil's economy include (Barro, 1991; Agenor and Canuto, 2015; Nakabashi and Salvato 2007; Postali, 2009; Bartlett, 2007; Van den Berg, 2017; Cravo et al., 2012; Bertola and Porcile, 2006; Lau et al., 1993). The theoretical and empirical relationship between *HC* and economic growth in Brazil has been studied by (Osiobe 2019; 2020; 2020b; & 2020c). The theoretical formulation of the relationship between *HC* and growth consistently predicts that knowledge embodied in humans is essential for innovation, productivity, and economic growth. However, this relationship does not hold in all cases; for example (Quiggin, 1999 & 2002).

REFERENCE

Agenor, P.-R., & Canuto, O. (2015). Gender equality and economic growth in Brazil: A long-run analysis. Journal of Macroeconomics, 43, 155-172. https://doi.org/10.1016/j.jmacro.2014.10.004

Barro, J. R. (1991). Human Capital and Growth in Cross-Country Regressions. The Quarterly Journal of Economics, 407-443. https://doi.org/10.2307/2937943

Bartlett, L. (2007). Human Capital or Human Connections? The Cultural Meanings of Education in Brazil. Teachers College Record, 109(7), 1613-1636.

Bertola, L., & Porcile, G. (2006). Convergence, trade and industrial policy: Argentina, Brazil, and Uruguay in the international economy, 1900-1980. Revista de Historia Economica-Journal of Iberian and Latin American Economic History, 24(1), 37-67. https://doi.org/10.1017/S021261090000046X

Bertola, L., & Porcile, G. (2012). Argentina, Brazil, Uruguay, and the World Economy: An approach to different convergence and divergence regimes.

Cravo, A. T., Gourlay, A., & Becker, B. (2012). SMEs and regional economic growth in Brazil. Small Business Economics, 38(2), 217-230. https://doi.org/10.1007/s11187-010-9261-z

Google Earth. (2019, 3 5). Google Earth. (Google) Retrieved 3 5, 2019, from https://www.google.com/earth/

International Monetary Fund. (2019, 5 1). IMF Groups and Clubs. (IMF) Retrieved 9 13, 2019, from https://www.imf.org/en/About/Factsheets/A-Guide-to-Committees-Groups-and-Clubs

Lau, A. L., Jamison, T. D., Liu, S.-C., & Rivkin, S. (1993). Education and economic growth some cross-sectional evidence from Brazil. Journal of Development Economics, 41(1), 45-70. https://doi.org/10.1016/0304-3878(93)90036-M

Library of Congress - Federal Research Division. (2006). Country Profile: Bolivia. Washington, D.C.: Library of Congress.

Loman, H. (2014). RaboResearch - Economic Research. (Rabobank) Retrieved 9 13, 2019, from https://economics.rabobank.com/publications/2014/january/brazils-macro-economy-past-and-present/

Nakabashi, L., & Salvato, A. M. (2007). Human Capital Quality in the Brazilian States. Economica, 8(2), 211-229.

Osiobe, E. U. (2019). A Literature Review of Human Capital and Economic Growth. Business & Economic Review, 179-196. https://doi.org/10.5296/ber.v9i4.15624

Osiobe, E. U. (2020). Human Capital and Economic Growth in Latin America: A Cointegration and Causality Analysis. The Economics and Finance Letters, 218-235. https://doi.org/10.18488/journal.29.2020.72.218.235

Osiobe, E. U. (2020). Human Capital, Capital Stock Formation, and Economic Growth: A Panel Granger Causality Analysis. Economics and Business, 569-582. https://doi.org/10.31014/aior.1992.03.02.221

Osiobe, E. U. (2020). Understanding Latin America's Educational Orientations: Evidence from 14 Nations. Higher Education Quarterly, 249-260. https://doi.org/10.31014/aior.1993.03.02.137

Osiobe, Ejiro U. (2021). An Overview of Brazil's Educational Policies. Economic Development Educational Research, Abuja: The Ane Osiobe International Foundation.

Postali, S. A. (2009). Petroleum royalties and regional development in Brazil: The economic growth of recipient towns. Resources Policy, 34(4), 205-213. https://doi.org/10.1016/j.resourpol.2009.03.002

Quiggin, J. (1999). Human capital Theory and Education Policy in Australia. Australian Economic Review, 32(2), 130-44. https://doi.org/10.1111/1467-8462.00100

Quiggin, J. (2002). Human Capital Theory and Education Policy in Australia. Australian Economic Review, Volume 32, Issue 2. https://doi.org/10.1111/1467-8462.00100

Relations Council on Foreign. (2019, Jan 12). CFR. (Council on Foreign Relations)

Retrieved 9 12, 2019, from
https://www.cfr.org/backgrounder/mercosur-south-americas-fractious-trade-bloc

Schwab, K. (2018). The Global Competitiveness Report. Geneva: World Economic Forum.

Van den Berg, H. (2017). Economic Growth and Development 3rd edition. Singapore: World Scientific Publishing Co. Pte. L.td.

World Development Index Group (2019, June 11). The World Bank. (World Development Indicators) Retrieved 3 18, 2019, from
https://data.worldbank.org/region/latin-america-and-caribbean

Yale Center for Environmental Law & Policy; Center for International Earth Science Information Network; World Economic Forum. (2018). The 2018 Environmental Performance Index. Environmental Performance Index.

Ejiro U. Osiobe

PERU

INTRODUCTION

Peru is located in western South America. The nation shares its border with Lake Titicaca, the South Pacific Ocean, Colombia, Brazil, Bolivia, Chile, and Ecuador (Google Earth (GE), 2019). The country is the 19th largest country globally and the 3rd largest in South America (GE, 2019). With 31.9 million people in 2018, the nation ranks 43rd by population (World Development Index (WDI), 2019). Peru was derived from a Quechua Indian word, which means abundant land. Resources like minerals, agriculture, and marine have served as the country's economic foundation, and by the late 20th century, tourism had become a significant sector of Peru's economic growth and development. Regarding the Global Competitive Index (GCI), Peru ranks 63rd out of 140 (Schwab, 2018). In the

Figure 1:
Peru on the continental map of Latin America

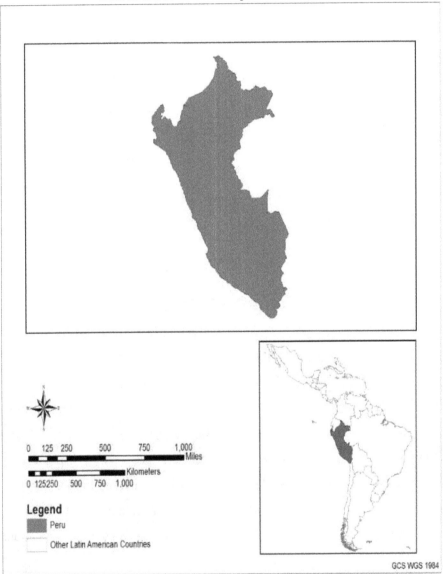

Author's creation (GE, 2019).
*Gray - specific country of interest

2018 Environmental Performance Index (EPI), Peru is ranked 64th in the world and 6th in Latin America (Yale Center for Environmental Law & Policy (YCELP), 2018).

Today, Peru is less-developed, and its economy depends on exporting its raw materials to the international market. The nation ranks among the world's largest bismuth, silver, copper, and fish farming producers. The government has struggled for decades to modernize its economy by promoting nontraditional export products to the international market and supporting local businesses to the needs of residents. With all these efforts made, serious social-economic problems persist in the nation. The country suffers from landslides, earthquakes, El Niño rains, and other natural

UNESCO World Heritage Site *Machu Picchu*, a major tourist attraction © Melinda B Hipple

disasters that have destroyed the nation's agriculture and transportation industries. Because of the natural disasters that plague the land, the agriculture industry can no longer support the country's rapidly growing population. As a result of food shortages this has led to a rise in the prices of imported food products. The food shortage has also created difficulties for the federal government in solving the farming industry problem. In the study, the Selected Latin America and the Caribbean (SLAC) countries that will be studied as a comparison benchmark are Argentina, Bolivia, Brazil, Chile, Colombia, Costa Rica, Honduras, Mexico, Nicaragua, Panama, Peru (excluded), El Salvador, Uruguay, and Venezuela.

Figure 2 shows Peru's Real Gross Domestic Product purchasing power parity (*RGDPppp*) 1981 = 100 index from 1950–2014 as it compares

Figure 2:
A comparison of our SLAC *RGDPppp* at chained
(in Mil. 2011 USD (average)) with that of Peru (1950 – 2014) 1981 = 100

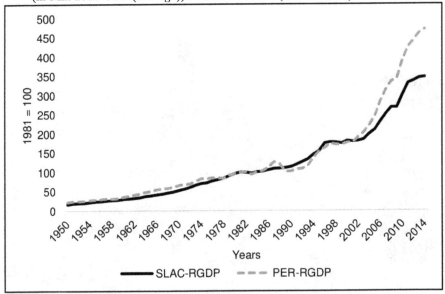

Source: (Penn World Tables (PWT), 2019).
Author's creation

with that of our SLAC. Figure 2 depicts Peru being at par with our bench-mark moving average from 1950–2001, and from 2002–2014, Peru outperformed the SLAC moving average. This implies that the numbers in

Figure 3 are converted to an index of 1981 = 100 to measure the changes in the value of their *RGDPppp* to see the direction of production in the economy. However, the nationalization of their economy created more social-economic problems, including but not limited to high unemployment, high inflation rate, large trade deficit, massive government debt, and strained relationships with the nation's trading partners in the international market.

© Melinda B Hipple

In the 21st century, the country experienced rapid economic growth due to restructuring the national economy from a government-controlled system to a private, more capitalist system. The educational system in Peru has been challenged by a steady percentage increase in young people in its population. As the government spending on compulsory education for ages 6–15 increased, this has weighed a considerable burden on the state's budget. Although enacted in society by law, compulsory education is challenging to enforce, especially outside central business districts. Because of enormous class sizes, unqualified teachers, and inadequate facilities, the standard of education received by children in publicly run schools is of low quality. As a result of the public schools' standards, the middle- and upper class in society send their children to run schools privately.

Figure 3:
A comparison of our SLAC $RGDP_{ppp}$ at chained
(in Mil. 2011 USD (average)) with that of Peru (1950 – 2014)

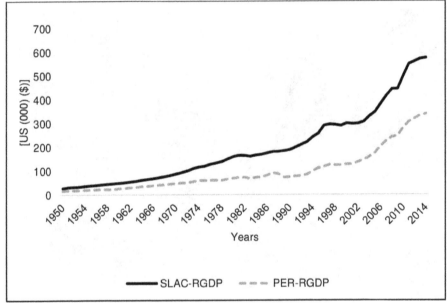

Source: (PWT, 2019).
Author's creation

Figure 3 shows Peru's $RGDPppp$ actual numbers compared to our SLAC moving average from 1950–2014. Figure 3 depicts Peru marginally doing worse than the benchmark moving average from 1950–2014. After the 1980s and 1990s hyperinflation and political revolution, the country has blossomed economically in the last few decades and is a significant tourist attraction.

On the other hand, after the revolution, the educational system has seen a transformation. This is reflected by an ever-increasing number of study-abroad students coming to the country to study for short and long-term

Lima, Peru © Melinda B Hipple

programs. Today, there are more US students in Peru than Peruvian students in US universities. Despite this, Peru still faces challenges in offering equal essential educational opportunities to its citizens. In 1996, Peru's government passed an academic bill that reformed the system by extending free and compulsory primary education to all students between 5–16. The law is called *educación básica* (general stream) *y técnico productive* (technical). But, the second period of mandatory education is somewhat aspirational, as about one-quarter of the secondary education age group doesn't currently enroll in the senior secondary educational level United Nations Educational, Scientific and Cultural Organization (UNESCO), 2019). This trend is especially seen in the rural areas of the country. While the public educational system is accessible in Peru, privately run schools operate at all levels of the educational system. The publicly run and privately run schools abide by the national curriculum the federal government sets.

Figure 4:
A comparison of our SLAC % change of $RGDP_{ppp}$ at chained (in Mil. 2011 USD (Average)) with that of Peru (1951 – 2014)

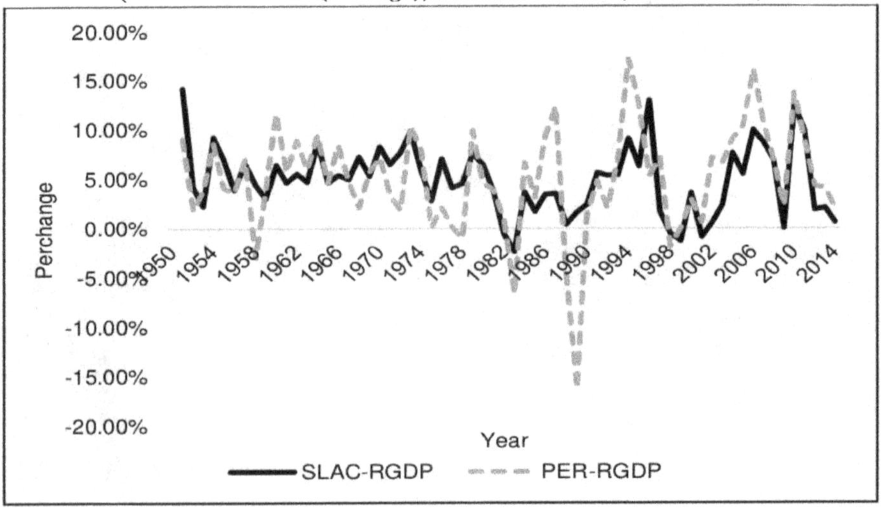

Source: (PWT, 2019).
Author's creation

Figure 4 shows Peru's economic volatility as it compares to that of our SLAC. Figure 4 depicts Peru somewhat at par with our benchmark moving average, with some unique spikes between 1986–1989, 1990–1993, and 1994–1996. The Peru Ministry of Education (ME) sets the educational policies, legislations, and curriculum guidelines—the overseeing authority from preschool education through higher education. On the other hand, the local education authorities in the 25 states of the country administer and implement ministry policies at the primary and secondary education levels.

Figure 5:
A comparison of our LAC *HDI* (average) with that of Peru (1950 – 2014)

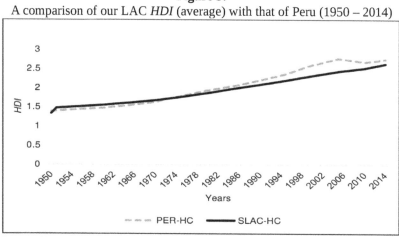

Source: (PWT, 2019).
Author's creation

In 2015, a new higher education authority was created, the Peru Superintendencia Nacional de Educación Superior Universitaria (SUNEDU), or the National Superintendence of University Higher Education. This new office replaced the Asamblea Nacional de Los Rectores (ANR), or the National Assembly of Rectors. The new higher education law seeks to improve educational quality standards within all levels of the educational system. This new body was charged with conducting quality assurance procedures and approving new public and private university licenses. The SUNEDU also had the responsibility of setting higher education policies under the instruction of the ME.

191

SUMMARY

Education Policy Orientation Main Findings:

- Free and compulsory essential education for all residents in the country.
- Public education is free in the nation.
- The nation also provides special education services for its students.

Policies that Moved the Country Forward:

- In 1996, the Peruvian government passed an education reform law that extended the free and mandatory basic education policy to all residents aged 5–16; the program was called *educacion basica y tecnico productiva.*
- The country has a mandated education policy passed in 2008 to ensure private and public schools follow the national curriculum.
- The ME oversees all education levels in the nation.

Policies Implication and Recommendation:

The Peruvian education system is one of the best in South America. It serves its residents from shortly after birth through university levels.

- Although the Peruvian government has improved its education accessibility gaps, its educational system still suffers from performance issues. It is recommended that more student support programs be introduced into the school system, especially for rural students.

- Teachers, teacher training, teaching methodology, and incentives continue to hold back the education system in Peru. It is recommended that these services be improved.

Contribution to Peru's Literature on Human Capital and Economic Growth:

This study contributes to the literature on the role of Human Capital *(HC)* in economic growth and development by highlighting the critical educational policies passed by Peru's government and how these policies affected the *HDI* level of Peru's economy. Studies that have delved into Peru's economy include (Keefer et al., 1998; Burns, 1999; Babb, 1989; Padoch, 1988; Orlove, 1977; Wilson, 2004; Ibarra et al., 2000). The theoretical formulation of the relationship between *HC* and economic growth in Peru has been studied by (Fitzgerald, 1976; Chicoine, 2011; Painter, 1991; Zenon, 2000; Leon, 2014; Urrunaga & Aparicio, 2012; Vinod & Kaushik, 2007; Falaris, 1979; Klein, 2011; Escobal, 2001; Attanasio et al., 2017; Urrutia & Paz, 2015; Escobal & Torero, 2005; Raju & Fitzpatrick, 2010; Charles & Zegarra, 2014; Qadri & Waheed, 2013; Saavedra & Chong, 1999; Behrman et al., 2017). The theoretical formulation of the relationship between *HC* and economic growth consistently predicts that knowledge embodied in humans is essential for innovation, productivity, and economic growth. However, this relationship was not true in all studies (Bils & Klenow, 2000; Levine & Renelt, 1992; Temple, 1999).

REFERENCE

Attanasio, O., Meghir, C., Nix, E., & Salvati, F. (2017). Human capital growth and poverty: Evidence from Ethiopia and Peru. Review of Economic Dynamics, 25, 234-259. https://doi.org/10.1016/j.red.2017.02.002

Babb, F. E. (1989). Between Field and Cooking Pot: The Political Economy of Market women in Peru. Austin: The University of Texas Press.

Behrman, J. R., Schott, W., Mani, S., Crookston, B. T., Dearden, K., Duc, L. T., . . . Stein, A. D. (2017). Intergenerational Transmission of Poverty and Inequality: Parental Resources and Schooling Attainment and Children's Human Capital in Ethiopia, India, Peru, and Vietnam. Economic Development and Cultural Change, 65(4), 657-697. https://doi.org/10.1086/691971

Bils, M., & Klenow, J. P. (2000). Does Schooling Cause Growth? American Economic Review, 90(5), 1160-1183. https://doi.org/10.1257/aer.90.5.1160

Burns, K. (1999). Colonial Habits: Convents and the Spiritual Economy of Cuzco, Peru. Durham and London: Duke University Press. https://doi.org/10.1515/9780822396192

Charles, V., & Zegarra, L. F. (2014). Measuring regional competitiveness through data envelopment analysis: A Peruvian case. Expert System with Application, 41(11), 5371-5381. https://doi.org/10.1016/j.eswa.2014.03.003

Chicoine, D. (2011). Feasting landscapes and political economy at the Early Horizon center of Huambacho, Nepean Valley, Peru. Journal of Anthropological Archaeology, 30(3), 432-453. https://doi.org/10.1016/j.jaa.2011.06.003

Escobal, J. (2001). The determinants of Nonfarm Income Diversification in Rural Peru. World Development, 29(3), 497-508. https://doi.org/10.1016/S0305-750X(00)00104-2

Escobal, J., & Torero, M. (2005). Measuring the Impact of Asset Complementarities: The Case of Rural Peru. Cuadernos de Economia, 42(125), 137-164. https://doi.org/10.4067/S0717-68212005012500007

Falaris, E. M. (1979). The Determinants of Internal Migration in Peru: An Economic

Analysis. Economic Development and Cultural Change, 27(2), 327-341. https://doi.org/10.1086/451096

Fitzgerald, E. V. (1976). Peru: The Political Economy of an Intermediate Regime. Journal of Latin American Studies, 8(1), 53-71. https://doi.org/10.1017/S0022216X00018162

Google Earth. (2019, 3 5). Google Earth. (Google) Retrieved 3 5, 2019, from https://www.google.com/earth/

Ibarra, A. A., Reid, C., & Thorpe, A. (2000). The Political Economy of Marine Fisheries Development in Peru, Chile, and Mexico. Journal of Latin American Studies, 32(2), 503-527. https://doi.org/10.1017/S0022216X00005824

Keefer, D. K., deFrance, S. D., Moseley, M. E., Richardson III, J. B., Satterlee, D. R., & Day-Lewis, A. (1998). Early Maritime Economy and El Nino Events at Quebrada Tacahuay Peru. Science, 281(5384), 1833-1835. https://doi.org/10.1126/science.281.5384.1833

Klein, T. (2011). Military expenditure and economic growth: Peru 1970-1996. Defense and Peace Economics, 15(3), 275-288. https://doi.org/10.1080/102426903200035101

Leon, G. (2014). Civil Conflict and Human Capital Accumulation: The Long-term Effects of Political Violence in Peru. The Journal of Human Resource, 49(3), 634-662.

Levine, R., & Renelt, D. (1992). A Sensitivity Analysis of Cross-Country Growth Regressions. The American Economic Review, 82(4), 942-963.

Orlove, B. S. (1977). Alpacas, Sheep, and Men: The Wool Export Economy and Regional Society in Southern Peru. New York: Academic Press.

Osiobe, E. U. (2019). A Literature Review of Human Capital and Economic Growth. Business and Economic Research, 9(4), 179-196. https://doi.org/10.5296/ber.v9i4.15624

Osiobe, E. U. (2020). Human Capital and Economic Growth in Latin America: A Cointegration and Causality Analysis. The Economics and Finance Letters, 218-235. https://doi.org/10.18488/journal.29.2020.72.218.235

Osiobe, E. U. (2020). Human Capital, Capital Stock Formation, and Economic Growth: A Panel Granger Causality Analysis. Journal of Economics and Business, 569-580. https://doi.org/10.31014/aior.1992.03.02.221

Osiobe, E. U. (2020). Understanding Latin America's Educational Orientations: Evidence from 14 Nations. Education Quarterly Review, 249-260. https://doi.org/10.31014/aior.1993.03.02.137

Osiobe, Ejiro U. (2021). An Overview of Peru's Educational Policies. Economic Development Educational Research, Abuja: The Ane Osiobe International Foundation. DOI:10.47752/aneosiobe.16.170.186

Padoch, C. (1988). Aguaje (Mauritia flexuosa L. F.) in the Economy of Iquitos, Peru. New York: Botanical Garden Press.

Painter, M. (1991). Re-creating Peasant Economy in Southern Peru. In Golden Ages, Dark Ages: Imagining the Past in Anthropology and History (pp. 81-106). Los Angeles: University of California Press. https://doi.org/10.1525/9780520327450-005

Penn World Table Equation: Human Capital in PWT 9.0. (2019). PWT 9.0. (Penn World Table) Retrieved 10 6, 2019, from https://www.rug.nl/ggdc/docs/human_capital_in_pwt_90.pdf

Qadri, F. S., & Waheed, A. (2013). Human capital and economic growth: Cross-country evidence from low, middle, and high-income countries. Progress in Development Studies, 13(2), 89-104. https://doi.org/10.1177/1464993412466503

Raju, S., & Fitzpatrick, B. (2010). Financial Market Development, Economic Development and Growth Diagnostics: An Application to Peru. International Business and Economic Research Journal, 9(9), 39-52. https://doi.org/10.19030/iber.v9i9.624

Saavedra, J., & Chong, A. (1999). Structural reform, institutions, and earnings: Evidence from the formal and informal sectors in urban Peru. The Journal of Development Studies, 35(4), 95-116. https://doi.org/10.1080/00220389908422582

Schwab, K. (2018). The Global Competitiveness Report. Geneva: World Economic Forum.

Temple, J. (1999). A Positive Effect of Human Capital on Growth. Economic Letter, 65(1), 131-134. https://doi.org/10.1016/S0165-1765(99)00120-2

UNESCO Institute for Statistics; Sustainable Development Goals, (2019). UNESCO Institute for Statistics. (United Nations) Retrieved 9 11, 2019, from http://uis.unesco.org/

Urrunaga, R., & Aparicio, C. (2012). Infrastructure and economic growth in Peru. CEPAL Review(107), 145-163. https://doi.org/10.18356/8537fd57-en

Urrutia, C., & Paz, P. (2015). Economic Growth and Wage Stagnation in Peru: 1998-2012. Review of Development Economics, 19(2), 328-345. https://doi.org/10.1111/rode.12145

Vindo, H. D., & Kaushik, S. K. (2007). Human Capital and Economic Growth: Evidence from Developing Countries. The American Economist, 51(1), 29-39. https://doi.org/10.1177/056943450705100103

Wilson, F. (2004). Towards a Political Economy of Roads: Experiences from Peru. Development and Change, 35(3), 525-546. https://doi.org/10.1111/j.1467-7660.2004.00364.x

World Development Index Group, (2019, June 11). The World Bank. (World Development Indicators) Retrieved 3 18, 2019, from https://data.worldbank.org/region/latin-america-and-caribbean

Yale Center for Environmental Law & Policy; Center for International Earth Science Information Network; World Economic Forum. (2018). The 2018 Environmental Performance Index. Environmental Performance Index.

Zenon, Q. M. (2000). Monetary policy in a dollarized economy: The case of Peru. Munich Personal RePEc Archive Paper No. 35530.

Ejiro U. Osiobe

BOLIVIA

INTRODUCTION

Bolivia is a landlocked country in west-central South America. It is the 28th largest country globally by landmass and the 5th largest South American nation (Google Earth (G.E.), 2019). With a 2018 population of 11.3 million people, the country ranks 81st globally by population (World Development Index (WDI), 2019). In the 2018 Environmental Performance Index (EPI), Bolivia is ranked 92nd in the world and 13th in the Latin Americas (Yale Center for Environmental Law & Policy (YCELP), 2018).

Bolivia is among the few countries in the world with two capitals, Sucre and La Paz. The constitutional capital is Sucre, where the Supreme Court is located (World Atlas (W.A.), 2019), while the administrative capital is La Paz, where the nation's executive and legislative branches are located

Figure 1
Bolivia on the continental map of Latin America

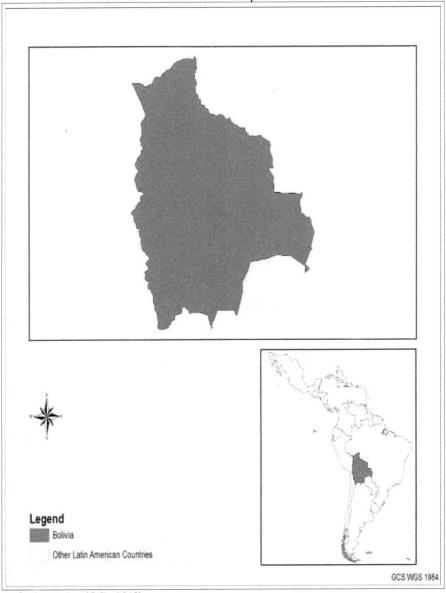

Author's creation (G.E., 2019)
*Gray - specific country of interest

(WA, 2019). In the 20th century, less than one-tenth of Bolivians lived in urban areas, and by 1950, the number had more than doubled (Library of Congress – Federal Research Division (LoC—FRD), 2006). Today, the country's rate of urbanization has more than doubled, with 50% of the population living in cities; this growth has a positive relationship with the nation's population growth (LoC—FRD, 2006). Bolivia is a rich country with

Alternative energy production © Angeoribeiro

many natural resources, including but not limited to mineral deposits, hydrocarbons, petroleum, and natural gas (LoC—FRD, 2006). The nation has shown a steady growth pattern in some economic indicators (see Figures 2, 3, and 4) that helped with economic prosperity and opportunities (Schwab, 2018; Penn World Table (PWT), 2019; Abdullah et al., 2015; WDI, 2019). In

Figure 2 depicts Bolivia marginally outperforming

the study, the Selected Latin America and the Caribbean (SLAC) countries that will be studied as a comparison benchmark are Argentina, Bolivia (excluded), Brazil, Chile, Colombia, Costa Rica, Honduras, Mexico, Nicaragua, Panama, Peru, El Salvador, Uruguay, and Venezuela.

Figure 2 shows Bolivia's (Real Gross Domestic Product purchasing power parity (*RGDPppp*) 1981 = 100 index from 1950–2014 compared to the SLAC's moving average. Figure 2 depicts Bolivia marginally outperforming the SLAC's moving average between 1950 and 1993; from 1994 to 2014, Bolivia exceeded the moving average. When the value in Figure 3 is converted to an index of 1981 = 100 to measure the changes in the value of their *RGDPppp* to see the direction of production in the economy, Bolivia outperformed the SLACs by a significant margin.

Figure 2
A comparison of our SLAC *RGDPppp* at chained (in Mil. 2011 USD (average)) with that of Bolivia (1950 – 2014) 1981 = 100

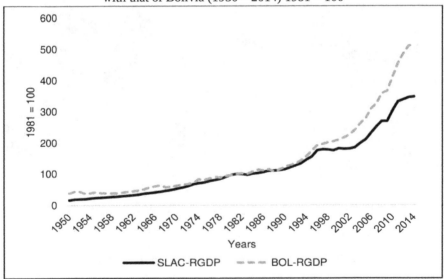

Source: (PWT, 2019).
Author's creation

In the international market, the country is known for its renewable natural resources, including agricultural and forest products, soybeans, and Brazil nuts (LoC—FRD, 2006). Despite its rich renewable and non-renewable natural resources, the nation's growth has been minimal (WDI, 2019). Issues such as production costs and lack of Foreign Direct Investment (FDI) have contributed to the nation's slow growth. The nation's Gross Domestic Product per capita *(GDPper capita)* is 3,500 current USD, and it has a Gross Domestic Product *(GDP)* of 40.3 Bil current USD (WDI, 2019). The country's economy grew by 4.7% in 2018 (WDI, 2019), and as an emerging market, its economy benefits from its literate population's Human Development Index *(HDI)*, which is 69% (PWT, 2019). Today, the nation ranks as the 105th most competitive nation in the world out of 140 countries listed in the 2018 Global Competitiveness Index Report (GCIR) (Schwab, 2018).

Figure 3

A Comparison of our LAC *RGDPppp* at chained (in Mil. 2011 USD (average)) with that of Bolivia (1950 – 2014)

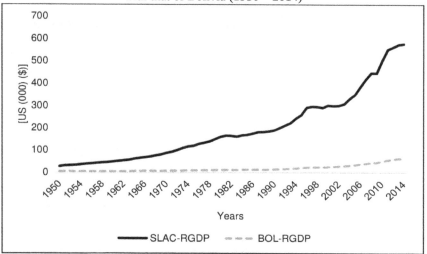

Source: (PWT, 2019).
Author's creation

Figure 3 shows Bolivia's *RGDPppp* actual numbers compared to the SLAC's moving average from 1950–2014. Figure 3 depicts Bolivia underperforming the benchmarked moving average from 1950–2014. This implies that the Bolivian economic well-being and total market value (adjusted for inflation) of domestic goods and services produced in each year from 1950–2014 underperformed that of the moving average of the SLAC.

Bolivia is an impoverished country in Latin America. The economy depends mainly on tin exportation (LoC—FRD, 2006). Its currency fluctuations in the international market have affected its national earnings (WDI, 2019). In the early 1980s, Bolivia's businesses stagnated due to the international market's falling prices for tin production (LoC—FRD, 2006). Also, due to falling prices in the global market and bad harvests, debt default rates went up, and the country's inflation status was rated as hyperinflation. In 1985, the administration of President Víctor Paz Estenssoro passed some of the continent's strictest austerity measures that reduced the nation's inflation rate from 24,000% to less than 10% (LoC—FRD, 2006).

Figure 4 shows Bolivia having similar positive changes to that of the SLAC. In contrast, the negative changes made the nation more volatile to adverse shocks than the SLAC moving average. Due to the adverse shocks, a 1985 bill was passed to foster growth in the country, and the economy rapidly grew in the '90s, which attracted billions of FDIs into the nation (LoC—FRD, 2006).

The administration of president Gonzalo Sánchez de Lozada Bustamente (1993 – 1997) led to the privatization of nearly the entire state-run sectors, but by 2006 president Juan Evo Morales Ayma introduced his socialist ideology that shifted the nation back toward the nationalization of the private industries (World Education News + Review (WEN+R), 2019; LoC—FRD, 2006). Today, the country of Bolivia continues to receive

Foreign Technical Assistance (FTA) and long-term loans from the World Bank (WB), International Monetary Fund (IMF), the International American Development Bank (IADB), and other sovereign nations (Schwab, 2018).

Figure 4

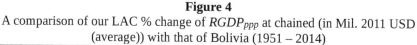
A comparison of our LAC % change of $RGDP_{ppp}$ at chained (in Mil. 2011 USD (average)) with that of Bolivia (1951 – 2014)

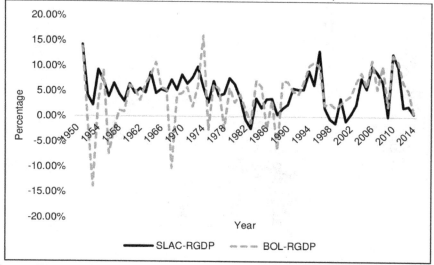

Source: (PWT, 2019).
Author's creation

Like other Latin American nations' educational systems, the Bolivian National Education System (NES) comprises both formal and non-formal sectors. The formal education sector is organized in four cycles: initial or pre-primary (mandatory), primary (compulsory), secondary (optional), and higher education (optional) (WEN+R, 2019). Another policy that has affected the Bolivian education system is the 1990 Mercosur Free Trade Agreement (MFTA). The economic implications of the MFTA to economy extend to the school systems; since the agreement impacts; political relations, technology, and globalization. The Ministry of Education and Culture (MEC) is responsible for all levels of the nation's educational system (Relations Council on Foreign (RCF), 2019).

Bolivian children with llama. © Adam Jones

Figure 5 shows Bolivia's *HDI* compared to the SLAC's moving average from 1950–2014. Figure 5 depicts Bolivia marginally under-performing the benchmark moving average from 1950–1974, being at equilibrium with the benchmark moving average between 1975–1982 and slightly outperforming the moving average from 1983–2014. Bolivia's *HDI* showed a steady upward trend on the actual *HDI*, and the growth rate trend was similar to that of the actual *HDI*, with some steady state growth between 1950–1955, 1981–1990, …, and 2011–2014. This implies that Bolivia's *HDI* growth pattern shows that the national literacy rate in the country underperformed that of the SLAC moving average from 1950–1974, was at equilibrium from 1975–1982, and marginally outperformed the benchmarked moving average from 198 –2014 based on residents' years of schooling and returns to education (PWT, 2019).

Figure 5

A comparison of our LAC *HDI* (average) with that of Bolivia (1950 – 2014)

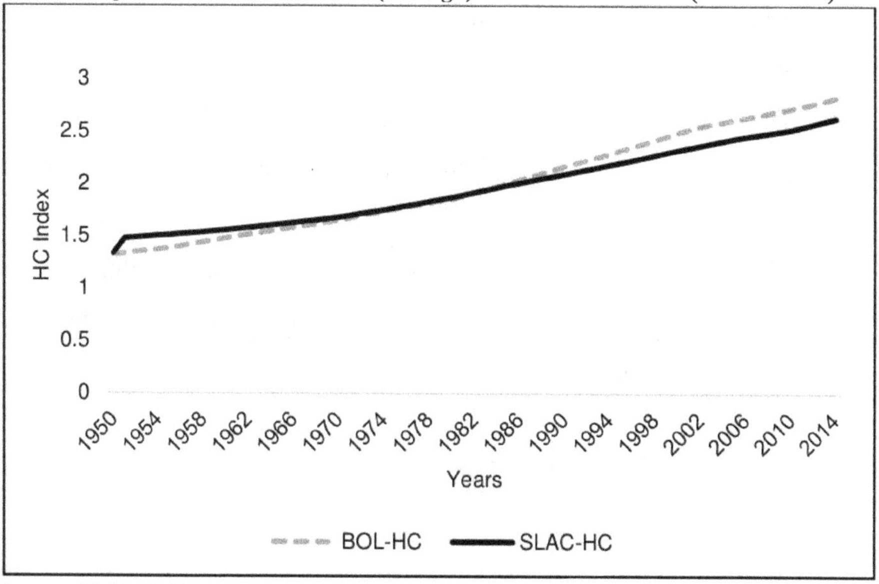

Source: (PWT, 2019)
Author's creation

SUMMARY

Education Orientation Main Finding:

- About 23% of Bolivia's annual budget is spent on the educational system.
- Spanish is the predominant language used in Bolivia's education system.
- The Bolivian Ministry of Education (ME) implemented the plurinational curricula 2013 for the primary and secondary education system.
- Childhood education for children aged 0–6 years, including family and community-basic non-formal education services, is mandatory for children under three years.

Policies that Moved the Country Forward:

- Non-formal education service is free for children under three.
- Education is compulsory for children between the ages of 0–6 years.
- The Bolivian ME has a subdivision called the MEC, which provides program guidelines and standards information.
- The 1994 decentralization education reform helped with educational funding at the local level by improving teachers' training, meeting rural communities' needs, formalizing intercultural bilingual education, and changing the local schools' grading system.
- The nation passed a 2010 Education Law, Avelino Sinani-Elizardo Perez, to make learning more inclusive.

- Easy access to primary education. One notable reform that moved the nation forward is the country's easy access to primary school education, leading to an all-time high enrollment rate of 82% with little difference between gender. As a result of this enrollment increase, children's literacy rate between the ages of 15 and above has reached 95% compared to 80% in 1992, according to the (WDI —Microdata Library, 2019).

Policies Implication and Recommendations:

From our descriptive analysis, one can identify the 2013 plurinational curricula law, the 2010 inclusivity law Avelino Sinani-Elizardo Perez, the 1990 Mercosur Free Trade Agreement, the free childcare service for children three years and under, and the mandatory education are educational growth policies other nations can imitate. Regardless, these policies come with their challenges.

- The mandated 23% of the nation's annual budget to be spent on education was mainly spent on the operating budget and personnel costs. It is recommended that the money be spent on other activities like capital programs and expansions of the schools' infrastructures and acquiring state-of-the-art equipment.

- The country's easy access to primary school education led to an all-time high enrollment rate of 82%, with little difference between gender. As a result of this enrollment increase, the literacy rate of children between the ages of 15 and above has reached 95% compared to 80% in 1992, according to the WDI Microdata Library (WDI—Microdata Library, 2019). Yet, the disparities in the educational system by minority groups persisted. In most cases, whether a child received quality education depended on their residency, gender, ethnicity, and economic status United Nations International Children's Emergency Fund (UNICEF, 2019). It is recommended that the nation takes action to reduce these inequalities in the school system by ensuring inclusivity to promote economic growth and Development.

- Increased enrollment rate has hurt rural school districts in Bolivia. The quality of education became a significant concern to the Bolivian ME as many rural schools lacked adequate infrastructure and essential educational facilities, including but not limited to water and electricity. It is recommended that the Bolivian ME allocate a significant amount of 60% of the annual budget is assigned to the rural schools' education system.

Contribution to Bolivia's Literature on Human Capital and Economic Growth:

Although an aggregate model was used for all 14 countries in the study, this study contributes to the literature on the role of Human Capital *(HC)* in economic growth and development by highlighting the critical educational policies passed by the Bolivian government and how these policies affected the *HDI* level of the Bolivian economy. Studies that have delved into Bolivia's economy include (the World Institute for Development Economics Research of the United Nations University (WIDER/UNU), 2002; Barro, 1991; Mayer, 2001; Osiobe, 2019; 2020a). The theoretical formulation of the relationship between *HC* and economic growth in Bolivia has been studied (Mayer-Foulkes, 2008; Osiobe, 2020b; 2020c). The theoretical formulation of the relationship between *HC* and economic growth consistently predicts that knowledge embodied in humans is essential for innovation, productivity, and economic growth. The theoretical formulation of the relationship between *HC* and growth always indicates that knowledge embodied in humans is necessary for innovation, productivity, and economic development. However, this relationship does not hold in all cases; for example (Quiggin, 1999 & 2002).

USAID volunteer helping school children

REFERENCE

Abdullah, A., Doucouliagos, H., & Manning, E. (2015). Does Education Reduce Income Inequality? A Meta-Regression Analysis. Journal of Economic Surveys, 29(2), 301-316. https://doi.org/10.1111/joes.12056

Barro, J. R. (1991). Human Capital and Growth in Cross-Country Regressions. The Quarterly Journal of Economics, 407-443. https://doi.org/10.2307/2937943

Google Earth. (2019, 3 5). Google Earth. (Google) Retrieved 3 5, 2019, from https://www.google.com/earth/

Levine, R., & Renelt, D. (1992). A Sensitivity Analysis of Cross-Country Growth Regressions. The American Economic Review, 82(4), 942-963.

Library of Congress - Federal Research Division. (2006). Country Profile: Bolivia. Washington, D.C. Library of Congress.

Mayer, J. (2001). Technology Diffusion, Human Capital and Economic Growth in Developing Countries. UNCTAD Discussion Paper.

Mayer-Foulkes, D. (October 21, 2008). Economic Geography of Human Development: Stratified Growth in Bolivia, Brazil, Guatemala, and Peru. centro de Investigacion y Docencia Economicas (CIDE). https://doi.org/10.2139/ssrn.1287952

Osiobe, E. U. (2019). A Literature Review of Human Capital and Economic Growth. Business and Economic Research, 9(4), 179-196. https://doi.org/10.5296/ber.v9i4.15624

Osiobe, E. U. (2020). Human Capital and Economic Growth in Latin America: A Cointegration and Causality Analysis. The Economics and Finance Letters, 218-235. https://doi.org/10.18488/journal.29.2020.72.218.235

Osiobe, E. U. (2020). Human Capital, Capital Stock Formation, and Economic Growth: A Panel Granger Causality Analysis. Journal of Economics and Business, 569-580. https://doi.org/10.31014/aior.1992.03.02.221

Osiobe, E. U. (2020). Understanding Latin America's Educational Orientations: Evidence from 14 Nations. Education Quarterly Review, 249-260. https://doi.org/10.31014/aior.1993.03.02.137

Osiobe, Ejiro U. (2021). An Overview of Bolivia's Educational Policies. Economic Development Educational Research, Abuja: The Ane Osiobe International Foundation.

Penn World Table Equation: Human Capital in PWT 9.0. (2019). PWT 9.0. (Penn World Table) Retrieved 10 6, 2019, from https://www.rug.nl/ggdc/docs/human_capital_in_pwt_90.pdf

Relations Council on Foreign. (2019, January 12). CFR. (Council on Foreign Relations) Retrieved 9 12, 2019, from https://www.cfr.org/backgrounder/mercosur-south-americas-fractious-trade-bloc

Schwab, K. (2018). The Global Competitiveness Report. Geneva: World Economic Forum.

Temple, J. (1999). A Positive Effect of Human Capital on Growth. Economic Letter, 65(1), 131-134. https://doi.org/10.1016/S0165-1765(99)00120-2

The World Institute for Development Economics Research of the United Nations University. (2002). Resource Abundance and Economic Development. New York: Oxford University Press.

UNICEF. (2019, February 5). United Nations International Children's Emergency Fund. (The United Nations) Retrieved 10 13, 2019, from United Nations International Children's Emergency Fund: https://www.unicef.org/bolivia/03_UNICEF_Bolivia_CK_-_concept_note_-_Education_low.pdf

World Atlas. (2019). (World Atlas) Retrieved 9 11, 2019, from https://www.worldatlas.com/articles/what-is-the-capital-of-bolivia.html https://doi.org/10.1016/S0262-1762(19)30253-6

World Development Index Microdata Library. (2019, February 21). National Census of Housing and Population 2001 - IPUMS Subset. (The World Bank) Retrieved 10 13, 2019, from World Bank: https://microdata.worldbank.org/index.php/catalog/449

World Development Index Group, (2019, June 11). The World Bank. (World Development Indicators) Retrieved 3 18, 2019, from https://data.worldbank.org/region/latin-america-and-caribbean

World Education News + Review. (2019). (World Education Services) Retrieved 9 5, 2019, from https://wenr.wes.org/

Yale Center for Environmental Law & Policy; Center for International Earth Science Information Network; World Economic Forum. (2018). The 2018 Environmental Performance Index. Environmental Performance Index.

CHILE

INTRODUCTION

The Republic of Chile occupies a long South American coastal strip between the Andes mountains and the Pacific Ocean. It is the 38th largest nation globally and the 7th largest country, and the longest country in South America (Google Earth (GE), 2019). With 18.7 million people as of 2018, the nation ranks 62nd worldwide by population (World Development Index (WDI), 2019). Chile is ranked 84th in the world and 11th in the Latin Americas in the 2018 Environmental Performance Index (EPI)--(Yale Center for Environmental Law & Policy (YCELP) 2018). Chile is an emerging economy with a small elite who controls most of the land, wealth, and political life. Compared to the country's regional neighbors, Chile has enjoyed long and modest economic growth, development, and prosperity

215

Figure1:
Chile on the continental map of Latin America

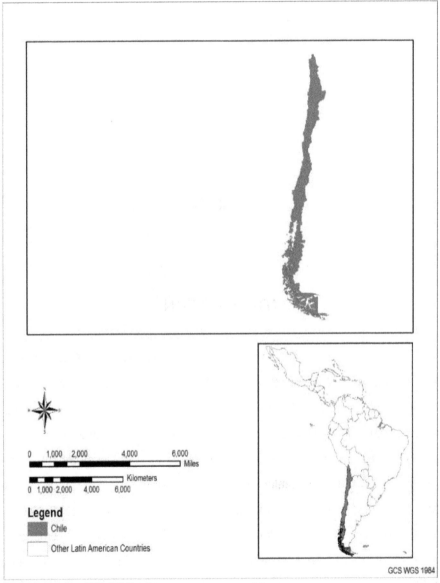

Author's creation (GE, 2019)
*Gray - specific country of interest

216

period. Making the country one of the most affluent nations in Latin America by most economic indicators, ranking 33rd out of 140 countries in the 2018 Global Competitiveness Index Report (GCI) (Schwab, 2018).

Concerning education, this growing national prosperity has led to rapidly increasing enrollments at the tertiary level, which led to more economic opportunities in different sectors. In the study, the Selected Latin America and the Caribbean (SLAC) countries that will be studied as a comparison benchmark are Argentina, Bolivia, Brazil, Chile (excluded), Colombia, Costa Rica, Honduras, Mexico, Nicaragua, Panama, Peru, El Salvador, Uruguay, and Venezuela.

Figure 2:
A comparison of our SLAC *RGDPppp* at chained (in Mil. 2011 USD (average)) with that of Chile (1950 – 2014) 1981 = 100

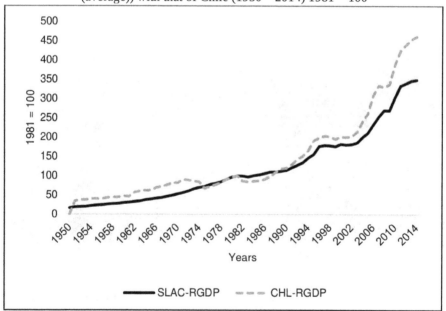

Source: (Penn World Tables (PWT), 2019).
Author's creation

Figure 2 shows Chile's Real Gross Domestic Product purchasing power parity (*RGDPppp*) 1981 = 100 index from 1950–2014 compared to the SLAC's moving average from 1950–2014. Figure 2 depicts Chile marginally outperforming the benchmark moving average from 1952–1974, at par with the SLAC's moving average from 1975–1982, then slightly underperforming the moving average from 1983–1989, and outperforming the SLAC's moving average from 1990–2014. This implies when the numbers in Figure 3 are converted to an index of 1981 = 100 to measure the change in the value of their *RGDPppp* to see the direction of production in the economy, the nation of Chile outperforms that of the SLAC by a significant margin on aggregate.

Santiago, Chile © Victor San Martin

Due to the nation's robust macroeconomic framework, the country was able to crush the effects of a volatile international context and reduce the number of people living in poverty (5.5 USD per day) from 30% of the total population in 2000 to less than 6.4% in 2018 (WDI, 2019). Because of the country's large cities and industrial centers, the nation attracts a steady flow of internal migrants. Most migrants move to the central business district of Santiago, the country's capital, while the rest head to smaller cities like Concepción–Talcahuano and Valparaíso–Viña del Mar. These migrants come from the rural regions of the Central Valley and some from north-central Chile. In recent years, Chile has seen an outflow of migrants to Punta Arenas, Lake District, and Argentina, where Chileans work in the mines.

Figure 3:
A comparison of our SLAC *RGDPppp* chained (in Mil. 2011 USD (Average)) with that of Chile (1950 – 2014)

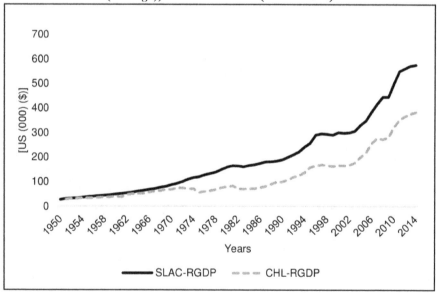

Source: (PWT, 2019).
Author's creation

Figure 3 shows Chile's *RGDPppp* actual numbers compared to our SLAC's moving average from 1950–2014. Figure 3 depicts Chile's underperforming benchmark moving average from 1950–2014. The Chilean economy is primarily based on agricultural, fishing, forest, and mining natural resources. Historically, the nation developed based on agriculture and the exportation of mineral resources. Today, the Chilean economy is dependent on the importation of manufactured products while resources and factors of production like, but not limited to, land, wealth, and power are concentrated in the hands of the elite few in society.

During the 19th century, Chile's economy grew based on agricultural export, nitrates, and copper. After the nitrate market crashed during World War I, Chile's economy took a downturn, leading to depression. These events prompted Chile to adopt socialistic programs that furthered the government's control of the economy.

Figure 4:
A comparison of our LAC % change of *RGDP*$_{ppp}$ at chained (in Mil. 2011 USD (Average)) with that of Chile (1951 – 2014)

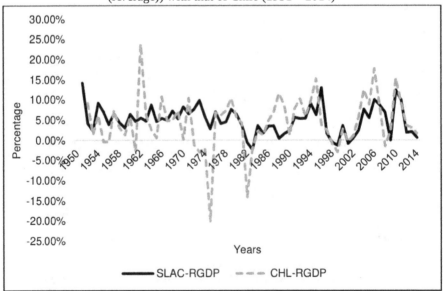

Source: (PWT, 2019).
Author's creation

Figure 4 shows Chile to be more volatile than the SLAC. The volatility on the chart implies that Chile was more affected by economic shocks (positive and negative), especially when the changes came from the agricultural sector. Developing a broader export-based economy improved Chile's economic growth and reduced the inflation rate in the 1990s (WDI, 2019). During the 1990s and to date, the country entered into many bilateral and regional trade agreements, which fostered economic growth and development in the region and further increased Foreign Direct Investment (FDI) in Chile's industries (Organization of American States (OAS), 2019).

Santa Cruz High School. © Diego Grez Cañete

By the early 21st century, the Chilean government had one of the most successful economies in South America. The economic implications of the 1990 Mercosur Free Trade Agreement (MFTA), a free trade market agreement created in the 1990s between six South American countries:

Argentina, Bolivia, Brazil, Chile, Paraguay, and Uruguay. MFTA to the nation extended to the educational systems; since the agreement impacts political relations, technology, and globalization. The Ministry of Education and Culture (MEC) is responsible for all the nation's educational system levels. Chile's economy faces severe economic issues, reflected in periodic high inflation, fluctuating trade policies, unemployment, and heavy dependence on a single primary export product, copper, in the international market.

Figure 5:
A comparison of our LAC *HDI* (average) with that of Chile (1950 – 2014)

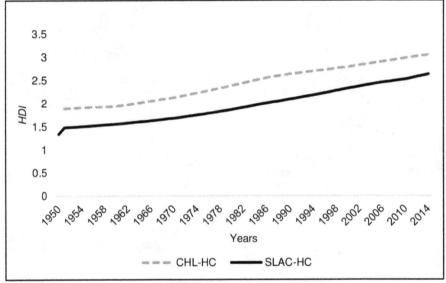

Source: (PWT, 2019).
Author's creation

Figure 5 shows Chile's *HDI* compared to the SLAC's' moving average from 1950–2014. Figure 5 depicts Chile outperforming the benchmark moving average from 1950–2014. This implies that Chile's national literacy rate is higher than the benchmark moving average based on residents' years of schooling and return to education. The educational system in Chile is one of the most privatized systems globally, both in terms of funding and total enrollment. A recent study done by the Organisation for Economic Co-operation and Development (OECD) and the WDI showed that public spending on higher education in Chile is the lowest as a percentage of Gross Domestic Product *(GDP)* compared to other OECD countries (OECD – Chile, 2018). On average, public universities in Chile receive over 80% of their operating budgets from external sources other than the government of Chile. As a result, the operating cost of the universities is moved to the student, leading to high tuition in public universities, meaning that the less affluent students face more challenges in covering the cost of going to school (OECD – Chile, 2018).

University of San Sebastian. © Rodrigo Fernández

SUMMARY

Education Policy Orientation Main Findings:

- The nation has eight years of free and compulsory primary education.
- Mandatory secondary education.
- Because of its robust education policies, Chile's university education is renowned throughout Latin America.
- In 2015, the government committed 4.9% of its *GDP* to education.

Policies That Moved the Country Forward:

- The MEC in Chile is responsible for pre-primary, primary, and secondary curricula and standards.
- The primary and secondary education system is mandatory in the country.
- The Chilean government-sponsored programs—like the Corporación de Fomento de la Producción, Sistema de Medición de la Calidad de la Educación, and Ingles Abre Puertas—support the English-language learning, scholarship, and testing of its citizens.
- In 2015, President Michelle Bachelet passed an education reform that strengthened the education system in the country.

Policies Implication and Recommendations:

From our descriptive analysis, one can identify the MFTA, the 2006 NEF bill, and the compulsory kindergarten through the primary free education system offered in the nation. These different education growth policies provide enormous lessons that other economies can imitate. These lessons come with challenges regarding how economic growth, development, and sustainability strategies can affect Human Capita *(HC)* and Capital Formation Structure *(CS)* formation enhancement in an economy.

- Although notable efforts have been made to increase the influx of students into the primary and secondary education system, an OECD/ World Bank (WB) report on the nation inferred that the country still had a long way to improve the Chilean education system. The already exciting education programs are recommended to provide chapters for low-income family loans, meal programs, and grant mechanisms to increase the percentage of rural demography in the education system.

- The MEC is responsible for Chile's pre-primary, primary, and secondary curricula and standards. To ensure the quality of *HC*, there is a need for the Chilean MEC to analyze and adjust the relationship between the higher education system and the job market to achieve coherence between the skills that the system produces and critical areas of economic growth and development.

- The country's mandatory primary and secondary education system has led to approximately 40% of Chilean students enrolling in technical schools responding to students' varying interests. The education system should become more flexible to accommodate the students' needs.

- In 2015, the Chilean government committed 4.9% of its *GDP* to education. Still, the whole exercise of the right to education cannot occur unless substantive changes are made in teaching policies and curricula. It is recommended that the roles and training of teachers must focus on effective teaching and generating conditions that allow students to exercise the right to learn.

Contribution to Chile's Literature on Human Capital and Economic Growth:

Although an aggregate model was used as the benchmark measuring tool, in the study, this study contributes to the literature on the role of *HC* in economic growth and development by highlighting the critical educational policies passed by the Chilean government and how these policies affected the *HDI* level of the Chilean economy. Studies that have delved into Chile's economy include (Barro, 1991; Chumacero and Fuentes, 2004; Harald and Rodrigo, 2002; Contreras, 2003; Olavarria-Gambi, 2003; Marotta et al., 2007; Castaneda, 1999).

The theoretical formulation of the relationship between *HC* and economic growth in Chile has been studied by (Agiomigianakis et al. 2002; Chumacero and Fuentes, 2004; Ibarra et al., 2000; Cavallo & Mondino, 1995; Kiran, 2014; Osiobe, 2020a, 2020b, & 2020c)). It is consistently predicted that knowledge embodied in humans is essential for innovation, productivity, and economic growth. However, this relationship did not hold in all studies (Bils and Klenow, 2000; Devarajan et al., 1996; Benhabib and Spiegel, 1994 & 2005; Temple, 1999).

REFERENCE

Agiomirgianakis, G., Asteriou, D., & Monastiriotis, V. (2002). Human Capital and Economic Growth Revisited: A Dynamic Panel Data Study. International Advances in Economic Research, 8(3), 177-187. https://doi.org/10.1007/BF02297955

Barro, J. R. (1991). Human Capital and Growth in Cross-Country Regressions. The Quarterly Journal of Economics, 407-443. https://doi.org/10.2307/2937943

Benhabib, J., & Spiegel, M. M. (1994). The role of human capital in economic development evidence from aggregate cross-country data. Journal of Monetary Economics, Elsevier, vol. 34(2), pages 143-173. https://doi.org/10.1016/0304-3932(94)90047-7

Benhabib, J., & Spiegel, M. M. (2005). Chapter 13 Human Capital and Technology Diffusion. Handbook of Economic Growth, 1(A), 935-966. https://doi.org/10.1016/S1574-0684(05)01013-0

Bils, M., & Klenow, J. P. (2000). Does Schooling Cause Growth? American Economic Review, 90(5), 1160-1183. https://doi.org/10.1257/aer.90.5.1160

Castaneda, B. E. (1999). An index of sustainable economic welfare (ISEW) for Chile. Ecological Economics, 28(2), 231-244. https://doi.org/10.1016/S0921-8009(98)00037-8

Cavallo, F. D., & Mondino, G. (1995). Argentina's Miracle? From Hyperinflation to Sustained Growth. The International Bank for Reconstruction and Development.

Chumacero, R. A., & Fuentes, R. J. (2004). On the Determinants of Chilean Economic Growth. The Global Development Network.

Contreras, D. (2003). Poverty and Inequality in a Raid Growth Economy: Chile 1990-1996. The Journal of Development Studies, 39(3), 181-200. https://doi.org/10.1080/00220380412331322871

Devarajan, S., Swaroop, V., & Zou, H.-f. (1996). The Composition of Public Expenditure and Economic Growth. Journal of Monetary Economics, 37(2), 313-344. https://doi.org/10.1016/S0304-3932(96)90039-2

Google Earth. (2019, 3 5). Google Earth. (Google) Retrieved 3 5, 2019, from https://www.google.com/earth/

Harald, B. B., & Rodrigo, V. M. (2002). Productivity and Economic Growth: The Case of Chile. Working Paper No. 174.

Ibarra, A. A., Reid, C., & Thorpe, A. (2000). The Political Economy of Marine Fisheries Development in Peru, Chile, and Mexico. Journal of Latin American Studies, 32(2), 503-527. https://doi.org/10.1017/S0022216X00005824

Kiran, B. (2014). Testing the impact of educational expenditures on economic growth: new evidence from Latin American countries. Quality & Quantity: International Journal of Methodology, vol. 48, issue 3, 1181-1190. https://doi.org/10.1007/s11135-013-9828-2

Marotta, D., Mark, M., Blom, A., & Thorn, K. (2007). Human Capital and University-Industry Linkages' Role in Fostering Firm Innovation: An Empirical Study of Chile and Colombia. The World Bank Group Policy Research Working Papers. https://doi.org/10.1596/1813-9450-4443

OECD-Chile. (2018). OECD Economic Surveys Chile. The Economic and Development Review Committee of the OECD.

Olavarria-Gambi, M. (2003). Poverty Reduction in Chile: Has economic growth been enough? Journal of Human Development, 4(1), 103-123. https://doi.org/10.1080/1464988032000051504

Organization of American States. (2019). Foreign Trade Information System. (SICE) Retrieved 11 3, 2019, from http://sice.oas.org/ctyindex/CHL/CHLagreements_e.asp

Osiobe, E. U. (2019). A Literature Review of Human Capital and Economic Growth. Business and Economic Research, 9(4), 179-196. https://doi.org/10.5296/ber.v9i4.15624

Osiobe, E. U. (2020). Human Capital and Economic Growth in Latin America: A Cointegration and Causality Analysis. The Economics and Finance Letters, 218-235. https://doi.org/10.18488/journal.29.2020.72.218.235

Osiobe, E. U. (2020). Human Capital, Capital Stock Formation, and Economic

Growth: A Panel Granger Causality Analysis. Journal of Economics and Business, 569-580. https://doi.org/10.31014/aior.1992.03.02.221

Osiobe, E. U. (2020). Understanding Latin America's Educational Orientations: Evidence from 14 Nations. Education Quarterly Review, 249-260. https://doi.org/10.31014/aior.1993.03.02.137

Osiobe, Ejiro U. (2021). An Overview of Chile's Educational Policies. Economic Development Educational Research, Abuja: The Ane Osiobe International Foundation.

Quiggin, J. (1999). Human capital Theory and Education Policy in Australia. Australian Economic Review, 32(2), 130-44. https://doi.org/10.1111/1467-8462.00100

Quiggin, J. (2002). Human Capital Theory and Education Policy in Australia. Australian Economic Review, Volume 32, Issue 2. https://doi.org/10.1111/1467-8462.00100

Schwab, K. (2018). The Global Competitiveness Report. Geneva: World Economic Forum.

Temple, J. (1999). A Positive Effect of Human Capital on Growth. Economic Letter, 65(1), 131-134. https://doi.org/10.1016/S0165-1765(99)00120-2

Yale Center for Environmental Law & Policy; Center for International Earth Science Information Network; World Economic Forum. (2018). The 2018 Environmental Performance Index. Environmental Performance Index.

ARGENTINA

INTRODUCTION

Argentina is in the southern part of South America. It is the 8th largest country globally and the 2nd largest country in South America after Brazil (Google Earth (GE), 2019); with about 44.5 million people as of 2018, the country ranks 31st in the world by population (World Development Index (WDI), 2019). Argentina ranks 74th globally and 9th in the Latin Americas in the 2018 Environmental Performance Index (EPI)--(Yale Center for Environmental Law & Policy (YCELP) 2018).

In the early 20th century, the nation of Argentina was among the world's top ten wealthiest countries, with a Gross Domestic Product per capita $(GDP_{per\ capita})$ higher than countries like France and Germany (Organization for Economic Cooperation and Development (OECD)-

Figure1:
Argentina on the continental map of Latin America

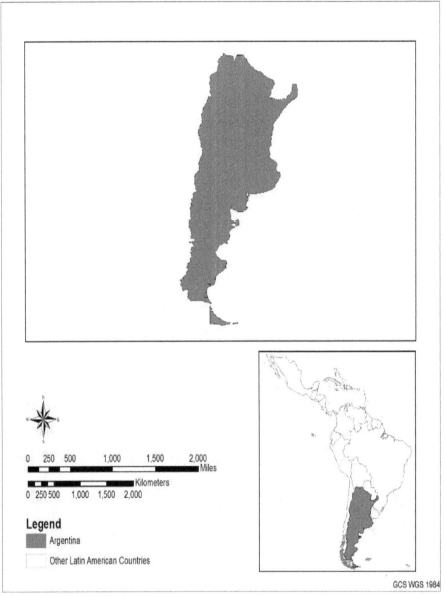

*Gray - specific country of interest
Author's creation (GE, 2019)

Argentina, 2019; OECD, United Nations Economic Commission for Latin America and the Caribbean (ECLAC), & CAF—Development Bank of Latin America (CAF), 2016). The nation showed a steady growth pattern (see Figures 2, 3, and 5) that helped with economic prosperity and created boundless opportunities (OECD-Argentina, 2019). This prosperity trend (Figures 3 and 5) made Argentina a magnet for immigrants from Africa, Europe, Latin America, and the Caribbean (LAC) (Schwab, 2018). In the study, the Selected Latin America and the Caribbean (SLAC) countries that will be studied as a comparison benchmark are Argentina (excluded), Bolivia, Brazil, Chile, Colombia, Costa Rica, Honduras, Mexico, Nicaragua, Panama, Peru, El Salvador, Uruguay, and Venezuela.

Figure 2:
A comparison of our SLAC *RGDPppp* at chained (in Mil. 2011 USD (average)) with that of Argentina (1950 – 2014) 1981 = 100

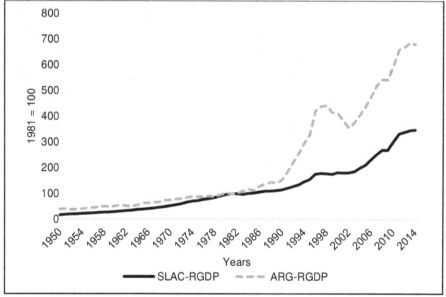

Source: (Penn World Tables (PWT), 2019).
Author's creation

Figure 2 shows Argentina's *RGDPppp* 1981 = 100 index from 1950–2014 compared to that of the SLAC's moving average, and it depicts Argentina performing marginally better than the benchmark moving average from 1950–1980 and outperforming the moving average from 1981–2014. This implies when comparing the SLAC economic indicator index (1981 = 100) to measure the changes in the value of their *RGDPppp* to see the direction of production in the economy, Argentina outperformed the SLAC by a significant margin.

Avenida de Mayo, Buenos Aires © Alexis González Molina

It is estimated that about 7 million people migrated to Argentina between 1870 and 1930 (Schwab, 2018). Until the nation's democratization in 1983, Argentina suffered from dictatorship governments and various military coups (Argentina-Profile International Monetary Fund, 2019). Although the country's democratization brought political stability, this movement did not stop the nation's economic woes as the influx of working people grew. Still, the number of jobs in the country remained the same. As a member of the G – 15 economies (Lekatis, 2019), the nation's *GDPper capita* is 11,652 USD, with a *GDP* of 518.47 billion USD (WDI, 2019).

The country's economy grew by 2.5% in 2018 (WDI, 2019) as an emerging market, and its economy benefits from its abundant natural resources, and literate population, which in this study will be measured using the Human Development Index *(HDI)* 83% (United Nations Development Programme (UNDP), 2018), trade openness, and a diversified industrial base. Argentina's economy is among the most stable economies in the region. The nation depends on its services and manufacturing industry for the most part, although the agricultural sector was the dominant industry in the 19th and 20th centuries. The nation still produces more grain than any other country in Latin America; it is the second-largest cattle-raising country in Latin America, with Brazil ranked #1, and its tourism sector is second in the region, with Mexico ranked #1.

Figure 3 shows Argentina's *RGDPppp* actual numbers compared to the SLAC's moving average from 1950–2014. It depicts Argentina performing marginally better than that of the benchmark moving average from 1950–1974, and from 1975–1990, Argentina slightly underperformed below the benchmarked moving average; however, after 1991, Argentina experienced a rapid growth period, outperforming the set benchmark moving average from 1991–2014.

According to (Schwab, 2018), in 1914, Argentina's capital was a booming city with an active migrant population of about 50% of its total population. Since the spike in migrant inflow into the nation, Argentina has been viewed as a rising economic star/emerging market while not attaining the status of a developed nation/first-world nation. Its extensive periods of financial-economic volatility and corruption, the stated plagues, have led to the fall of the nation's economic status, resulting in Argentina's government not living up to its full economic potential (World Education News + Review (WEN+R), 2019).

Figure 3:
A comparison of our SLAC *RGDPppp* at chained (in Mil. 2011 USD (average)) with that of Argentina (1950 – 2014)

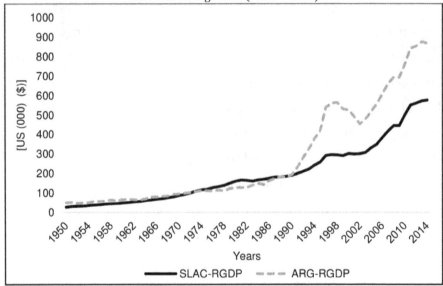

Source: (PWT, 2019).
Author's creation

The (Economist Magazine (TEM), 2019) described Argentina's economic performance as "a century of declining economic performance (TEM, 2019). Today, the nation ranks 81st most competitive nation globally, out of 140 countries listed in the 2018 Global Competitiveness Index Report (GCIR) (Schwab, 2018).

Figure 4 shows Argentina to be more volatile than that of the SLACs. The chart's volatility implies that the nation was quickly impacted by economic shocks (positive and negative), especially when the change came from industries that are the nation's stronghold, like the oil and gas industry and the tourism industry. Due to the Great Depression in 1930 and the Depression in 1980, the country lost its economic ranking as one of the world's wealthiest nations and its emerging market category.

Figure 4:

A comparison of our SLAC % change of *RGDPppp* at chained (in Mil. 2011 USD (average)) with that of Argentina (1951 – 2014)

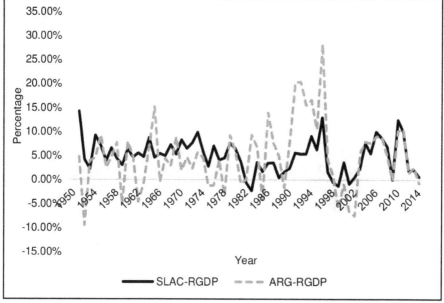

Source: (PWT, 2019).
Author's creation

The overall educational system in Argentina is grouped into four distinct training levels (WEN+R, 2019). The nursery school/pre-primary/ kindergarten enrolls children between the ages of 3–5 years old (optional); the primary school/elementary enrolls children between the ages of 6–12 years old and some adults (mandatory); the secondary school/high school enrolls children within the ages of 12–17 years old and some adults (compulsory), and the higher education includes private and public institutions, with program lengths varying from 3–12 years (optional).

There is a significant discrepancy between schools in the rural and urban regions of the country. The provinces are geographically isolated, and about 50% of the population lives in the capital (OECD-Argentina, 2019;

School in Yerevan

OECD, 2017). This demographic distribution leaves the rural school with very little or no power to pass educational bills and policies at the national level that would be of benefit to their school districts and residences. This conundrum has led to a low academic attainment rate in rural areas. But in

general, the educational system in the nation has seen a lot of improve-
ment(s) with rural education expanding.

Argentina outperforms most of South America's countries in
educational standards (WDI, 2019). Advancing access to education has been
a historical priority for the nation. The National Education Finance (NEF)
Law passed in 2006 mandated that a minimum of 6% of the nation's *GDP*
should be spent on education (WEN+R, 2019). Although the NEF bill was
passed in 2006, the nation's educational spending was below the set target,
ranging from 4.1% in 2006 to 5.6% in 2016 (WEN+R, 2019). In South
America, Argentina has a high net enrollment rate in secondary education
(89.5 % in 2016) (WDI, 2019) and tertiary/university education second only
to Chile (UNESCO Institute for Statistics, 2019).

Figure 5:
A comparison of our SLAC *HDI* (average) with that of Argentina (1950 – 2014)

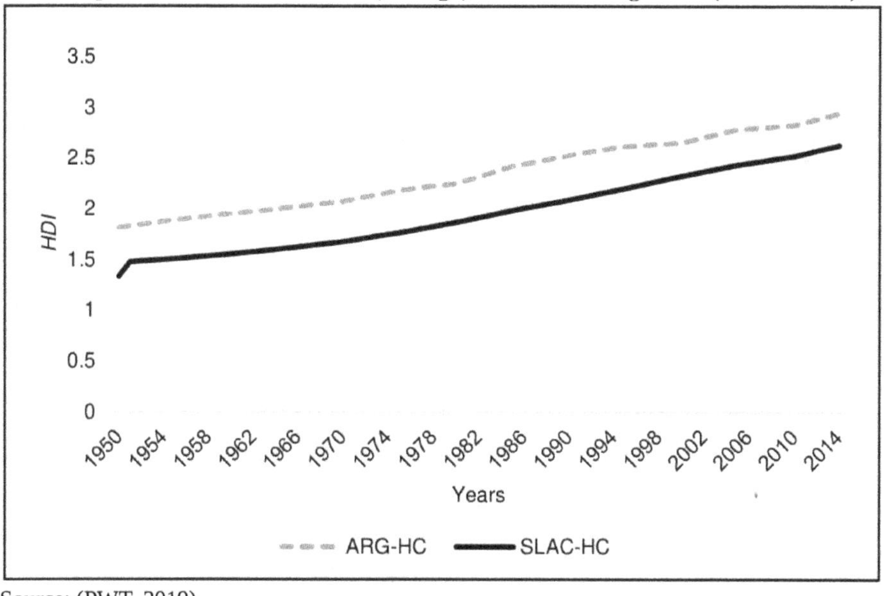

Source: (PWT, 2019).
Author's creation

Another policy affecting the Argentine education system is the 1990 Mercosur Free Trade Agreement (MFTA), a free trade market agreement created in the 1990s between six South American countries: Argentina, Bolivia, Brazil, Chile, Paraguay, and Uruguay. The economic implications of MFTA to the economy extend to the school systems since the agreement impacts political relations, technology, and globalization. The Ministerio de Educación y Cultura (The Ministry of Education and Culture (MEC)) is responsible for all levels of the nation's educational system (Relations Council on Foreign (RCF), 2019).

Figure 5 shows Argentina's *HDI* compared to the SLAC's moving average from 1950–2014. It depicts Argentina outperforming the benchmark moving average. The figure implies that Argentina's *HDI* growth pattern shows that its national literacy rate exceeded the SLAC's moving average based on residencies' years of schooling and returns to education (PWT, 2019).

SUMMARY

Education Policy Orientation Main Findings:

- Spanish is the predominant language used in Argentina's education system.
- Kindergarten-level education is not compulsory.
- A mandated NEF Law dictates 6% of the country's *GDP* be spent on the nation's education system.

Policies that Moved the Country Forward:

- Primary education is compulsory and accessible for everyone ages six and above.
- Secondary education is mandatory and free.
- National Education Law No. 26206 established Intercultural Bilingual Education (EIB) as one of the eight modalities under Chapter XI, article 52.
- The NEF Law was passed in 2006
- The National Institute for Education was established to develop a nationwide standard and coherent teacher training structure.

Policies Implication and Recommendations:

From our descriptive analysis, one can identify that the MFTA, the NEF bill, and the compulsory kindergarten through the nation's primary free education system provide enormous lessons that other economies can learn.

241

These lessons come with new challenges regarding how economic growth, development, and stability policies can affect Human Capital *(HC)* and Capital Structure *(CS)* enhancement in an economy.

- The mandatory free basic education in the country has allowed many low-income families to send their children to school, hence increasing the overall *HDI* of the nation (see Figure 5). On the other hand, this has also led to the subsidization of basic education for the rich in the country who can afford it (Rozada & Menedez, 2002). For there to be equity and efficiency in mandatory free basic education-economic development programs, it is recommended that a branch program be created that offers complimentary, comparative, and low-income household scholarships and loans for students who plan on attending the university.

- Due to the urban-rural regional divide in the country, children from rural areas are less represented in the decision-making process and distribution of the NEF budget, making it less likely for them to attend college (Parrado, 1998). It is recommended that entrepreneurs and private- and government-sector jobs consider employing and training candidates without a college degree but competent in doing the job.

- In Argentina, there is a gap between the law on paper and the law in practice (Lodi, 2009). The divergence between the formal and informal institutions in the country is vast. It has led to the lack of implementation of many economic growth policies, such as the 2006 NEF bill. It is recommended that the rule of law in the country be upheld in all areas, especially with government policies that promote economic growth, development, and sustainability in the long run, like allocating a 6% National Education Budget to the education system.

- The MFTA shifted the educational system from an elite to a mass higher education (Larrechea & Castro, 2009). Although a good idea, as more people will have access to a degree, it is recommended that Argentina concentrate more on the degree's quality than the number of enrollments in the school system at every level of the educational system.

Contribution to Argentina's Literature on Human Capital and Economic Growth:

Although an aggregate economic indicator model is used (Figure 2 – 5), this study contributes to the literature on the role of Argentina's *HC* in economic growth and development by highlighting the importance of educational growth policies. Studies that have delved into Argentina as a country include but are not limited to (Dinda, 2006; Narula & Marin, 2003; Bertola & Porcile, 2006 & 2012; Spruk, 2018; Dana, 1997; Artana et al., 2010). The theoretical and empirical relationship between *HC* and economic growth in Argentina has been studied (Cavallo & Mondino, 1995; Kiran, 2014; Osiobe, 2020a, 2020b, & 2020c). The theoretical formulation of the relationship between *HC* and growth consistently predicts that knowledge embodied in humans is essential for innovation, productivity, and economic growth. However, this relationship does not hold in all cases (Quiggin, 1999 & 2002).

REFERENCE

Argentina-Profile-International Monetary Fund; (2019). (International Monetary Fund) Retrieved 9 5, 2019, from https://www.imf.org/en/Countries/ARG

Artana, D., Bour, E., Bour, L. J., & Susmel, N. (2010). Strengthening long-term growth in Argentina. Seminar Paper.

Bertola, L., & Porcile, G. (2006). Convergence, trade and industrial policy: Argentina, Brazil, and Uruguay in the international economy, 1900-1980. Revista de Historia Economica-Journal of Iberian and Latin American Economic History, 24(1), 37-67. https://doi.org/10.1017/S021261090000046X

Bertola, L., & Porcile, G. (2012). Argentina, Brazil, Uruguay, and the World Economy: An approach to different convergence and divergence regimes.

Cavallo, F. D., & Mondino, G. (1995). Argentina's Miracle? From Hyperinflation to Sustained Growth. The International Bank for Reconstruction and Development.

Dana, L. P. (1997). A contrast of Argentina and Uruguay: The Effects of government policy on entrepreneurship. Journal of Small Business Management, 35(2), 99-104.

Dinda, S. (2006). Social Capital in the creation of human capital and economic growth: A productive consumption approach. MPRA Paper No. 50586.

Google Earth. (2019, 3 5). Google Earth. (Google) Retrieved 3 5, 2019, from https://www.google.com/earth/

Kiran, B. (2014). Testing the impact of educational expenditures on economic growth: new evidence from Latin American countries. Quality & Quantity: International Journal of Methodology, vol. 48, issue 3, 1181-1190. https://doi.org/10.1007/s11135-013-9828-2

Larrechea, M. E., & Castro, C. A. (2009). New Demand and Policies on Higher Education in the Mercosur: A comparative study on challenges, resources, and trends. Policy Futures in Education, 7(5). https://doi.org/10.2304/pfie.2009.7.5.473

Lekatis, G. (2019). Understanding the Groups: G7, G8, G10, G15, G20, G24 Countries. Retrieved 3 18, 2019, from https://www.scribd.com/doc/50098701/Under-standing-the-Groups-G7-G8-G10-G15-G20-G24-countries

Lodi, L. M. (2009). Rule of Law: The Missing Link of the Argentine Democracy. Conference Paper: 21st World Congress of Political Science-Santiago, Chile, July 12 – 16.

Narula, R., & Marin, A. (2003). FDI spillover, absorptive capacities, and human capital development: evidence from Argentina. Second Draft Paper.

OECD. (2017). Argentina Multi-dimensional Economic Survey. OECD.

OECD; ECLAC; CAF. (2016). Latin American Economic Outlook 2017: Youth, Skills, and Entrepreneurship. Paris: OECD Publishing. https://doi.org/10.1787/leo-2017-en

OECD-Argentina. (2019). OECD Economic Surveys on Argentina. OECD.

Osiobe, E. U. (2019). A Literature Review of Human Capital and Economic Growth. Business and Economic Research, 9(4), 179-196. https://doi.org/10.5296/ber.v9i4.15624

Osiobe, E. U. (2020). Human Capital and Economic Growth in Latin America: A Cointegration and Causality Analysis. The Economics and Finance Letters, 218-235. https://doi.org/10.18488/journal.29.2020.72.218.235

Osiobe, E. U. (2020). Human Capital, Capital Stock Formation, and Economic Growth: A Panel Granger Causality Analysis. Journal of Economics and Business, 569-580. https://doi.org/10.31014/aior.1992.03.02.221

Osiobe, E. U. (2020). Understanding Latin America's Educational Orientations: Evidence from 14 Nations. Education Quarterly Review, 249-260. https://doi.org/10.31014/aior.1993.03.02.137

Osiobe, Ejiro U. (2021). An Overview of Argentina's Educational Policies. Economic Development Educational Research , Abuja: The Ane Osiobe International Foundation.

Parrado, A. E. (1998). Expansion of Schooling, Economic Growth, and Regional Inequalities in Argentina. Comparative Education Review, 42(3), 338-364. https://doi.org/10.1086/447511

Penn World Table Equation: Human Capital in PWT 9.0. (2019). PWT 9.0. (Penn World Table) Retrieved 10 6, 2019, from https://www.rug.nl/ggdc/docs/human_capital_in_pwt_90.pdf

Quiggin, J. (1999). Human capital Theory and Education Policy in Australia. Australian Economic Review, 32(2), 130-44. https://doi.org/10.1111/1467-8462.00100

Quiggin, J. (2002). Human Capital Theory and Education Policy in Australia. Australian Economic Review, Volume 32, Issue 2. https://doi.org/10.1111/1467-8462.00100

Relations Council on Foreign. (2019, January 12). CFR. (Council on Foreign Relations) Retrieved 9 12, 2019, from https://www.cfr.org/backgrounder/mercosur-south-americas-fractious-trade-bloc

Rozada, G. M., & Menedez, A. (2002). The Public University in Argentina: Subsidizing the rich? Economic of Education Review, 21(4), 341-351. https://doi.org/10.1016/S0272-7757(01)00030-9

Schwab, K. (2018). The Global Competitiveness Report. Geneva: World Economic Forum.

Spruk, R. (2018). The Rise and Fall of Argentina. Mercatus Working Paper. https://doi.org/10.2139/ssrn.3242408

The Economist Magazine. (2019, 8 22). The Economist. (The Economist) Retrieved 9 5, 2019, from https://www.economist.com/the-americas/2019/08/22/argentinas-crisis-shows-the-limits-of-technocracy

The World Development Index. (2019). Retrieved from http://data.worldbank.org/country/australia

UNESCO Institute for Statistics; Sustainable Development Goals, (2019). UNESCO Institute for Statistics. (United Nations) Retrieved 9 11, 2019, from http://uis.unesco.org/

United Nations Development Programme, (2018). Human Development Indices and Indicator. New York, NY: United Nations Development Program (UNDP).

World Development Index Group, (2019, June 11). The World Bank. (World Development Indicators) Retrieved 3 18, 2019, from https://data.worldbank.org/region/latin-america-and-caribbean

World Education News + Review. (2019). (World Education Services) Retrieved 9 5, 2019, from https://wenr.wes.org/

World Penn Tables. (2019). Retrieved from http://datacentre2.chass.utoronto.ca/pwt/alphacountries.html

Yale Center for Environmental Law & Policy; Center for International Earth Science Information Network; World Economic Forum. (2018). The 2018 Environmental Performance Index. Environmental Performance Index.

Ejiro U. Osiobe

URUGUAY

INTRODUCTION

The nation of Uruguay, officially the Oriental Republic of Uruguay, is the 89th largest country in the world, the 11th largest country in South America (google (GE), 2019), and with a population of about 3.4 million people in 2018, ranks 168th in the world by population (World Development Index (WDI), 2019). Regarding the GCI, Uruguay ranks 53rd out of 140 countries (Schwab, 2018). Uruguay is ranked 47th in the world and 3rd in Latin America in the 2018 Environmental Performance Index (EPI) (Yale Center for Environmental Law & Policy (YCELP), 2018).

Compared to other Selected Latin America and the Caribbean (SLAC), the country's landmass and low population density have afforded Uruguay many economic growth and development opportunities. The

Figure 1:
Uruguay on the continental map of Latin America

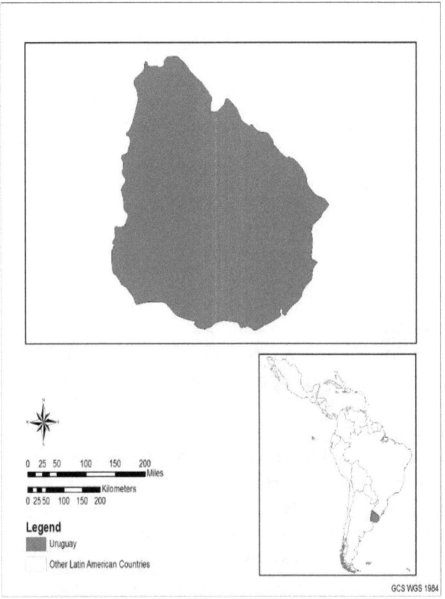

Author's creation (GE, 2019).
*Gray - specific country of interest

country has strong ties to the United Kingdom, Italy, and France in the international market. This relationship helped Uruguay grow and develop throughout the 20th century as one of Latin America's most progressive nations, known for its political and social-economic stability, middle and working-class growth, and the advancement of social legislation. After the military rule in 1973–1985, Uruguay was troubled by economic decline and financial struggles in the decades dating to when a civilian democratic government took over the country's governance. The SLAC countries studied as a comparison benchmark are Argentina, Bolivia, Brazil, Chile, Colombia, Costa Rica, Honduras, Mexico, Nicaragua, Panama, Peru, El Salvador, Uruguay (excluded), and Venezuela.

Figure 2:
A comparison of our SLAC *RGDPppp* at chained
(in Mil. 2011 USD (average)) with that of Uruguay (1950 – 2014) 1981 = 100

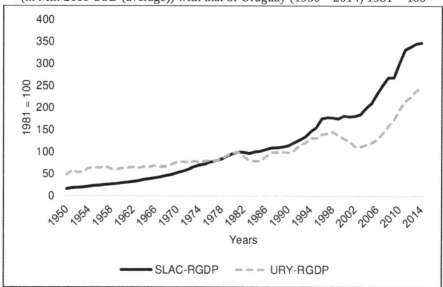

Source: (Penn World Table (PWT), 2019).
Author's creation

Figure 2 shows Uruguay's Real Gross Domestic Product purchasing power parity (*RGDPppp*) 1981 = 100 compared to the average SLAC moving from 1950 to 2014. Figure 67 depicts Uruguay marginally outperforming our SLAC moving average from 1950–1975 and underperforming the benchmark moving average from 1976–2014. This implies that when the numbers in Figure 3 are converted to an index 1981 = 100 to measure the changes in the value of their *RGDPppp*, to see the direction of production in the economy, Uruguay underperforms our SLAC moving average.

The capitol city of Montevideo © Leandro Neumann Ciuffo

Such social-economic adversities have caused many Uruguayans to emigrate out of the country to places like the US and many European countries, giving the nation a negative slur, "We export our young." The country's government strives in the tourism sector of the economy, as it is a popular destination to tour around the world. The nation's Gross National Product per capita *(GNP per capita)* is among the highest in Central and South America, with a growing middle class. The nation's high standard of living comes from the earnings generated by the agricultural industry's exports, which have been volatile on the international market. Governments have encouraged domestic manufacturing and services to grow by passing economic-friendly business policies to reduce the country's high dependence on global products. These generous business policies have led to the diversification of the nation's economy. Uruguay's government nationalized many of its corporations that produce products like but are not limited to petroleum, electricity, alcohol, cement, processed meat, processed fish, the railway industry, and the nation's largest telephone company.

Figure 3:
A comparison of our SLAC *RGDPppp* at chained
(in Mil. 2011 USD (Average)) with that of Uruguay (1950 – 2014)

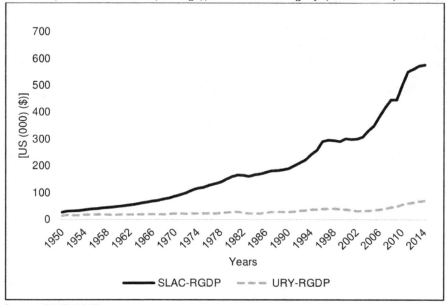

Source: (PWT, 2019).
Author's creation

Figure 3 shows Uruguay's *RGDPppp* actual numbers compared to the SLAC moving average from 1950–2014. Figure 3 depicts Uruguay underperforming the benchmark moving average from 1950–2014 with a somewhat flat upward slope. The country's literacy rate is high compared to the literacy rate of other SLAC, and its educational system policy includes compulsory free basic education for students between the ages of 6–14 years.

Kindergarten students in Montevideo. © Vince Alongi

The country has boasted about the nation's high levels of compliance with required basic education for its citizens, also bragging about its large number of students enrolled in the secondary school educational level. As a result, the national literacy rate is approximately 96%, which is very high compared to other Latin American nations. In the 1990s, the Administration Nacional de la Educación Pública (National Administration of Public Education) proposed several educational reforms, which were not passed until 2001. The new educational reform provided new guidelines for new school facilities and curricula. After these changes, the WB approved a 28 Mil. USD loan to the nation to improve its primary education system.

Figure 4 shows Uruguay to be more volatile than that of the SLAC. The volatility on the chat implies that both positive and negative economic shocks heavily impacted the nation from 1950–2014. Another policy affecting the Argentine education system is the 1990 Mercosur Free Trade Agreement (MFTA), a free trade market agreement created in the 1990s between six South American countries: Argentina, Bolivia, Brazil, Chile, Paraguay, and Uruguay. The socioeconomic implications of the MFTA to the economy extend to the school systems since the agreement impacts political relations, technology, and globalization. The MEC is responsible for all levels of the nation's educational system.

Figure 4:
A comparison of our SLAC % change of *RGDPppp* at chained (in Mil. 2011 USD (Average)) with that of Uruguay (1951 – 2014)

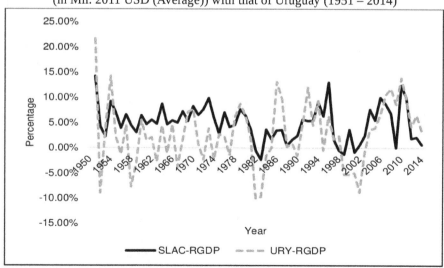

Source: (PWT, 2019).
Author's creation

Figure 5 shows Uruguay's Human Development Index (*HDI*) compared to the SLAC moving average from 1950–2014. Figure 5 depicts Uruguay outperforming the benchmark moving average from 1950–2014. Uruguay's *HDI* showed a steady upward trend on the actual *HDI*, and the growth rate trend was like that of the actual *HDI*. The figure implies Uruguay's *HDI* in the country outperformed the SLAC moving average based on residencies, years of schooling, and returns to education.

Figure 5:
A comparison of our SLAC *HDI* (average) with that of Uruguay (1950 – 2014)

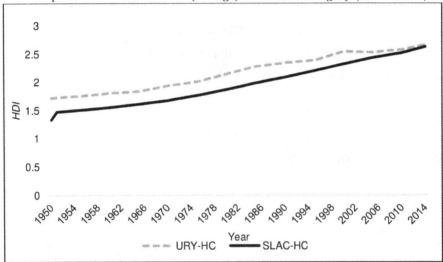

Source: (PWT, 2019).
Author's creation

SUMMARY

Education Policy Orientation Main Findings:

- Primary, secondary, and university education are free. This has resulted in Uruguay having a 98.6% literacy rate, comparable to that of the US.
- The education system in the nation is highly centralized, unlike other Latin and Central American countries.
- Education is compulsory, from ages 6–11.
- Spanish is the predominant language used in the Uruguayan education system.

Policies that Moved the Country Forward:

- The enforcement of a low student-to-teacher ratio. The nation has an average teacher-to-student ratio of 13:1, one of the lowest in the world.
- The Uruguayan education department expanded the school material program, including free laptops and Wi-Fi connections for every student nationwide.

Policies Implication and Recommendation:

The Uruguayan education system has some remarkable and applicable policies from which the rest can learn. However, the system is still imperfect, which their government can improve. But overall, their education system has achieved great success, and their educational attainment rate has steadily increased for years.

- Although the country has a free education system from preschool through the university level, students from low-income families graduate much less than middle- and upper-income families. It is recommended that the Uruguayan government provide programs to support these families and reduce this gap in the graduate rate of low-income households.

- Another recommendation in the school system will be to increase teacher hire standards and improve the teacher's training programs.

Contribution to Uruguay Literature on Human Capital and Economic Growth:

This study contributes to the literature on the role of Human Capital *(HC)* in economic growth and development by highlighting the essential educational policies passed by the Uruguayan government and how these policies affected the *HDI* level of the Uruguayan economy. Studies that have delved into Uruguay's economy include (Finch, 1981; Winters & Martin, 1995; Teixeira, 1998; Panizza, 2004; Bertola & Porcile, 2006; Harmsen, 1995; de Brun & Licandro, 2006). The theoretical formulation of the relationship between *HC* and economic growth in Uruguay has been studied by (Hoffmeister & Vegh, 1996; Francois et al., 1994 & 1996; Moraes et al., 2005; Kirby, 1975; Bertola & Porcile, 2012; Finger, 2001; Harrison et al., 1997; Khan & Kazmi, 1994; Blandford, 1996; Dana, 1997; Yap, 1996; Runge & Stanton, 1988; Lopez-Alves, 1993). The theoretical formulation of the relationship between *HC* and economic growth consistently predicts that knowledge embodied in humans is essential for innovation, productivity, and

258

economic growth. However, this relationship didn't hold true in every study (Devarajan et al., 1996; Levin & Renelt, 1992).

Students from all over Uruguay celebrating the country's bicentennial.
© Karin Porley von Bergen

REFERENCE

Bertola, L., & Porcile, G. (2006). Convergence, trade and industrial policy: Argentina, Brazil, and Uruguay in the international economy, 1900-1980. Revista de Historia Economica-Journal of Iberian and Latin American Economic History, 24(1), 37-67. https://doi.org/10.1017/S021261090000046X

Bertola, L., & Porcile, G. (2012). Argentina, Brazil, Uruguay, and the World Economy: An approach to different convergence and divergence regimes.

Blandford, D. (1996). The political economy of post-Uruguay round agricultural policies in the United States and the European Union: Discussion. American Journal of Agricultural Economics, 78(5), 1324-1326. https://doi.org/10.2307/1243514

Dana, L. P. (1997). A contrast of Argentina and Uruguay: The Effects of government policy on entrepreneurship. Journal of Small Business Management, 35(2), 99-104.

De Brun, J., & Licandro, G. (2006). To Hell and Back - Crisis Management in a Dollarized Economy: The Case of Uruguay. In Financial Dollarization (pp. 147-176). London: Palgrave Macmillan. https://doi.org/10.1057/9780230380257_7

Devarajan, S., Swaroop, V., & Zou, H.-f. (1996). The Composition of Public Expenditure and Economic Growth. Journal of Monetary Economics, 37(2), 313-344. https://doi.org/10.1016/S0304-3932(96)90039-2

Finch, M. H. (1981). A Political Economy of Uruguay Since 1870. London: The Macmillan Press. https://doi.org/10.1007/978-1-349-16623-7

Finger, J. M. (2001). Implementing the Uruguay round agreements: Problems for developing countries. The World Economy, 24(9), 1097-1108. https://doi.org/10.1111/1467-9701.00402

Francois, J., McDonald, B., & Nordstrom, H. (1994). The Uruguay Round: A global general equilibrium assessment. CEPR Discussion Paper 1067.

Francois, J., McDonald, B., & Nordstrom, H. (1996). A user's guide to Uruguay round assessments. CEPR Discussion Papers 1410.

Harmsen, R. (1995). The Uruguay Round: A Boon for the world economy. Finance and Development, 32(1).

Harrison, G. W., Rutherford, T. F., & Tarr, D. G. (1997). Quantifying the Uruguay Round. The Economic Journal, 107(444), 1405-1430. https://doi.org/10.1111/j.1468-0297.1997.tb00055.x

Hoffmaister, A. W., & Vegh, C. A. (1996). Disinflation and the recession-now-versus-recession-later hypothesis: Evidence from Uruguay. IMF Staff Paper, 43(2), 355-394. https://doi.org/10.2307/3867401

Khan, A. H., & Kazmi, A. A. (1994). The Impact of the Uruguay Round on the World Economy. The Pakistan Development Review, 33(4), 1191-1203. https://doi.org/10.30541/v33i4IIpp.1191-1203

Kirby, J. (1975). On the viability of small countries: Uruguay and New Zealand Compared. Latin American Politics and Society, 17(3), 259-280. https://doi.org/10.2307/174724

Levine, R., & Renelt, D. (1992). A Sensitivity Analysis of Cross-Country Growth Regressions. The American Economic Review, 82(4), 942-963.

Lopez-Alves, F. (1993). Between the economy and the polity in the river plate: Uruguay, 1811-1890. University of London Institute of Latin American Studies Research Papers, 1-92.

Moraes, J. A., Chasquetti, D., & Bergara, M. (2005). The political economy of the budgetary process in Uruguay. Departamento de Economia: Documento No. 19/05, 1-52.

Osiobe, E. U. (2019). A Literature Review of Human Capital and Economic Growth. Business and Economic Research, 9(4), 179-196. https://doi.org/10.5296/ber.v9i4.15624

Osiobe, E. U. (2020). Human Capital and Economic Growth in Latin America: A Cointegration and Causality Analysis. The Economics and Finance Letters, 218-235. https://doi.org/10.18488/journal.29.2020.72.218.235

Osiobe, E. U. (2020). Human Capital, Capital Stock Formation, and Economic Growth: A Panel Granger Causality Analysis. Journal of Economics and Business, 569-580. https://doi.org/10.31014/aior.1992.03.02.221

Osiobe, E. U. (2020). Understanding Latin America's Educational Orientations: Evidence from 14 Nations. Education Quarterly Review, 249-260. https://doi.org/10.31014/aior.1993.03.02.137

Osiobe, Ejiro U. (2021). An Overview of Uruguay's Educational Policies. Economic Development Educational Research, Abuja: The Ane Osiobe International Foundation. DOI:10.47752/aneosiobe.16.187.201

Panizza, F. (2004). A Reform without Losers: The Symbolic Economy of Civil Service Reform in Uruguay 1995-96. Latin American Politics and Society, 46(3), 1-28. https://doi.org/10.1353/lap.2004.0035

Penn World Table Equation: Human Capital in PWT 9.0. (2019). PWT 9.0. (Penn World Table) Retrieved 10 6, 2019, from https://www.rug.nl/ggdc/docs/human_capital_in_pwt_90.pdf

Runge, C. F., & Stanton, G. H. (1988). The political economy of the Uruguay round negotiations: A view from Geneva. American Journal of Agricultural Economics, 70(5), 1146-1152. https://doi.org/10.2307/1241753

Schwab, K. (2018). The Global Competitiveness Report. Geneva: World Economic Forum.

Teixeira, E. C. (1998). Impact of the Uruguay Round Agreement and Mercosul on the Brazilian Economy. Rio de Janeiro, 52(3), 441-462.

Winters, A., & Martin, W. (1995). The Uruguay Round and the Developing Economies. The World Bank Discussion Paper. https://doi.org/10.1596/0-8213-3469-7

World Development Index Group, (2019, June 11). The World Bank. (World Development Indicators) Retrieved 3 18, 2019, from https://data.worldbank.org/region/latin-america-and-caribbean

Yap, C. L. (1996). The implication of the Uruguay Round on the world rice economy. Food Policy, 21(4-5), 377-391. https://doi.org/10.1016/0306-9192(96)00014-0

COINTEGRATION

INTRODUCTION

This chapter investigates the causal relationship between government spending on education and economic growth in eight selected Latin American countries using a panel unit root test and panel cointegration analysis from 2000-2014. A three-variable model was formulated with trade volume as the second independent variable. The findings conclude that government spending on education and economic growth in the selected countries is positively and significantly associated, in the long and short-run, with evidence of a bidirectional Granger causal relationship between the dependent and the variable of interest, a unidirectional Granger causal relationship between trade volume and economic growth. Our results imply that government secondary school spending on education positively impacts the selected countries, and our analysis can be replicated with other countries. Today fostering educational practices, increasing enrollment, and improving learning are central to most economic development strategies. Most economists from the 20th and early 21st century see the idea of increasing the public's aggregate per capita investment in human capital as a controversial topic; the expansion of education has not guaranteed improved economic conditions in some regions. The variables used in the study include 14 Latin American countries that have been analyzed, and the results show a strong causal relationship between real gross domestic product per capita–purchasing power parity and human capital. Although the study doesn't find a direct Granger causal relationship moving from human capital to real gross domestic product per capita-purchasing power parity, there is an indirect Granger causal relationship between our variables of interest. The association can be found in the bidirectional Granger causal relationship between human capital and trade balance. The chapter's main contribution to the existing literature is investigating the cointegration and Granger causal relationship between human capital and economic growth for eight selected Latin American countries: Argentina, Brazil, Chile, Colombia, Costa Rica, Mexico, Peru, and El Salvador.

The concept of human capital emerged from recognizing that the investment in human capital by an individual or a firm has an increasing return to scale on productivity. Human capital can be split into three concepts: talent (natural given ability), acquired qualification(s), and expertise. Human capital was first used in the late '50s and early '60. Before the '50s and '60s, the term was a suggestive phrase in economics and played no role in the decision-making algorithm when recommending, passing, and implementing educational policies. Upon empirical and practical evidence that there was a high return on quality education and it helped promote a nation's national goals, academics, policymakers, and practitioners advocated new ideas on public spending on education as a form of a nation's domestic investment. The chapter contributes to the research of economic growth, that is, human capital and how it fosters economic growth following Lucas Jr (1988); Barro (1991); Mankiw, Romer, and Weil (1992). The chapter's main contribution to the existing literature is it analyzes the cointegration and Granger Causal Relationship *(GCR)* between human capital proxied as Secondary School Government Expenditure ($SGE_{i,t}$), which is the variable of interest and economic growth proxied as ($RGDP_{per\ capitapppi,t}$) for eight Selected Latin American Countries (SLAC): Argentina, Brazil, Chile, Colombia, Costa Rica, Mexico, Peru, and El Salvador; suggesting that there is:

1. a bidirectional *GCR* between $SGEi,t$ and $RGDP_{per\ capitapppi,t}$ both in the short and long run

2. an increase in $RGDP_{per\ capitapppi,t}$ will boost the nation's trade volume ($Vt_{i,t}$)

3. a unidirectional *GCR* between $RGDP_{per\ capitapppi,t}$ and $Vt_{i,t}$, moving from $RGDP_{per\ capitapppi,t}$ to $VT_{i,t}$

Understanding Human Capital

This chapter defines human capital as human labor expertise used to produce other goods and services. Schultz (1961) defined human capital as a value measuring human potential. Smith (1776) "[stated that] the improvement to human capital through training, education, and experience makes the individual enterprise more profitable while adding to the collective wealth of the nation. Human capital can be seen as the collective wealth of a society in terms of judgment, skills, training, knowledge, experiences, and talent for a population (Schultz, 1961; Schultz., 1960).

Return on Human Capital

In a standard growth economic model (Mankiw et al., 1992; Romer, 1989, 1990; Romer, 1996; Romer, 1994), human capital accumulation is seen as a (private and public) investment undertaken to promote economic growth and development. The principle of opportunity cost is implemented in the model where the individual trades (some initial proportion of) his/her current income during their education and training period in return for and the hopes of higher future earnings. This trade-off will only be done if the additional schooling or training (i.e., investment in human capital) that translates to higher future earnings compensates the current costs (tuition and training course fees, forgone earnings while at school, and reduced wages during the training period) of the sacrifices.

LATIN AMERICA

In the last two decades, our SLAC and Latin America, in general, have achieved remarkable socio-economic progress. The lower and middle class has grown to historic levels; access to education and health care has expanded; poverty has been cut almost in half; property rights are recognized, and prosperity is being shared (World Economic Forum, 2016). As a result, most Latin American countries have achieved "middle-income" and emerging nation status, but the work(s) is far from done. Suppose our SLAC is to move onto a path of first-world countries, achieving sustained socio-economic growth. In that case, these nations will have to address numerous challenges–beginning with their lack of high-quality human capital

(World Economic Forum, 2016). Today, Latin America's young population has enormous potential, with 67% of the region's total population being counted in the labor force. Population aging is not yet a significant concern, as in developed economies – many workers lack the skills required to fulfill the demand for labor (World Economic Forum, 2016). Unskilled human capital makes much-needed productivity growth challenging in these regions. Companies in the productive sectors– which should be creating more and better-quality jobs – struggle to grow due to this human capital crisis, much less compete in the global economy (World Economic Forum, 2016). The continued worldwide technological advancement threatens to increase the gap between available skills, and those demanded worldwide. Suppose our SLAC and other Latin American countries are to or want to compete effectively and efficiently with those based in developed or emerging economies. In that case, the nations' must remedy this by raising the skill level of their workforce (World Economic Forum, 2016).

CHRONICLES

Kögel and Prskawetz (2001) analyzed how the advancement of human capital affected the industrialized world and escaped the Malthusian trap characterized by low economic and high population growth to the post-Malthusian regime characterized by high economic and low population growth. The authors' examined the transition between these regimes by constructing a growth model with two types of consumer goods (an agricultural and manufacturing product), endogenous fertility, and endogenous technological progress in the manufacturing sector. In their paper, Gibbons and Waldman (2004), which built on Becker (1964), expressed the economic implications of the third type of human capital Task-Specific, which is as essential as the general-purpose and firm-specific. The team Task-Specific human capital is when a person acquires the skills for a particular job instead of the firm or the industry. This type of human capital is based on the simple—plausible ideology that most human capital accumulation is due to Task-Specific learning by doing. The authors concluded by discussing how the concept of human capital can explain the cohort effects and provide an essential perspective regarding job-design issues. Becker's (1964) work on human capital focused on the presupposition of general-purpose and firm-specific human capital. Becker (1964) developed one of the most significant strands of research that focused on human capital and the economic approach to human capital. Teixeira (2014) explored (Becker, 1964) early work on human capital, which Becker considered a method of analysis rather than an assumption about human emotions because, an attempt to explain various facets of human behavior through a set of simplified assumptions regarding human behavior, a result of individual choices characterized by utility maximization a forward-looking stance, consistent rationality, and stable and persistent preferences (Becker, 1964). Asserting that the decisions were constrained by income, calculating capabilities, time, opportunities, and imperfect memory (Becker, 1993). Nerdrum and Erikson (2001) analyzed intellectual capital and found complementary capacities of competence and commitment. Based on theoretically and empirically robust human capital theory, Nerdrum and Erikson (2001) found that intellectual capital generates added value and creates wealth. The authors viewed resources to be perceived to be both tangible and intangible; and an extension of the human capital theory to be included in the intangible capacities of people.

METHODOLOGY, MODEL, AND RESULTS

As the world transitions from the millennial generation (1980 – 1995) to generation Z (1996 – 2010) in colleges, it is safe to conclude that the increasing enrollment rate can be attributed to the primary and secondary school net favorable educational policies implemented by educational policymakers. Over the decades, education, which for this chapter and book will be defined as the successful completion of a formal primary school system, has led to the effective use of physical and financial capital leading to the efficient use of units of labor in the production process (Smith, 1776) an overall increase in production.

Data Definition and Source

The chapter employs panel data between 2000 – 2014 for eight SLAC: Argentina, Brazil, Chile, Colombia, Costa Rica, Mexico, Peru, and El Salvador. These countries were selected due to data availability. The data was collected from (World Penn Tables, 2019) Real Gross Domestic Product-per capita-purchasing power parity ($RGDP_{per\ capitapppi,t}$), which is Gross Domestic Product (GDP) converted to international dollars using purchasing power parity rates divided by total population; return on education $\equiv$ human capital $\equiv$ ($HC_{i,t}$) is based on years of schooling and returns to education. The second source of our data is (the World Development Index (World Penn Tables, 2019) Volume of Trade ($VT_{i,t}$) is net export + net import; Primary School Government Expenditure ($PGE_{i,t}$), which is the average general government expenditure (current, capital, and transfers) per student in the given level of education, expressed as a percentage of Gross Domestic Product per capita

(*GDP*$_{per\ capita}$); Secondary School Government Expenditure (*SGE*$_{i,t}$) is the average general government expenditure (current, capital, and transfers) per student in the given level of education, expressed as a percentage of *GDP* $_{per\ capita}$, where i = countries and t = years.

Correlation analysis:

The correlation coefficient (r) was applied to measure the relationships between *HC*$_{i,t}$, *PGE*$_{i,t}$, and *SGE*$_{i,t}$ in our data set and r is given as:

$$r = \frac{n(\sum HC_{i,t}\, PGE_{i,t}\, SGE_{i,t}) - (\sum HC_{i,t})(\sum PGE_{i,t})(\sum SGE_{i,t})}{\sqrt{[n \sum HC_{i,t}^2 - (\sum HC_{i,t})^2][n \sum PGE_{i,t}^2 - (\sum PGE_{i,t})^2][n \sum SGE_{i,t}^2 - (\sum SGE_{i,t})^2]}} \qquad (1)$$

Table 1: Correlation analysis

Correlation *T-Stat* (P-Value)	$HC_{i,t}$	$PGE_{i,t}$	$SGE_{i,t}$
$HC_{i,t}$	1.00 n/a n/a		
$PGE_{i,t}$	0.96 36.66 (0.00)***	1.00 n/a (n/a)	
$SGE_{i,t}$	0.96 37.69 (0.00)***	0.85 17.12 (0.00)***	1.00 n/a (n/a)

Note:
* indicates significance level at 10%
** indicates significance level at 5%
*** indicates significance at 1%

Given the strong relationship between *HC*$_{i,t}$, *PGE*$_{i,t}$, and *SGE*$_{i,t}$, *HC*$_{i,t}$, and *PGE*$_{i,t}$ were dropped from the base model. Equation one shows the correlation coefficient between *HC*$_{i,t}$, *PGE*$_{i,t}$, and *SGE*$_{i,t}$. Table 1 shows the correlation relationship (see equation one); our result shows a significant relationship between *PGE*$_{i,t}$, and *SGE*$_{i,t}$, while Figure 1 shows the graphical representation of our results. $SGE_{i,t}$ was selected as the base model because, according to Feinstein, Robertson, and Symons (1999), parental interest in education is the most potent parental input. Building on this parental input will lead a child to achieve more in their educational career.

Figure 1: Line graph of the cross-correlation between $HC_{i,t}$, $PGE_{i,t}$, and $SGE_{i,t}$

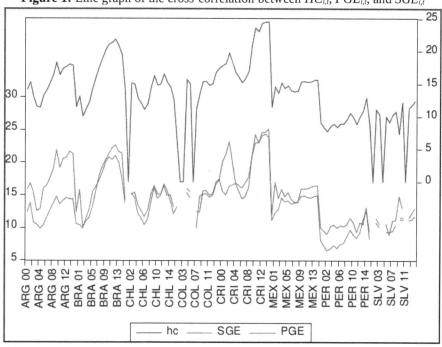

Note:
HC: Left Axis
SGE & PGE: Right Axis

Estimation Concerns

To test the Panel Unit Root (*PUR*) among the explained and explanatory variables, the first step is to examine the unit root properties of the data because stationarity is required for our variables to be integrated in the same order. For this study, the unit root test by Levin, Lin, and Chu (2002), Breitung and Das (2005), and Im, Pesaran, and Shin (2003) were implemented. The Levin et al. (2002) test is based on the Augmented Dickey-Fuller (*ADF*) test. The null hypothesis of our unit root test is non-stationary of the data. The Pedroni panel cointegration test was adopted for the panel cointegration test (Pedroni, 2002, 2004). The test allows various cross-sectional interdependencies and other different individual effects to establish cointegration. Then, the Panel Granger Causality Vector Error Correction Model (*VECM*) test will be analyzed.

Model Specification

The theoretical structure of the study will be based on the new endogenous theory of Romer (1994). The Romer model argues that the main factor for economic growth is the accumulation of knowledge, asserting that economic growth is dependent on human capital, labor, physical capital, and technology. Romer's production function is as follows:

$$Y(t) = K(t) \, H(t) p \, Y[A(t) \, L(t)], 1 > x > 0, p > 0, a + p < 1 \quad (2)$$

Romer's production function is as follows:

$$Y_t = K_t^a \, (A, L)^\beta l^\varepsilon \quad (3)$$

$$0 < \alpha < 1$$

Then we normalize (*L*) the simple endogenous growth model, where *K* embodies physical and human capital.

$$Y = AK$$

$$\frac{Y}{L} = A. \frac{K}{L}$$

$$y = Ak$$

EDUCATION IN LATIN AMERICA

The model implicitly assumes that $A > 0$. It also assumes that the labor force is growing at a constant rate of (n), and that there is no capital depreciation. ($= 0$). For the study and following Mankiw et al. (1992); Romer (1989); Romer (1990); Romer (1994), and Vieira (2013), the differential equation of the neoclassical growth model is the chapter defines the total factor productivity (A) as

$$A = f(SGE_{i,t} \text{ and } VT_{i,t}) = SGE_{i,t}^{\beta_1} VT_{i,t}^{\beta_2} \tag{4}$$

Where $Y_t = RGDP_{per\ capitappp}$ $SGE_{i,t}$ = human capital and $VT_{i,t}$ = volume of trade

Substituting y = Ak

$$Y_t = {}^nK_t^\alpha \left(SGE_{i,t}^{\beta_1} VT_{i,t}^{\beta_2} \right) l^\varepsilon \tag{5}$$

Taking the logarithm of the variables, differencing $RGDP_{per\ capita_{ppp}}$ we get:

$$lnY_t = \beta_0 + \beta_1 lnSGE_{i,t} + \beta_2 lnVT_{i,t} + \varepsilon_t \tag{6}$$

Where: $ln^n = \beta_0$, $ln l^\varepsilon = 1$, and ln = natural logarithm. Where: K = Physical capital, H = Human capital, A = Technology, L = Labor. The assumption of K, H, and L are as follows:

$$\dot{K}(t) = S_K Y(t), \quad \dot{H}(t) = S_H Y(t), \text{ and } \dot{L}(t) = nL(t)$$

Where S_K = The portion of output assigned to physical capital accumulation for K, S_H = the portion of output assigned to human capital accumulation for H, and n is the growth rate.

The Dynamics of the Model

Where equation seven represent the Cobb-Douglas production function, showing physical and human capital that is defined as

$$k = \frac{K}{AL}, h = \frac{H}{AL}, and\ y \tag{7}$$

Which implies:

$$y(t) = f(k(t, h(t))$$

Differentiating with respect to time, we get:

$$\Delta y(t) = \Delta f_k k(t) + \Delta f_h h(t)$$

The model will be estimated using the stated/base equation/model of the study:

$$lnRGDP = \beta_0 + \beta_1 SGE_{i,t} + \beta_2 lnVT_{i,t} + \varepsilon_{i,t} \tag{8}$$

EMPIRICAL RESULTS

Panel Unit Root Test

Conventionally, macroeconomics time series are non-stationary (Nelson, 1982). It is necessary to test the stationary properties of the data. This requires examining the order of integration of the data set, which is the unit root test. A time series is stable if its mean, variance, and autocovariance are independent of time (Gujarati, 2012). The panel data technique referred to above has appealed to the researchers because of its weak restrictions. It captures the country-specific effects, allows for heterogeneity in the direction and magnitude of the parameters across the panel, and provides a high degree of freedom in the model selection. Following the methodology used in earlier works (Al-Yousif, 2002), we test for the trend and intercept stationary for our variables. With a null of non-stationary, the test is a residual-based test that explores the performance of three different statistics. These three statistics reflect a combination of Levin et al. (2002), Breitung (2000), and Im et al. (2003). The Levin et al. (2002) test is based on the ADF test, which assumes homogeneity in the dynamics of the autoregressive coefficients for all panel units with cross-sectional independence. The *LLC* equation is as follows:

$$\Delta X_{it} = \alpha_i + \beta_i X_{i,t-1} + \delta_i t + \sum_{j=1}^{k} \gamma_{ij} X_{i,t-j} + \theta_{it}$$

Where: Δ = Is the first difference operator, X_{it} = Is the dependent variable, = Is the white-noise disturbance with a variance of σ^2, $i = 1,2,.....,n$ indexes countries, and $t = 1,2,.....,$ T indexes time. According to Levin et al. (2002), the hypothesis to test the stationarity of the panel data is

$$H_o: \beta_i = 0 \quad \text{and} \quad H_1: \beta_i < 0$$

Where the alternative hypothesis; corresponds to Y_{it} being stationary. The test also finds that while comparing with the single equation of the ADF test, the panel approach substantially increases its power in finite samples. Levin et al. (2002) also specified another equation, which restricts β_i while keeping it identical across countries.

$$\Delta X_{it} = \alpha_i + \beta_i X_{i,t-1} + \delta_i t + \sum_{j=1}^{k} \gamma_{ij} \Delta X_{i,t-j} + \theta_{it}$$

In the equation, it is assumed that:

$$H_o: \beta_1 = \beta_2 = \cdots = \beta_n = 0 \quad \text{and} \quad H_1: \beta_1 = \beta_2 = \cdots = \beta_n < 0$$

Where:

$t - statistics = t_{\hat{\beta}}/\sigma(\hat{\beta})$ and

$\Delta X_{it} = \alpha_i + \beta_i X_{i,t-1} + \delta_i t + \sum_{j=1}^{k} \gamma_{ij} \Delta X_{i,t-j} + \theta_{it} = \hat{\beta}$ and its standard error $= \sigma(\hat{\beta})$

The Breitung unit root test is based on Breitung (2000); Breitung and Das

(2005) developed a pooled panel unit root test that does not require bias correction factors. This is achieved by (depending upon the case considered) variable transformation. The Breitung unit root test has better small-sample performance; it is pre-whitening[1].

$$\Delta y_{it} = \alpha_i + \sum_{j=1}^{P_i} y_{ij} \Delta y_{it} -j + v_{it}$$

In which the residuals

$\widetilde{e_{it}}$ and $\widetilde{f_{it}}$ are computed as follows:

$$\widetilde{e_{it}} = \Delta y_{it} - \sum_{j=1}^{P_i} \widehat{y_{ij}} \Delta y_{it} - j$$

$$\widetilde{f_{it}-1} = y_{it} - 1 - \sum_{j=1}^{P_i} \widehat{y_{ij}} y_{it} - j - 1$$

The residuals at the base model are

$$\Delta y_{it} = \alpha_i + \sum_{j=1}^{P_i} y_{ij} \Delta y_{it} -j + v_{it}$$

Then standardized by the regression standard error to $\widetilde{e_{it}}$ and $\widetilde{f_{it}}-1$
Then, the residuals of
$\widetilde{e_{it}}$ and $\widetilde{f_{it}}$ are orthogonalized as follows:

$$e_{it}^{*} = \sqrt{\frac{T-t}{T-(t+1)}} \left(\Delta \widehat{e_{it}} - \frac{1}{T-t} (\Delta \hat{e}_{it+1} + \cdots + \Delta \hat{e}_{iT}) \right)$$

$$f_{it}^{*} = \hat{f}_{it-1} - \hat{f}_{i1} + \frac{t-1}{T} (\hat{f}_{iT} - \hat{f}_{i1})$$

Where: T = The sample size after the auxiliary regressions. Then the unit root is performed in the pooled regression.

$$e_{it}^* = \emptyset^* f_{it}^* + v_{it}^*$$

Where our hypothesis is:

$H_o: \emptyset^* = 0$ and $H_1: -1 < p_i < 1$ Where $i = 1, ..., N_1$ and $p_i = 1$ for $i = N_1,....,N$. The Breitung unit root test shows the test's t-statistic with a standard Normal limiting distribution (for a sequential limit of the first $T \rightarrow \infty$ followed by $N \rightarrow \infty$). The *IPS* is based on Im et al. (2003), which uses the average of the $t_{\beta i}$ statistics from

$$\Delta X_{it} = \alpha_i + \beta_i X_{i,t-1} + \delta_i t + \sum_{j=1}^{k} \gamma_{ij} \Delta X_{i,t-j} + \theta_{it}$$

Then it's used to perform the following $\bar{Z}$ statistic. Where:

$$\bar{Z} = \sqrt{N} \left[\bar{t} - E(\bar{t}) \right] / \sqrt{V(\bar{t})} \qquad \bar{t} = \left(\frac{1}{N} \right) \Sigma_{i=1}^{N} t_{\beta i} \qquad E(\bar{t}) \text{ and } V(\bar{t}) =$$

are the man and variance of each $t_{\beta i}$ statistic. Eventually, the Z converges to a standard normal distribution. So, the IPS test is based on the average individual unit root test, and it is expressed by

$$\bar{t} = \left(\frac{1}{N} \right) \Sigma_{i=1}^{N} t_{\beta i}$$

The result of the *PUR* test is in Table 2. The table includes Levin et al. (2002), Breitung (2002), Breitung and Das (2005), and Im et al. (2003).

Table 2: Panel Unit Root Table (Trend and Intercept).

Variable	LLC	IPS	Breitung	LLC	IPS	Breitung
	Levels			1st Difference		
$RGDP_{per\ capita_{PPP_{i,t}}}$	0.00***	0.13	0.09*	n/a	0.00)***	(0.01)***
$SGE_{i,t}$	0.04**	0.11	0.76*	n/a	(0.00)***	(0.04)**
$VT_{i,t}$	0.00***	0.49	0.23	n/a	(0.00)***	(0.00)***

Notes:
* indicates significance level at 10%
** indicates significance level at 5%
*** indicates a significance level at 1%

Ejiro U. Osiobe

Lag Selection Criteria Test

We test for a cointegrating relationship since our variables are now rendered stationary. The lag length is first determined using the Lag Selection Criteria test to analyze the cointegration test. Five lag length selection criteria have been employed in this study to assess our variables' Autoregressive (AR) lag length. The *AR* lag length p is unknown and can be estimated using the lag selection criteria. The analysis would be carried out using the likelihood ratio (*LR*) test, according to Sims (1980).

$$LR = (T - c)|\log|\Omega_1| - \log|\Omega_2||$$

Where T = Sample size, c = Total number of parameters estimated in the model Ω_1 = Is the maximum likelihood estimate of the variance-covariance matrix of the residuals in the Vector Autoregression (*VAR*) model under the null hypothesis, and Ω_2 = Is the maximum likelihood estimate of the variance-covariance matrix of the residuals in the VAR model under the alternative hypothesis. The *LR* test is a chi-square distributed with the degrees of freedom equal to the number of restrictions that are tested. Final Prediction Error (*FPE*) is given as:

$$FPE(p) = |\check{\Sigma}(p)| + (\frac{\hat{T} + M_p + 1}{\hat{T} - M_p - 1})^2$$

Akaike Information Criterion (*AIC*), according to Akaike (1974), is given as

$$AIC(p) = \ln|\hat{\Sigma}_p| + \frac{2k^2 p}{T}$$

Where T = Is the number of observations, k = is the time series dimension, p = Is the estimated number of lags, Σ_p = Is the estimated white noise covariance matrix. Shibata (1976) proves that the *AIC* criterion, in the univariate *AR(p)* representation, is inconsistent in that asymptotically, it overestimates the exact order with a nonzero probability. Schwarz

278

Information Criterion (*SC*), according to Schwarz (1978), the equation is given as

$$SC(p) = \ln|\hat{\Sigma}_p| + \frac{k^2 p \ln T}{T}$$

and Hannan-Quinn Criterion (*HQ*) is given as

$$HQ(p) = \ln|\hat{\Sigma}_p| + \frac{2pk^2 \ln \ln T}{T}$$

Table 3 shows the lag length selection results.

Table 3: Lag length selection criteria test.

Lag	LogL	LR	FPE	AIC	SC	HQ
0	-229.34	N/A	1.27e-05	8.59	8.85	8.69
1	517.05	1275.65	1.25e-16*	-16.77	-14.72*	-15.97*
2	566.07	71.31*	1.36e-16	-16.77*	-12.93	-15.28
3	604.18	45.73	2.55e-16	-16.37	-10.75	14.20

Note:
*Indicates lag order selected by the criterion.
LR: sequential modified LR test statistic (each test at 5% level).
FPE: Final prediction error. / AIC: Akaike information criterion.
SC: Schwarz information criterion. / HQ: Hannan-Quinn information criterion.

Panel Cointegration Test

Our study identifies two kinds of test statistics the pooling residuals within the dimension of the panel and the other without the dimension. The long-run equilibrium equations are as follows:

Panel V-Statistic

$$Z_v = \left(\sum_{i=1}^{N} \sum_{t=1}^{T} \hat{L}_{11i}^{-2} \hat{e}_{it-1}^2 \right)^{-1}$$

Panel rho-Statistic

$$Z_p = \left(\sum_{i=1}^{N} \sum_{t=1}^{T} \hat{L}_{11i}^{-2} \hat{e}_{it-1}^2 \right)^{-1} \sum_{i=1}^{N} \sum_{t=1}^{T} \hat{L}_{11i}^{-2} (\hat{e}_{it-1}^2 \Delta \hat{e}_{it} - \hat{\lambda}_i)$$

Panel PP-Statistic

$$Z_t = \left(\sum_{i=1}^{N} \sum_{t=1}^{T} \hat{L}_{11i}^{-2} \hat{e}_{it-1}^2 \right)^{-1/2} \sum_{i=1}^{N} \sum_{t=1}^{T} \hat{L}_{11i}^{-2} (\hat{e}_{it-1}^2 \Delta \hat{e}_{it} - \hat{\lambda}_i)$$

Panel ADF-Statistic

$$Z_t^* = \left(\hat{\sigma}^{*2} \sum_{i=1}^{N} \sum_{t=1}^{T} \hat{L}_{11i}^{-2} \hat{e}_{it-1}^2 \right)^{-1/2} \sum_{i=1}^{N} \sum_{t=1}^{T} \hat{L}_{11i}^{-2} (\hat{e}_{it-1}^* \Delta \hat{e}_{it}^*)$$

Group rho-Statistic

$$\check{Z}_p = \sum_{i=1}^{N} \left(\sum_{t=1}^{T} \hat{e}_{it-1}^2 \right)^{-1} \sum_{t=1}^{N} (\hat{e}_{it-1}^2 \Delta \hat{e}_{it} - \hat{\lambda}_i)$$

Group PP-Statistic

$$\check{Z}_t = \hat{\sigma}^2 \left(\sum_{t=1}^{T} \hat{e}_{it-1}^2 \right)^{-1/2} \sum_{t=1}^{T} (\hat{e}_{it-1} \Delta \hat{e}_{it} - \hat{\lambda}_i)$$

Group ADF-Statistic

$$\check{Z}_t^* = \sum_{i=1}^{N} \left(\sum_{t=1}^{T} \hat{s}_i^2 \hat{e}_{it-1}^{*2} \right)^{-1/2} \sum_{t=1}^{T} (\hat{e}_{it-1}^* \Delta \hat{e}_{it}^*)$$

Where $\hat{e}_{it}$ = Is the estimated residual from our primary equation

$$lnRGDP_{per\ capita_{ppp_{i,t}}} = \beta_0 + \beta_1 lnSGE_{i,t} + \beta_2 lnVT_{i,t} + \varepsilon_{i,t}$$

Where

$\hat{L}_{11i}^{-2}$ = Is the estimated long-run covariance matrix for

$$\Delta \hat{e}_{it}^* \quad \hat{\sigma}_i^2 = \hat{s}_i^2(\hat{S}_i^{*2}) =$$

are the long run and contemporaneous variance for the country t. The Panel V-Stat, Panel rho-Stat, Panel PP-Stat, Panel ADF-Stat, Group rho-State, Group PP-Stat, and Group ADF-Stat are normally and asymptotically distributed. The results are as follows:

Table 4: Pedroni panel cointegration test.

Panel Group Statistics	Statistic	Prob
Panel V–Statis tic	5.90	0.00***
Panel rho–Statis tic	3.33	0.99
Panel PP–Statis tic	-2.64	0.00***
Panel ADF–Statis tic	-2.84	0.00***
Group rho–Statis tic	4.01	1.00
Group PP–Statis tic	-5.74	0.00***
Group ADF Statis tic	-3.03	0.00***

Note:
* indicates significance at 10%
** indicates significance at 5%
*** indicates significance at 1%

Fully Modified Ordinary Least Squares (FMOLS)

The Fully Modified Ordinary Least Squares *FMOLS* technique to determine the coefficients of the long-run relationship between the explained and the explanatory variables. The *FMOLS* estimates show the cointegration regression by accounting for serial correlation effects and endogeneity in the regression (Phillips, 1995). Pedroni (2002); Pedroni (2004) *FMOLS* can accommodate considerable heterogeneity across individual members of the panel. Pedroni (2002) further stated that the cointegration test determines

Ejiro U. Osiobe

whether our variables are cointegrated without providing estimated co-efficients for the individual variables in the panel.

Table 5: Results of long-term coefficient estimates by FMOLS

Variables	Model
$SGE_{i,t}$	0.005 $(0.00)^{***}$
$VT_{i,t}$	0.36 $(0.00)^{***}$
R-squared (Adj-R)	87% (86%)

Note:
p-value in parenthesis
* indicates significance level at 10%
** indicates significance level at 5%
*** indicates significance at 1%

Table 5 shows a positive, statistically significant long-run relationship between $RGDP_{per\ capitapppi,t}$ and $SGE_{i,t}$ with a coefficient of 0.005. This indicates a 1% increase in $RGDP_{per\ capitapppi,t}$ in our LAC. The 0.005%-point associated with $SGE_{i,t}$ implies an incentive for a nation to increase its expenditure on secondary school education as it will translate to improved skillsets, knowledge, and innovative ideas. In the long run, this improvement will lead to the creation of new jobs, (an) increase in productivity, the disposable income of employees, and the consumption of consumer goods and services. This result indicates that the incentive to increase expenditure on $SGE_{i,t}$ of a nation would yield a positive outcome as it translates to an increase in $RGDP_{per\ capitappp}$. This result is consistent with Edrees (2016), Mehrara and Musai (2013); Khembo and Tchereni (2013); Rahman (2011) and Sharma and Sahni (2015), and Osiobe (2020) which is a similar vein study that analyzes the relationship among $RGDP_{per\ capitapppi,t}$ (as a proxy for economic growth) and the examined variable, $Hc_{i,t}$, (as a proxy for human

282

capital) $CS_{i,t}$ (as a proxy for physical capital), and $TB_{i,t}$ as the explanatory variables between 1950-2014, and expands on the countries used in the book, by adding Bolivia, Honduras, Nicaragua, Panama, Uruguay, and Venezuela. The $VT_{i,t}$ showed a positive, statistically significant result with a coefficient of 0.36. This implies that a 1% increase in the $VT_{i,t}$ is associated with a 0.36%-point increase in $RGDP_{per\ capitapppi,t}$ in our LAC as the nation becomes more trade-friendly.

Panel Granger Causality (VECM)

The chapter of the causal relationship among economic variables has been one of the main objectives of empirical econometrics. Engle (1987) states that cointegrated variables must have an error correction representation. One of the implications of the Granger representation theorem is that if non-stationary series are cointegrated, one must cause the other (Gujarati, 2012). To examine the direction of causality in the presence of cointegrating vectors, the GC test is estimated using the following specifications:

$$(10)$$

$$\begin{pmatrix} \Delta lnRGDP_{per\ capita_{ppv}\ i,t} \\ \Delta SGE_{i,t} \\ \Delta lnVT_{i,t} \end{pmatrix} = \begin{pmatrix} \emptyset_{i,1} \\ \emptyset_{i,2} \\ \emptyset_{i,3} \end{pmatrix} + \sum_{i=1}^{m} \begin{pmatrix} \theta_{1,2,3,4,k} \\ \theta_{2,1,3,4,k} \\ \theta_{3,1,2,4,k} \end{pmatrix} \begin{bmatrix} \Delta lnRGDP_{i,t} \\ \Delta SGE_{i,t} \\ \Delta lnVT_{i,t} \end{bmatrix} + \begin{pmatrix} \lambda_1 \\ \lambda_2 \\ \lambda_3 \end{pmatrix} ECT_{i,t-1} + \begin{pmatrix} \varphi_{1,i,t} \\ \varphi_{2,i,t} \\ \varphi_{3,i,t} \end{pmatrix}$$

Where Δ = the first differences, $\emptyset_{i,j}$ (j, k = 1, 2) = fixed country effect, $I(I = 1,....m)$ = Is the lag length determined by SIC, $ECT_{i,t-1}$ = Is the estimated lagged error correction term (ECT) derived from the long-run cointegrating relationship, λ_i = Is the adjustment coefficient, and $\emptyset_{1,l,t}$ = Is the disturbance term, which is assumed to have a zero mean.

Table 6: The estimate of the panel vector error correction model.

Explained Variable	Explanatory Variables – Chi-square value (Wald test)			
	$RGDP_{per\ capita_{ppp_{i,t}}}$	$SGE_{i,t}$	$VT_{i,t}$	ECT (-1) t-Test
$RGDP_{per\ capita_{ppp_{i,t}}}$		7.98 (0.04)**	2.51 (0.47)	-0.031 [-2.44]
$SGE_{i,t}$	7.32 (0.02)**		1.83 (0.40)	-1.12 [-3.67]
$VT_{i,t}$	6.22 (0.10)*	2.01 (0.57)		-0.00 [-0.24]

Note:
*indicates significance level at 10%
** indicates significance level at 5%
*** indicates significance at 1%

Table 6 and 7 shows our estimates indicate a significant bidirectional GCR between $RGDP_{per\ capitapppi,t} \leftrightarrow SGE_{i,t}$ and unidirectional GCR between $RGDP_{per\ capitapppi,t} \rightarrow VT_{i,t}$. The bidirectional GCR between $RGDP_{per\ capitapppi,t} \leftrightarrow SGE_{i,t}$ implies a chicken and egg GCR, but the $VECM$ doesn't tell us which of our variables comes first. If it is the dependent variable ($RGDP_{per\ capitapppi,t}$) or the independent ($SGE_{i,t}$). In light of this dilemma, our results can be associated with; the following interpretation as a nation's $RGDP_{per\ capitapppi,t}$ increases, this will lead to a rise in the country's real gross domestic product, increasing the nation's net expenditure on $SGE_{i,t}$ which will increase the supply and the demand for quality blue-collar and Artisan jobs. The unidirectional GCR between $RGDP_{per\ capitapppi,t} \rightarrow VT_{i,t}$ implies ceteris paribus as $RGDP_{per\ capitapppi,t}$ starts to rise, Marginal Propensity to Consume (MPC) will increase, as well as Marginal Propensity to Save (MPS), which in turn will increases net investment, creating more jobs in the domestic market, increasing the total output of consumer and producers goods and services within the country, which will translate and expand into the international market, thus increasing the volume of trade (Import + Export) and boosting the wealth of the national real gross domestic product.

SUMMARY STATEMENT, CONCLUSION,
AND EDUCATIONAL POLICY RECOMMENDATIONS

The results contained in Table 6 support the long-term *GCR* between our explained and explanatory variables in all the selected countries. In contrast, the short-run *GCR* results from our variables can be found in Table 7. Our results imply that $SGE_{i,t}$ does Granger cause $RGDP_{per\ capitapppi,t}$ in the short and long run, and vice versa in the respective countries. Given the results obtained, the importance of $SGE_{i,t}$ in boosting economic growth can't be overemphasized. While $VT_{i,t}$ does not GC $RGDP_{per\ capitapppi,t}$ in the short-run, the reverse holds to be true, and in the long-run, it does *GC* economic growth in the respective countries. This study investigates the *GCR* between $SGE_{i,t}$ and economic growth in SLAC. The study employs a time series of annual data between 2000–2014 for a panel of eight SLAC: Argentina, Brazil, Chile, Colombia, Costa Rica, Mexico, Peru, and El Salvador.

Table 7: Summary of main findings of short-run causality.

Variables	Direction of Causality	Implication
$RGDP_{per\ capita_{ppp_{i,t}}} \leftrightarrow SGE_{i,t}$	Bidirectional	Granger causality runs from $RGDP_{per\ capita_{ppp\ i,t}}$ to $SGE_{i,t}$
$RGDP_{per\ capita_{ppp_{i,t}}} \rightarrow VT_{i,t}$	Unidirectional	Granger causality runs from $RGDP_{per\ capita_{ppp\ i,t}}$ to $VT_{i,t}$

Note:
↔ indicates causality running in both direction
→ indicates causality from left to right
← indicates causality from right to left
↑ increase
↓ decrease
— leads too

The data was collected from World Penn Tables (2019). The empirical findings reveal that after controlling for $SGE_{i,t}$ $VT_{i,t}$ and $RGDP_{per\ capitapppi,t,}$ there is a positive statistically significant long-run relationship between $RGDP_{per\ capitapppi,t}$ and $SGE_{i,t}$ with a coefficient of 0.005. This indicates that a 1%-point increase in $SGE_{i,t}$ will lead to a 0.005%-point increase in $RGDP_{per\ capitapppi,t}$ in the SLAC. This result indicates that the incentive to improve a nation's secondary school attainment rates and levels (HDI) would yield a positive outcome as it translates to creating new blue-collar workers and an increase in $RGDP_{per\ capitapppi,t}$ in the SLAC. The $VT_{i,t}$ has a positive statistically significant long-run relationship with $RGDP_{per\ capitapppi,t}$, with a coefficient of 0.36%. That is, a one percent increase in $VT_{i,t}$ causes an increase in $RGDP_{per\ capitapppi,t}$ by 0.36%-point. Our results also indicate a significant causal link between $RGDP_{per\ capitapppi,t}$ and $SGE_{i,t}$ with a bidirectional GCR, moving from $RGDP_{per\ capitapppi,t}$ to $SGE_{i,t}$ and vice versa. While $RGDP_{per\ capitapppi,t,}$ and $VT_{i,t}$ have a unidirectional GCR, moving from $RGDP_{per\ capitapppi,t}$ to $Vt_{i,t}$. Further studies need to be examined using different methodologies to investigate how spending on education translates to higher economic growth, community development, and higher productivity. Notwithstanding, specific government spending on different tiers of education (higher education) needs to be investigated. The policy implications of this research involve the following: first, Our SLAC will provide incentives that would promote academic spending in the primary and secondary education levels and overall educational advancement in the region.

In conclusion, this chapter adopted the Mankiw et al. (1992) technique and supports that education is imperative for the economic growth and development of the SLAC. Despite this widespread belief that investment in education is a key determinant of economic growth and will shortly lead to economic development, the empirical estimations, especially focusing on low-income countries, are less than conclusive. Quiggin (2002); Devarajan, Swaroop, and Zou (1996); Benhabib and Spiegel (1994). This can be attributed to how schooling, investment, and success are measured.

Ejiro U. Osiobe

CAUSALITY

This chapter contributes to the literature on human capital, education, and Latin America studies by presenting our empirical results on the effect(s) of human capital and economic growth in Latin America grounded on Smith's (1776) learning by doing and Ricardo (1803) division of labor ideology and economic growth theory. The human capital theory focuses on health and the return on education investment as an input to economic production. In 1997, the United Nations (UN) defined human capital as productive wealth embodied in labor, skills, and knowledge (UN, 2016 and 2020). This study defines human capital as education and training (formal, informal, and cultural); knowledge; labor; skills (general, industry, firm, job, and task-specific); experience. They are incorporated and called human capital because people can't be separated from the stated factors in how they can be separated from their financial and physical capital during production.

Education affects the quality of labor and technical progress, affecting a country's economic growth, development, and stability. However, trade liberalization is often considered essential for increasing a nation's productivity. There is almost a unilateral concession among economists that liberal and open trade policies increase trade volume to Gross Domestic Product (*GDP*), resulting in a more favorable trade balance (+/-) as it is evaluated based on the differences between spending on consumer or producer goods. Today, developing nations are liberalizing their economies to become attractive to foreign direct investments. This chapters aims to analyze the impact of human capital on economic growth and development. The empirical analysis tries to determine the Granger Causal Relationship (*GCR*) between human capital and economic growth in 14 Selected Latin American Countries (LAC) by using the panel unit root test and panel cointegration analysis from 1950 to 2014.

Chronicle of Economic Growth Theory

Human capital's net impact(s) on economic growth, development, and stability has received significant attention in recent years, especially from emerging countries. But to address the underlying question of this study, there are two vital approaches to take. First, human capital is seen as an essential factor of production in the production process, and second, as a production facilitator. Smith (1776) argues that specialization, learning by doing, at all production line levels, can be enhanced by ensuring that each job position can be improved (production per capita and quality per unit) by reducing the job requirement. He asserted with empirical backing that the productivity of skilled workers is higher than the unskilled, and hence his justification for higher earnings per individual marginal productivity as a result of the individual (per workers') investment. Malthus (1798), a classic work, set two underlying assumptions. First, an increase in Gross Domestic Product per capita ($GCP_{per\ capita}$) above the economic equilibrium level of consumption will lead to a rise in the economy population size. Second, a country's increasing population size will reduce the nation's resources per capita; consequently, consumption per capita will fall back to equilibrium. As a result of these stated underlying assumptions, any economy will be trapped in economic stagnation. This view, now heavily criticized for not factoring in the effect of technological advancement, accurately described the demography and economic status of the 18th century. The author concludes his argument by saying that an increase in agricultural productivity leads to an increase in population size with zero long-run improvements in living standards. Ricardo (1817) discussed the division of labor and the consequences of technological progress in society. Ricardo Agreed with Smith's division of labor, specialization, and mechanization of the production process as a net benefit to any community, leading to a reduction in cost per unit and a net increase in total production. Later changing his position but not opposed to technology, he argued that introducing machinery in the production process might lead to permanent unemployment if the expenditure is financed with circulating fixed capital and not savings. He concludes that if the investment is made with net savings, entrepreneurs will search for more profits by increasing productivity through technological advancements or investing abroad.

Mill's (1871) view was contrasted to Ricardo's, arguing that lower prices don't bring additional investment because the demand for a good or service, although correlated, doesn't affect the demand for [its] labor. Marx's (1844 & 1867) sociological and philosophical critique of the market economy upon workers' life as distinct from economic well-being. Marx argues that private property and mechanization of production lead to the degrading and dehumanization of workers. But several scholars believe that Smith's Wealth of Nations (Smithian treatment of alienation) was an essential precursor of Marxist socialism (Marxian treatment of alienation) (West, 2020).

Empirical Foundation and Methods of Analysis

The study employs a time series annual data analysis between 1950–2014 for a panel of 14 LAC: Argentina, Bolivia, Brazil, Chile, Colombia, Costa Rica, Honduras, Mexico, Nicaragua, Panama, Peru, El Salvador, Uruguay, and Venezuela. The LAC was selected due to data availability compared to other countries that lacked comprehensive data from our data source (Penn World Table (PWT), 2019). Table 1 lists the variables used in the study and abbreviations.

Variables

Table 1: Variables used in our based Model

Variables	Meaning
$RGDP_{per\ capita_{ppp_{i,t}}}$	Real gross domestic product-per capita–purchasing power parity is gross domestic product converted to international dollars using purchasing power parity rates per individual.
$HC_{i,t}$ (lowest 0.1 – 13.4 highest)	Is based on years of schooling and returns to education
$CS_{i,t}$ at constant (2011 USD)	It is the plant, equipment, and other assets that help with production.
$TB_{i,t}$ as a % of $RGDP$	Trade Balance as a share of real gross domestic product

Source: (PWT, 2019)
i = countries
t = years

The descriptive statistic shows all variables' maximum, minimum, mean, and standard deviation (See Table 2). The variables used in the study are $RGDP_{per\ capitapppi,t}$; $HC_{i,t}$ our variable of interest, and an explanatory variable. $RGDP_{per\ capitapppi,t}$ from our econometric equation, is operationalized as Real Gross Domestic Product-purchasing power parity ($RGDPppp$) ≡ $RGDP_{per\ capitapppi,t}$ by dividing $RGDPppp$ by the total population. $HC_{i,t}$ it is measured as the number of years of schooling and the returns to education of the entire population. The Human Development Index (HDI) from (Barro & Lee, 2013) is based on the average years of schooling and an assumed rate of return to education, which comes from the Mincer equation estimates explained by (Psacharopoulos, 1994), is used as the measuring tool for $HC_{i,t}$. The HDI formula is:

$$\emptyset(s) = \begin{cases} 0.134.s & if\ s \leq 4 \\ 0.134.4 + 0.101(s-4) & if\ 4 < s \leq 8 \\ 0.134.4 + 0.101.4 + 0.068(s-8) & if\ s > 8 \end{cases} \tag{1}$$

Where s is the average years of schooling from the dataset.

The correlation of decadal growth rates, $\emptyset\frac{s_{it}}{\emptyset(s_{it-10})} - 1$ (PWT equation: human capital in PWT 9.0, 2019); $CS_{i,t}$ an explanatory variable, which measures the infrastructure of a nation (2011 USD); and $TB_{i,t}$ is an explanatory variable, which measures the monetary value of the net exports of a nation as a share of $RGDP$, where:

$$TB_{i,t} = \frac{Exports - Imports}{RGDP}.100.$$

Table 2: Descriptive Statistics of Variables (1950 – 2014)

Variables	$RGDP_{per\ capita_{ppp_{i,t}}}$	$HC_{i,t}$	$CS_{i,t}$	$TB_{i,t}$
Mean	196112	1.96	814383.10	-0.03
Median	419923.58	1.91	127792.50	-0.02
Maximum	3080764	3.05	13311433	0.43
Minimum	1328.68	1.22	6753.31	-0.40
Standard Dev.	402363.1	0.45	1798829	0.10

Source: (PWT, 2019)
Author's calculation

Model Specification

The theoretical structure of the study is based on the endogenous growth theory. The model supports the conclusion that an essential factor for economic growth is accumulating knowledge in the form of human capital. ((Mankiw et al., 1992, Romer, 1989, 1990, & 1994) modeled production as a function of human capital (*HC*), physical capital (*PC*), technology (*T*), and labor (*L*) in their growth theory. Holland et al. (2013) explained the production function similarly. Based on the following literature, our $HC_{i,t}$ using the Augmented Solow Growth Model (*ASGM*) is as follows:

$$Y_t = AH^\alpha K_t^\beta L^\gamma \tag{2}$$

where Y_t is output, H is human capital, K is physical capital, L is labor, A is technology, and the parameters α, β, and γ messages the return to scale. $0 < \alpha, \beta, \gamma < 1$. Restating in per capita terms:

$$\frac{Y}{L} = A\left(\frac{H}{L}\right)^\alpha \left(\frac{K}{L}\right)^\beta \equiv y_t \equiv Ah^\alpha k^\beta \tag{3}$$

To operationalize equation (3), we define the total factor productivity (*A*) as

$$A = f(T_i) = T_t^\delta \tag{4}$$

Substituting equation (3) into (4) and taking the natural log, we get:

$$lny_t = \beta_0 + \alpha lnh_t + \beta lnk + \delta lnT_t \tag{5}$$

To create the study's econometric-equation, the theoretical model was transformed into an empirical by using $RGDP_{per\ capitapppi,t}$, $HC_{i,t}$, $CS_{i,t}$, and $TB_{i,t}$ to represent y_t, h_t, k_t, and T_t where y_t is $RGDP_{per\ capitapppi,t}$, h is $HC_{i,t}$: k is $CS_{i,t}$; and T is $TB_{i,t}$. The econometrics equation is given as

$$lny_{i,t} = \beta_0 + \alpha HC_{i,t} + \beta lnCS_{i,t} + \delta TB_{i,t} + \varepsilon_{i,t} \tag{6}$$

where $\varepsilon_{i,t}$ = error term.

The Vector Error Correction Model (*VEC*) was employed in this study as the estimation technique. This technique was selected because it allows the exploration of the causal relationship between human capital and economic growth. The Vector Autocorrection has four steps one, the panel unit root test, which determines the stationarity of our data Using the (Levin–Lin–Chu (*LLC*), 2002), Breitung and Das (Breitung), 2005), and (Im–Pesaran–Shin (*IPS*), 2003) were implemented. The *LLC* test is based on the Augmented Dickey-Fuller (*ADF*) analysis, which assumes homogeneity in the dynamics of the autoregressive coefficients for all panel units with cross-sectional independence. The *LLC* equation is as follows:

$$\Delta X_{int} = \zeta_i + \eta_i X_{in,t-1} + \theta_i t + \sum_{j=1}^{k} \lambda_{ij} X_{i,t-j} + \mu_{ijt} \tag{7}$$

where: i is an index of variables: $RGDP_{per\ capitai,t}$, $HC_{i,t}$, $CS_{i,t}$, and $TB_{i,t}$; t is a time index from 1950 to 2014; n is a country index running across 14 LAC; Δ is the first difference operator; $X_{i,t}$ is $lnHC_{i,t}$, $lnCS_{i,t}$, and $lnTB_{i,t}$; and $\mu_{i,t}$ = the error term disturbance with a variance of σ_i^2. According to (Levin, Lin, & Chi, 2002), the hypothesis of the stationarity of the panel data is: $H_0 : \eta_i = 0$ and $H_1 : \eta_i < 0$, where the alternative hypothesis corresponds to X_{it} being stationary. (Levin, Lin, & Chi, 2002) also specified another equation as follows, which restricts β_i while keeping it identical across countries, which substantially increases the power of the test in panel data.

$$\Delta X_{it} = v_i + o_i X_{i,t-1} + \pi_i t + \sum_{j=1}^{\rho} \phi_{ij} \Delta X_{i,t-j} + \psi_{it} \qquad (8)$$

In equation (8), it is assumed that: $H_0 : o_1 = o_2 = \cdots = o_n = 0$ and $H_1 : o_1 = o_2 = \cdots = o_n < 0$, where $t - statistics = t_{\hat{o}}/\sigma(\hat{o})$. Equation (8) equals $\hat{o}$, and its standard error $= \sigma(\hat{o})$. The Breitung unit root test is based on (Breitung 2000), who developed a pooled panel unit root test that does not require bias correction factors. Table 5 includes the Levin et al. (Levin, Lin, & Chi, 2002), the (Breitung, 2000), and the (Kyung, Pesaran, & Shin, 2003) unit root results. Step two is the determination of the lag length; given our variables are now rendered stationary, we tested for the existence of a cointegrating relationship and to analyze the cointegration test. The lag length is first determined by using the Lag Selection Criteria (*LSC*) test. Five lag length selection criteria have been employed in this study to determine our variables' Autoregressive (AR) lag length. The *AR* lag length p^1 is unknown and can be estimated using the *LSC*. The analysis would be carried out using the likelihood ratio (*LR*) test, according to (Sims 1980).

$$LR = (T - c)||log|\Omega_1| - log|\Omega_2| \qquad (9)$$

where T is the sample size; c the total number of parameters estimated in the model; Ω_1 the maximum likelihood estimate of the variance-covariance matrix of the residuals in the Vector Autoregression (*VAR*) model under the null hypothesis; and Ω_2 is the maximum likelihood estimate of the variance-covariance matrix of the residuals in the *VAR* model under the alternative hypothesis. The *LR* test is a chi-square distributed with the degrees of freedom equal to the number of restrictions that are tested.

The *FPE* is given as

$$FPE(\omega) = |\breve{\Sigma}(\omega)| + \left(\frac{\hat{T}+M_\omega+1}{\hat{T}-M_\omega-1}\right)^2 = det\left(\frac{1}{N}\sum_i^N e(t,\widehat{\tau_N})\right)\left(e(t,\widehat{\tau_N})\right)^T\left(\frac{1+d/N}{1-d/N}\right) \qquad (10)$$

where N is the number of values in the estimates; $e(t)$ is the $ny - by - 1$ vector of prediction error; τ_N is the estimated parameters; and d is the number of estimated parameters.

The *AIC*, according to (Akaike, 1969 & 1974), is given as

$$AIC(\varrho) = \ln\left|\hat{\Sigma}_\varrho\right| + \frac{2k^2 p}{T} \tag{11}$$

where T is the number of observations; k is the dimension of the time series; ϱ is the estimated number of lags; and Σ_ϱ is the estimated error term covariance matrix.

Shibata (1976) proves that the *AIC*, in the univariate *AR(p)* representation, is inconsistent in the sense that, asymptotically, it overestimates the true order with a nonzero probability. In the Schwarz Information Criterion (*SIC*), according to (Schwarz, 1978), the equation is given as

$$SC(\varrho) = \ln\left|\hat{\Sigma}_\varrho\right| + \frac{k^2 \varrho \ln T}{T} \tag{12}$$

and the *HQC* is given as

$$HQC(\varrho) = \ln\left|\hat{\Sigma}_\varrho\right| + \frac{2\varrho k^2 \ln \ln T}{T} \tag{13}$$

Step three, the Padroni cointegration test using the panel, the Cointegration Test, the Kao Residual Cointegration Test (Kao, 1999), Pedroni Panel Cointegration Test (Pedroni, 2002) (Pedronic, 2004), and Fisher Panel Cointegration Test (Yate & Fisher, 1925) were used. These tests allow various cross-sectional interdependencies and other different individual effects to establish cointegration. Given that our variables are integrated in order one, we tested for a cointegration relationship. This was done using the Pedroni Cointegration Test, Kao Residual Cointegration Test, and Fisher Panel Cointegration Test. These tests enable us to investigate the long-run relationship between the variables. The Pedroni test allows various cross-sectional interdependencies and other individual effects to establish cointegration. Our study identifies two kinds of test statistics: the pooling residuals within the dimension of the panel and the other without the dimension. The long-run equilibrium equations are as follows:

where Panel V-Statistic: $T^2 N^{3/2} Z_{v\,N,T} \equiv \left(\sum_{i=1}^{N} \sum_{t=1}^{T} \hat{L}_{11i}^{-2} \hat{e}_{it-1}^{2}\right)^{-1}$; Panel rho-Statistic: $T\sqrt{N} Z_{p\,N,T-1} \equiv$

$T\sqrt{N} \left(\sum_{i=1}^{N} \sum_{t=1}^{T} \hat{L}_{11i}^{-2} \hat{e}_{it-1}^{2}\right)^{-1} \sum_{i=1}^{N} \sum_{t=1}^{T} \hat{L}_{11i}^{-2} (\hat{e}_{it-1}^{2} \Delta \hat{e}_{it} - \hat{\lambda}_i)$; Panel PP-Statistic: $Z_{t\,N,T} \equiv$

$\left(\sigma^2 N, T \sum_{i=1}^{N} \sum_{t=1}^{T} \hat{L}_{11i}^{-2} \hat{e}_{it-1}^{2}\right)^{-1/2} \sum_{i=1}^{N} \sum_{t=1}^{T} \hat{L}_{11i}^{-2} (\hat{e}_{it-1}^{2} \Delta \hat{e}_{it} - \hat{\lambda}_i)$; Panel ADF-Statistic: $Z_{t\,N,T}^{*} \equiv$

$\left(s_{N,T}^{*2} \sum_{i=1}^{N} \sum_{t=1}^{T} \hat{L}_{11i}^{-2} \hat{e}_{it-1}^{2}\right)^{-1/2} \sum_{i=1}^{N} \sum_{t=1}^{T} \hat{L}_{11i}^{-2} (\hat{e}_{it-1}^{*} \Delta \hat{e}_{it}^{*})$; Group rho-Statistic: $N^{-1/2} \tilde{Z}_{t\,N,T-1} \equiv$

$TN^{-1/2} \sum_{i=1}^{N} \left(\sum_{t=1}^{T} \hat{e}_{it-1}^{2}\right)^{-1} \sum_{t=1}^{N} (\hat{e}_{it-1}^{2} \Delta \hat{e}_{it} - \hat{\lambda}_i)$; Group PP-Statistic: $N^{-1/2} \tilde{Z}_{t}^{*} \equiv$

$N^{-\frac{1}{2}} \sum_{i=1}^{N} (\sigma_i^2 \sum_{t=1}^{T} e_{i,t-1}^{*2})^{-1/2} \sum_{t=l}^{T} (\hat{e}_{it-1} \Delta \hat{e}_{it} - \hat{\lambda}_i)$; and Group ADF-Statistic: $\tilde{Z}_{t\,N,T}^{*} \equiv$

$\sum_{i=1}^{N} (\sum_{t=1}^{T} \hat{s}_i^2 \hat{e}_{i,t-1}^{*2})^{-1/2} \sum_{t=1}^{T} (\hat{e}_{it-1}^{*} \Delta \hat{e}_{it}^{*})$ where λ_i is $\frac{1}{T} \sum_{s+1}^{k_i} (1 - \frac{2}{k_i+1}) \sum_{t=s+1}^{T} \widehat{\mu_{i,t}} \, \widehat{\mu}_{i}, t - s, s_i^2 \equiv$

$\frac{1}{T} \sum_{t=1}^{T} \hat{\mu}_{i,t} \, \widehat{\sigma_i^2} = \widehat{s_i^2} + 2\hat{\lambda}_i, \widehat{\sigma_{N,T}} \equiv \frac{1}{N} \sum_{i=l}^{N} \widehat{L_{1i}^{-2}\sigma_i^2}; \widehat{S_i^2} \equiv \frac{1}{t} \sum_{t=1}^{T} \widehat{\mu_{i,t}^2}, \ \widehat{s_{N,T}^{*2}} \equiv \frac{1}{N} \sum_{i=1}^{N} \widehat{s_i^{*2}}, \ \widehat{L_{11}^2} =$

$\frac{1}{T} \sum_{t=1}^{T} \widehat{\eta_{i,t}^2} + \frac{2}{T} \sum_{s=1}^{k_i} (1 - \frac{s}{k_i+1}) \sum_{t=s+1}^{T} \widehat{\eta_{i,t}} \, \widehat{\eta_i} \, t - s$ and where the residuals $\widehat{\mu_{i,t}}, \widehat{\mu_{i,t}^*},$ and $\widehat{\eta_{i,t}}$ are obtained from the following regressions: $\widehat{e_{i,t}} = \hat{\gamma}_i \, \widehat{e_{i,t-1}} + \widehat{\mu_{i,t}} \, \widehat{e_{i,t}} = \hat{\gamma}_i \widehat{e_{i,t-1}} + \sum_{k=1}^{k_i} \hat{\gamma}_i \, k\Delta \hat{e}_{i}, t - k + \widehat{\mu^*}i, t, \ \Delta y_{i,t} =$

$\sum_{m=1}^{M} \widehat{b_{m,i}} \Delta x_{mi,t} + \widehat{\eta_{i,t}}$ (Pedroni, 2002 & 2004).

The Panel V-Stat, Panel rho-Stat, Panel PP-Stat, Panel ADF-Stat, Group rho-State, Group PP-Stat, and Group ADF-Stat are normally and asymptotically distributed (see Table 6). Step four, the *VEC*, which estimates the long-run and short-run relationship ((E-view, 2019) (Batchelor, 2018) (Stata, 2019)). The study employed the Fully Modified Ordinary Least Squares (*FMOLS*) technique to determine the coefficients of the long-run relationship between the explained and the explanatory variables. The *FMOLS* estimates show the cointegration regression by accounting for serial correlation effects and endogeneity in the regression (Phillips, 1995). According to (Pedroni 2002 & 2004), the *FMOLS* can accommodate considerable heterogeneity across individual members of the panel. (Pedroni, 2002) further stated that the cointegration test determines whether our variables are cointegrated without providing estimated coefficients for individual variables in the panel.

Table 3: Panel Unit Root Results

Variable	Intercept						Trend and Intercept					
	Levels			1st Difference (2nd Difference)			Levels			1st Difference (2nd Difference)		
	LLC	IPS	Bretung	LLC	IPS	Bretung	LLC	IPS	Bretung	LLC	IPS	Bretung
$RGDP_{per\ capita_{PPP,t}}$	1.00	1.00	n/a	0.00*	0.00*	n/a	1.00	1.00	1.00	0.00*	0.00*	0.00*
$HC_{i,t}$	0.00**	0.00**	n/a	n/a	n/a	n/a	0.00**	0.00**	0.04**	n/a	n/a	n/a
$CS_{i,t}$	1.00	1.00	n/a	0.00*	0.00*	n/a	1.00	1.00	0.00*	0.00*	0.00*	0.00*
$TB_{i,t}$	0.00**	0.00*	n/a	n/a	n/a	n/a	0.00**	0.00*	0.00*	n/a	n/a	n/a

Notes: variables are in real terms
*** indicates significance level at 10%
** indicates significance level at 5%
* indicates a significance level at 1%
Source: Author's calculation

Table 4: Lag Length Selection Criteria Test

Lag	LogL	LR	FPE	AIC	SIC	HQC
0	-1838.11	NA	0.0007	4.13	4.15	4.13
1	2858.91	9341.44	2.04e-08	-6.36	-6.25*	-6.32
2	2902.01	85.34*	1.92e-08*	-6.42*	-6.23	-6.34*
3	2909.60	14.95	1.95e-08	-6.40	-6.12	-6.29
4	2917.86	16.21	1.99e-08	-6.38	-6.02	-6.24
5	2924.95	13.85	2.03e-08	-6.36	-5.91	-6.19
6	2930.96	11.69	2.07e-08	-6.34	-5.80	-6.14
7	2935.49	8.77	2.13e-08	-6.31	-5.69	-6.08
8	2940.79	10.21	2.18e-08	-6.29	-5.58	-6.02

*Indicates lag order selected by the criterion
LR: sequential modified LR test statistic (each test at 5% level)
FPE: Final prediction error
AIC: Akaike information criterion
SC: Schwarz information criterion
HQC: Hannan-Quinn information criterion
Source: Author's calculation

Table 5: Pedroni Panel Cointegration Test

Panel Group Statistics	Statistic	Prob
Panel V-Statistic	-1.17	0.43
Panel rho-Statistic	2.42	0.98
Panel PP-Statistic	-1.84	0.00***
Panel ADF-Statistic	-1.84	0.00***
Group rho-Statistic	2.62	2.00
Group PP-Statistic	-3.61	0.00***
Group ADF Statistic	-3.55	0.00***

* indicates significance at 10%
** indicates significance at 5%
*** indicates significance at 1%
Source: Author's calculation

Table 6: Kao Residual Cointegration Test

	T-Statistic	Prob
ADF	-1.97	0.02**

* indicates significance at 10%
** indicates significance at 5%
*** indicates significance at 1%
Source: Author's calculation

Table 7: Fisher Panel Cointegration Test

	Stat	Prob
None*	129.5	0.00***
At most 1*	53.20	0.00***
At most 2*	29.46	0.11
At most 3*	20.25	0.86

* indicates significance at 10%
** indicates significance at 5%
*** indicates significance at 1%
Source: Author's calculation

Table 8: Results of Long-term Coefficient Estimates by FMOLS

Variables	Model
$HC_{i,t}$	0.21 (0.00)***
$CS_{i,t}$	0.13 (0.00)***
$TB_{i,t}$	-0.43 (0.004)***
R-squared	36%
(Adj-R)	36%

Note
p-value in parenthesis
' indicates significance level at 10%
** indicates significance level at 5%
*** indicates significance at 1%
Source: Author's calculation

Results

Table 3 shows that $RGDP_{per\ capitapppi,t}$ and $CS_{i,t}$ are non-stationary at level terms. Hence, we fail to reject the null hypothesis indicating that the variables contain a unit root. However, after the first-order differentiation, the test statistic shows that we can reject the null hypothesis of non-stationarity for $RGDP_{per\ capitapppi,t}$, and $CS_{i,t}$ at the 1% significant level. In contrast, $HC_{i,t}$ and $TB_{i,t}$ were stationary at level terms. Hence, we rejected the null hypothesis of non-stationarity at the 1% significant level. Table 4 shows the lag length selection results. Four of the five statistics—*LR*, *FPE*, *AIC*, and *HQC*— indicate a lag length of two, while SIC suggested a lag length of one. Therefore, the study selected two lag lengths, viewing the loss of efficiency, which is less of an issue than bias. Tables 5, 6, and 7 show we can reject the null hypothesis of no cointegrating relationship between our variables. Hence, the Pedroni, Kao, and Fisher's cointegration tests provide a benchmark for a panel cointegration between our explained and explanatory variables in the study.

Table 8 shows a positive, statistically significant long-run relationship between $RGDP_{per\ capitapppi,t}$ and $HC_{i,t}$ with a coefficient of 0.21. This indicates that a 1% increase in $HC_{i,t}$ is associated with a 0.21%-point increase in $RGDP_{per\ capitapppi,t}$ in our LAC. $HC_{i,t}$ implies that there is an incentive for a nation to improve its citizens' skill-set, knowledge, and innovative ideas. This improvement will lead to the creation of new jobs, an increase in productivity, an increase in the disposable income of employees, and an increase in the consumption of consumer goods and services. This result indicates that the incentive to improve a nation's $HC_{i,t}$ index would yield a positive result as it translates to an increase in $RGDP_{per\ capitapppi,t}$. This result is consistent with (Edrees, 2016), (Mehrara & Musai, 2013), (Khembo & Tchereni, 2013), (Rahman, 2011), and (Sharma & Sahni, 2015). $CS_{i,t}$ was used as a proxy for domestic investment in private and public infrastructures. It showed a positive, statistically significant result with a coefficient of 0.13. This implies that a 1% increase in the $CS_{i,t}$ is associated with a 0.13%-point increase in $RGDP_{per\ capitapppi,t}$ in our LAC, and should increase their investments in the nation's plants and infrastructures. This will lead to the creation of new jobs in the construction sector of their economies, which will lead to an increase in the disposable income of the construction worker, which in turn, will lead to a rise in the consumption of more consumer goods and services in the economy, which will increase sales and have a positive impact on the economy. The results indicate that domestic investment, plants, and good infrastructures in our LAC contribute significantly to the economy's growth in terms of $RGDP_{per\ capitapppi,t}$.

$TB_{i,t}$ is a percentage of $RGDP$ (see Table 2) and has a negative and statistically significant long-run relationship with $RGDP_{per\ capitapppi,t}$. A 1% increase in $TB_{i,t}$ decreases $RGDP_{per\ capitapppi,t}$ by 0.43%-point. This implies that a negative trade balance affects economic growth in our LAC: an increase in TB will negatively affect the economic growth of the LAC. These countries are net importers of consumer goods and services; hence, they should substitute their current economic policy of importing consumer goods and services from the international market to importing more capital goods ($CS_{i,t}$ -materials) and services ($HC_{i,t}$). This consumption shift will increase the nations' opportunities for exporting more consumer goods and services in the future in the international market and improve their country's $RGDP_{per\ capitapppi,t}$. The chapter on causal relationships among economic variables has been one of the main objectives of empirical econometrics. According to (Engle & Granger, 1987), cointegrated variables must have an error correction representation. One of the implications of the Granger representation theorem is that if non-stationary series are cointegrated, then one of the series must GC the other (Gujarati et al., 2012). To examine the direction of GCR in the presence of cointegrating vectors, GC is conducted based on the following specifications:

Ejiro U. Osiobe

$$
\begin{pmatrix} \Delta lnRGDP_{per\ capita_{ppp_{i,t}}} \\ \Delta HC_{i,t} \\ \Delta lnCS_{i,t} \\ \Delta TB_{i,t} \end{pmatrix} = \begin{pmatrix} \emptyset_{i,1} \\ \emptyset_{i,2} \\ \emptyset_{i,3} \\ \emptyset_{i,4} \end{pmatrix} + \sum_{l=1}^{m} \begin{pmatrix} \theta_{1,2,3,4,k} \\ \theta_{2,1,3,4,k} \\ \theta_{3,1,2,4,k} \\ \theta_{4,1,2,3,k} \end{pmatrix} \begin{bmatrix} \Delta lnRGDP_{per\ capita_{ppp_{i,t-l}}} \\ \Delta HC_{i,t-l} \\ \Delta lnCS_{i,t-l} \\ \Delta TB_{i,t-l} \end{bmatrix} +
$$

$$
\begin{pmatrix} \lambda_1 \\ \lambda_2 \\ \lambda_3 \\ \lambda_4 \end{pmatrix} ECT_{i,t-1} + \begin{pmatrix} \varphi_{1,i,t} \\ \varphi_{2,i,t} \\ \varphi_{3,i,t} \\ \varphi_{4,i,t} \end{pmatrix} \tag{14}
$$

where Δ = the first differences, $\emptyset_{i,j}$ ($j, k = 1,2$) = the fixed country effect, $I(I = 1, \ldots m)$ = the lag length determined by SIC, $ECT_{i,t-1}$ = the estimated lagged error correction term (ECT) derived from the long-run cointegrating relationship, λ- = the adjustment coefficient, and $\emptyset_{1,I,t}$ = the disturbance term, which is assumed to have a zero mean.

Table 9: The estimate of the Panel Vector Error Correction Model
Explanatory Variables – Chi-square value (Wald test)

	$RGDP_{per\ capita_{ppp_{i,t}}}$	$HC_{i,t}$	$CS_{i,t}$	$TB_{i,t}$	ECT (-1) [t-Test]
$RGDP_{per\ capita_{ppp_{i,t}}}$		0.00 (0.99)	0.05 (0.95)	9.33 (0.00)***	-0.013 [-2.63]
$HC_{i,t}$	3.27 (0.04)**		2.05 (0.12)	5.43 (0.00)***	-0.05 [-1.95]
$CS_{i,t}$	2.92 (0.05)**	1.06 (0.35)		4.73 (0.00)***	-0.03 [-1.15]
$TB_{i,t}$	1.39 (0.25)	4.91 (0.00)***	5.13 (0.00)***		-0.01 [-5.31]

*indicates significance level at 10%
** indicates significance level at 5%
*** indicates significance at 1%
Source: Author's calculation

Table 9 and 10 shows our estimates indicate a significant uni-directional GCR between $RGDP_{per\ capitapppi,t} \rightarrow HC_{i,t}$, $RGDP_{per\ capitapppi,t} \rightarrow$

$CS_{i,t}$, and $RGDP_{per\,capitapppi,t} \leftarrow TB_{i,t}$, and a bidirectional GCR between $HC_{i,t} \leftrightarrow$ $TB_{i,t}$, and $CS_{i,t} \leftrightarrow TB_{i,t}$. The unidirectional causality link between $RGDP_{per}$ $_{capitapppi,t} \rightarrow HC_{i,t}$ implies that when an individual or nation invests in $HC_{i,t}$ (training people). It takes time to see any return on one's investment. For example, training an individual to become a world-class/skilled researcher or economist will take 12 years of formal education and 2–4 years of post-doctoral training (optional). The individual will need to have at least 5 years of industrial experience or more in some cases before the country/economy can reap the benefits of the initial investment in $HC_{i,t}$. The unidirectional causality link between $RGDP_{per\,capitapppi,t} \rightarrow CS_{i,t}$ implies that when a country invests in the construction of infrastructure, it takes time for these projects to be completed, such as the case of new roads, railways, dams with hydro-electric generators, and airports. These projects will take a minimum of 6–10 years before the nation can use them optimally. The unidirectional causality link between $RGDP_{per\,capitapppi,t} \leftarrow TB_{i,t}$ shows that these LAC heavily depend on importing consumer goods and services. The bidirectional is $HC_{i,t} \leftrightarrow TB_{i,t}$ and $CS_{i,t} \leftrightarrow TB_{i,t}$, which implies that our LAC lacks $HC_{i,t}$, and $CS_{i,t}$; hence, their importation on consumer goods and services is high. So, these countries must import more capital goods, $HC_{i,t}$ (skilled expatriate) and $CS_{i,t}$ (raw materials). Increased importation of $HC_{i,t}$ will translate into $HC_{i,t} \uparrow$ — productivity $\uparrow$ — exportation of consumer goods and services $\uparrow$ — importation of consumer goods and services $\downarrow$. Likewise, if $CS_{i,t} \uparrow$ — productivity $\uparrow$ — exportation of consumer goods and services $\uparrow$ — importation of consumer goods and services $\downarrow$. This implies that the variation in $RGDP_{per\,capitapppi,t}$ is useful in predicting the variation in $HC_{i,t}$ and $CS_{i,t}$. In contrast, the variation in $TB_{i,t}$ is useful in predicting the variation in $RGDP_{per}$ $_{capitapppi,t}$. In a bidirectional causality, the variation in the two variables is useful in predicting the variation in the other.

Table 10: Summary of Main Findings of Short-run Causality

Variables	Direction of Causality	Implication
$RGDP_{per\ capita_{ppp_{i,t}}} \rightarrow HC_{i,t}$	Unidirectional	Granger causality runs from $RGDP_{per\ capita_{ppp_{i,t}}}$ to $HC_{i,t}$
$RGDP_{per\ capita_{ppp_{i,t}}} \rightarrow CS_{i,t}$	Unidirectional	Granger causality runs from $RGDP_{per\ capita_{ppp_{i,t}}}$ to $CS_{i,t}$
$RGDP_{per\ capita_{ppp_{i,t}}} \leftarrow TB_{i,t}$	Unidirectional	Granger causality runs from $TB_{i,t}$ to $RGDP_{per\ capita_{ppp_{i,t}}}$
$HC_{i,t} \leftrightarrow TB_{i,t}$	Bidirectional	Granger causality runs from $HC_{i,t}$ to $TB_{i,t}$ vice versa
$CS_{i,t} \leftrightarrow TB_{i,t}$	Bidirectional	Granger causality runs from $CS_{i,t}$ to $TB_{i,t}$ vice versa

$\leftrightarrow$ indicates causality running in both direction
$\rightarrow$ indicates causality from left to right
$\leftarrow$ indicates causality from right to left
↑ increase
↓ decrease
− leads too
Source: Author's Calculation

Conclusion, and Overall Policy Recommendations

The results contained in Table 9 support the long-term *GC* between our explained and explanatory variables in all the selected countries. In contrast, the short-run *GC* results from our variables can be found in Table 10. Our results imply that $HC_{i,t}$ does not *GC* $RGDP_{per\ capitapppi,t}$ to increase in the short-run, while in the long-run, it does *GC* economic growth in the respective countries. Given the results obtained, the importance of $HC_{i,t}$ in boosting economic growth can't be overemphasized. Also, $CS_{i,t}$ does not *GC* $RGDP_{per\ capitapppi,t}$ to increase in the short-run, while in the long-run, it does *GC* economic growth in the respective countries. On the other hand, $TB_{i,t}$ does *GC* $RGDP_{per\ capitapppi,t}$ to increase both in the short-run and long-run. This book investigates the *GCR* between $HC_{i,t}$ and economic growth in LAC. The study employs a time series of annual data between 1950–2014 for a panel of 14 LAC: Argentina, Bolivia, Brazil, Chile, Colombia, Costa Rica, Honduras, Mexico, Nicaragua, Panama, Peru, El Salvador, Uruguay, and Venezuela. The data was collected from (PWT, 2019). The empirical findings reveal that after controlling for $CS_{i,t}$, $TB_{i,t}$, $HC_{i,t}$, and $RGDP_{per\ capitapppi,t}$, there is a positive statistically significant long-run relationship between $RGDP_{per\ capitapppi,t}$ and $HC_{i,t}$ with a coefficient of 0.21. This indicates that a 1%-point increase in $HC_{i,t}$ will lead to a 0.21%-point increase in $RGDP_{per\ capitapppi,t}$ in the LAC. This result indicates that the incentive to improve the HDI of a nation would yield a positive outcome as it translates to an increase in $RGDP_{per\ capitapppi,t}$. This result is consistent with (Edrees, 2016), (Mehrara & Musai, 2013), (Khembo & Tchereni, 2013), (Rahman, 2011), (Sharma & Sahni, 2015), and (Osiobe, 2020) which is a similar vein study that analyzes relationship among $RGDP_{per\ capitapppi,t}$ (as a proxy for economic growth) and the examined variable, $SGE_{i,t}$, ((Secondary School Government Expenditure) as a proxy for human capital), and $VT_{i,t}$ (Trade Volume) as the explanatory variables between 2000-2014. The study preceded this book with less countries analyzed (excluding Bolivia, Honduras, Nicaragua, Panama, Uruguay, and Venezuela).

$CS_{i,t}$ was used as a proxy for domestic investment in private and public infrastructures. It showed a positive, statistically significant result with a coefficient of 0.13. This implies that a 1%-point increase in the $CS_{i,t}$ will lead to a 0.13%-point rise in $RGDP_{per\ capitapppi,t}$ in the LAC. The results indicate that domestic investment, plants, and excellent infrastructures in our LAC contribute significantly to the economy's growth in terms of $RGDP_{per\ capitapppi,t}$. The $TB_{i,t}$ has a negative and statistically significant long-run relationship with $RGDP_{per\ capitapppi,t}$. A one percentage point increase in $TB_{i,t}$ causes a decrease in $RGDP_{per\ capitapppi,t}$ by 0.43%-point. This implies that a negative $TB_{i,t}$ affects economic growth in the LAC.   Our   results   also indicate a significant causal link between $RGDP_{per\ capitapppi,t}$ and $HC_{i,t}$ with a unidirectional a GCR, moving from $RGDP_{per\ capitapppi,t}$ to HC. $RGDP_{per\ capitapppi,t}$ and $CS_{i,t}$ with a unidirectional GCR, moving from $RGDP_{per\ capitapppi,t}$ to $CS_{i,t}$, and $RGDP_{per\ capitapppi,t}$ and $TB_{i,t}$ with a unidirectional GCR, moving from $TB_{i,t}$ to $RGDP_{per\ capitapppi,t}$. While a bidirectional significant GCB can be found between $HC_{i,t}$ and $TB_{i,t}$, and, $CS_{i,t}$ and $TB_{i,t}$. The results imply that the variation in $RGDP_{per\ capitapppi,t}$ is useful in predicting the variation in $HC_{i,t}$ and $CS_{i,t}$, while the variation in $TB_{i,t}$ is useful in predicting the variation in $RGDP_{per\ capitapppi,t}$. In a bidirectional causality, the variation in the two variables is useful in predicting the variation in the other.

Further studies need to be examined using different methodologies to investigate how spending on education translates to higher economic growth, community development, and higher productivity. Notwithstanding, specific government spending on different tiers of education (primary, secondary, and higher education) needs to be investigated. Although the chapter doesn't find a direct GCR moving from, $HC_{i,t} \rightarrow RGDP_{per\ capitapppi,t}$, there is an indirect causal relationship between our variables of interest. This association is the bidirectional GCR between $HC_{i,t} \leftrightarrow TB_{i,t}$. The relationship exists because $TB_{i,t}$ is an explanatory factor of $GDP \equiv RGDP \equiv RGDP_{per\ capita} \equiv RGDP_{per\ capitappp} \equiv RGDP_{per\ capitapppi,t}$ in this study and $TB-,.$ is derived from net exports. The result supports the long-term GCR between our explained and explanatory variables in all of the LAC. Meanwhile, the short-run GC results from our variables can be found, and our results imply that $HC_{i,t}$ does not GC $RGDP_{per\ capitapppi,t}$ to increase in the short-run, while in the long-run, it does GC economic growth in the respective countries. Given these results, HCi, t's importance in boosting economic growth confirmed our sample. Also, $CS_{i,t}$ does not $GC\ RGDP_{per\ capitapppi,t}$ to increase in the short-run, while in the long-run, it does GC economic growth in the respective countries. On the other hand, $TB_{i,t}$ does $GC\ RGDP_{per\ capitapppi,t}$ to increase both in the short-run and long-run. This study provides information that will guide future studies and the formulation and implementation of the Latin American region's short- and long-term development goals (not limited to the selected countries).

The policy implications of this research involve the following: first, Our Latin America study sample should provide incentives that would foster, attract, and retain public and private investment in $HC_{i,t}$ development, and educational advancement in the region. These incentives should be regulated at the regional level under the umbrella of a decentralized governing body for each country. Second, a legal framework regulating government expenditure on education and the educational sector in the region should be strengthened. This will create a conducive learning environment for both the students and teachers.

REFERENCES

Akaike, H. (1969). Fitting the Autoregressive Model for Prediction. *Annals of the Institute of Statistical Mathematics, 21*(1), 243-247. https://doi.org/10.1007/BF02532251

Akaike, H. (1974). A new look at the statistical model identification. *IEEE Transactions on Automatic Control, 19*(6), 716-723. Available at: https://doi.org/10.1109/TAC.1974.1100705.

Al-Yousif, Y. K. (2002). Financial development and economic growth: Another look at the evidence from developing countries. *Review of Financial Economics, 11*(2), 131-150. Available at: https://doi.org/10.1016/S1058-3300(02)00039-3.

Barro, J. R. (1991). Human capital and growth in cross-country regressions. *The Quarterly Journal of Economics, 106*(2), 407-443. Available at: https://doi.org/10.2307/2937943.

Barro, J. R., & Lee, J.-W. (2013). A new data set of educational attainment in the World, 1950 - 2010. *Journal of Development Economics, 104*, 184 - 198. https://doi.org/10.1016/j.jdeveco.2012.10.001

Batchelor, R. (2018). Retrieved 5 12, 2018, from http://www.eco.uc3m.es/~jgonzalo/teaching/PhDTimeSeries/CointeEviews.pdf

Becker, G. S. (1964). *Human capital: A theoretical and empirical analysis, with special reference to education.* Chicago, IL: University of Chicago Press.

Becker, G. S. (1993). Nobel lecture: The economic way of looking at behavior. *Journal of Political Economy, 101*(3), 385-409. Available at: https://doi.org/10.1086/261880.

Benhabib, J., & Spiegel, M. M. (1994). The role of human capital in economic development evidence from aggregate cross-country data. *Journal of Monetary Economics, 34*(2), 143-173. Available at: https://doi.org/10.1016/0304-3932(94)90047-7.

Breitung, J. (2000). The Local Power of Some Unit Root Test for Panel Data. *JAI, 15*, 161-178. https://doi.org/10.1016/S0731-9053(00)15006-6

Breitung, J., & Das, S. (2005). Panel unit root tests under cross-sectional dependence. *Dutch Statistics, 59*(4), 414-433. Available at: https://doi.org/10.1111/j.1467-9574.2005.00299.x.

Breitung, J. (2000). The local power of some unit root test for panel data. *JAI, 15,* 161-178. Available at: https://doi.org/10.1016/S0731-9053(00)15006-6.

Breitung, J., & Hashem, P. M. (2005). Unit Roots and Cointegration in Panels. Discussion Paper Series 1: Economic Studies No. 42.

Devarajan, S., Swaroop, V., & Zou, H.-f. (1996). The composition of public expenditure and economic growth. *Journal of Monetary Economics, 37*(2), 313-344. Available at: https://doi.org/10.1016/S0304-3932(96)90039-2.

Edrees, A. (2016). Human capital, infrastructure, and economic growth in Arab world: A panel granger causality analysis. *Business and Economics Journal.*

Engle, R. A. (1987). Co-integration and error correction: representation, estimation, and testing. *Econometrica, 55*(2), 251-276. Available at: Co-integration and error correction: representation, estimation, and testing.

Engle, R. F., & Granger, C. (1987). Co-Integration and Error Correction: Representation, Estimation, and Testing. *Econometrica, 55*(2), 251-276. https://doi.org/10.2307/1913236

E-Views (2019). E-views Help Intro Vector Autoregression And Error Correction Models. Retrieved 5 12, 2018, from http://www.eviews.com/help/helpintro.html#page/content/VAR-Vector_Autoregression_and_Error_Correction_Model.html

E-Views (2019). E-views help Intro Vector Error Correction (VEC) Models. Retrieved 5 12, 2018, from http://www.eviews.com/help/helpintro.html#page/content/VAR-Vector_Error_Correction_(VEC)_Models.html

Feinstein, L., Robertson, D., & Symons, J. (1999). Pre-school education and attainment in the national child development study and British cohort study. *Education Economics, 7*(3), 209-234. Available at: https://doi.org/10.1080/09645299900000019.

Gibbons, R., & Waldman, M. (2004). Task-specific human capital. *American Economic Review, 94*(2), 203-207. Available at: https://doi.org/10.1257/0002828041301579.

Gujarati, N. P. (2012). *Basic econometrics.*
Gujarati, N., Porter, D., & Gunasekar, S. (2012). *Basic Econometrics.* New York, NY: Mc Graw Hill Education.

Holland, M., Vieira, V. F., Da Silva, G. C., & Bottecchia, C. L. (2013). *Growth and Exchange rate Volatility: A Panel Data Analysis. Applied Economics, 45*(26). https://doi.org/10.1080/00036846.2012.730135

Im, K. S., Pesaran, M. H., & Shin, Y. (2003). Testing for unit roots in heterogeneous panels. *Journal of Econometrics, 115*(1), 53-74. Available at: https://doi.org/10.1016/S0304-4076(03)00092-7.

Kao, C. (1999). Spurious regression and residual-Based Test for Cointegration in Panel Data. *Journal of Econometrics, 90*(1), 1-44. https://doi.org/10.1016/S0304-4076(98)00023-2

Khembo, F., & Tchereni, B. H. (2013). The impact of human capital on economic growth in the SADC Region. *Developing Country Studies, 3*(4), 144-152.

Kögel, T., & Prskawetz, A. (2001). Agricultural productivity growth and escape from the Malthusian trap. *Journal of Economic Growth, 6*(4), 337-357. Available at: https://doi.org/10.1023/A:1012742531003.

Kyung, S. I., Pesaran, M. H., & Shin, Y. (2003). Testing for Unit Root in Heterogeneous Panels. *Journal of Econometrics, 115*(1), 53-74. https://doi.org/10.1016/S0304-4076(03)00092-7

Levin, A., Lin, C.-F., & Chu, C.-S. J. (2002). Unit root tests in panel data: Asymptotic and finite-sample properties. *Journal of Econometrics, 108*(1), 1-24. Available at: https://doi.org/10.1016/S0304-4076(01)00098-7.

Lucas Jr, R. E. (1988). On the mechanics of economic development. *Journal of Monetary Economics, 22*(1), 3-42. Available at: https://doi.org/10.1016/0304-3932(88)90168-7.

Mankiw, N. G., Romer, D., & Weil, D. N. (1992). A contribution to the empirics of economic growth. *The Quarterly Journal of Economics, 107*(2), 407-437. Available at: https://doi.org/10.2307/2118477.

Malthus, T. R. (1798). An Essay on the Principle of Population. 1st, Londo: William Pickering.

Mankiw, N. G., Romer, D., & Weil, N. D. (1992). A Contribution to the Empirics of Economic Growth. *The Quarterly Journal of Economics, 107*(2), 407- 437. https://doi.org/10.2307/2118477

Marx, K. (1844). Economic and Philosophic Manuscripts.

Marx, K. (1867). Capital: Critique of Political Economy.

Mehrara, M., & Musai, M. (2013). The relationship between economic growth and human capital in developing countries. *International Letters of Social and Humanistic Sciences, 5*(55), 55-62. Available at: https://doi.org/10.18052/www.scipress.com/ILSHS.5.55.

Mill, J. S. (1871). *Principle of Political Economy*. London: Longmans, Green, Reader, and Dyer.

Nelson, R. C. (1982). Trends and random walk in macroeconomics time series. *Journal of Monetary Economics*(10), 139-162. Available at: https://doi.org/10.1016/0304-3932(82)90012-5.

Nerdrum, L., & Erikson, T. (2001). Intellectual capital: A human capital perspective. *Journal of Intellectual Capital, 2*(2), 127-135. Available at: https://doi.org/10.1108/14691930110385919.

Osiobe, E. U. (2019). A Literature Review of Human Capital and Economic Growth https://doi.org/10.5296/ber.v9i4.15624

Osiobe, E. U. (2020). Human Capital and Economic Growth in Latin America: A Cointegration and Causality Analysis. Working Paper.

Osiobe, E. U. (2020). Understanding Latin America's educational orientations: Evidence from 14 nations. *Education Quarterly Review*, 249-260. Available at: https://doi.org/10.31014/aior.1993.03.02.137.

Pedroni, P. (2002). Critical value for cointegration test in heterogeneous panels with multiple regressors. *Oxford Bulletin of Economics and Statistics, 61*(S1). Available at: https://doi.org/10.1111/1468-0084.61.s1.14.

Pedroni, P. (2004). Panel cointegration: Asymptotic and finite sample properties of pooled time series test with an application to the PPP hypothesis. *Economic Theory, 20*(3), 325-597. Available at: https://doi.org/10.1017/S0266466604203073.

Penn World Table Equation: Human Capital in PWT 9.0. (2019). PWT 9.0. (Penn World Table) Retrieved 10 6, 2019, from https://www.rug.nl/ggdc/docs/human_capital_in_pwt_90.pdf

Penn World Tables, (2019). Retrieved 1 25, 2019, from http://datacentre2.chass.utoronto.ca/pwt/alphacountries.html

Phillips, C. P. (1995). Fully modified least squares and vector autoregression. *Econometrica, 63*(5), 1023 - 1078. Available at: www.jstor.org/stable/2171721.

Phillips, C. P. (1995). Fully Modified Least Squares and Vector Autoregression. Cowles Foundation Paper. https://doi.org/10.2307/2171721

Psacharopoulos, G. (1994). Return to investment in education: A global update. *World Development, 22*(9), 1325-1343. https://doi.org/10.1016/0305-750X(94)90007-8

Quiggin, J. (2002). Human capital theory and education policy in Australia. *Australian Economic Review, 32*(2). Available at: https://doi.org/10.1111/1467-8462.00100.

Rahman, M. M. (2011). Causal relationship among education expenditure, health expenditure and GDP: A case study for Bangladesh. *International Journal of Economics and Finance, 3*(3), 149-159. Available at: https://doi.org/10.5539/ijef.v3n3p149.

Ricardo, D. (1817). The Principle of Political Economy and Taxation.

Romer, P. (1989). Human capital and growth: Theory and evidence. NBER Working Paper No. 3173.

Romer, P. (1990). Endogenous technological change. *Journal of Political Economy, 98*(5), 71-102. Available at: https://doi.org/10.1086/261725.

Romer, D. (1996). *Advanced macroeconomics*. New York: Mc Graw Hill Education.

Romer, P. M. (1994). The origins of endogenous growth. *The Journal of Economic Perspective, 8*(1), 3-22. Available at: https://doi.org/10.1257/jep.8.1.3.

Schultz, T. (1961). Investment in human capital. *American Economic Review, 51*(1), 1-17.

Schultz., T. W. (1960). Capital formation by education. *Journal of Political Economy, 68*(6), 571-583. Available at: https://doi.org/10.1086/258393.

Schwarz, G. (1978). Estimating the dimension of a model. *The Annals of Statistics, 6*(2), 461-464. Available at: https://doi.org/10.1214/aos/1176344136.

Sharma, P., & Sahni, P. (2015). Human capital and economic growth in India: A cointegration and causality analysis. *Ushus Journal of Business Management - Journals, 14(2)*, 1-18. Available at: https://doi.org/10.12725/ujbm.31.1.

Shibata, R. (1976). Selection of the order of an autoregressive model by akaike's Information criterion. *Biometrika, 63*(1), 117-126. Available at: https://doi.org/10.1093/biomet/63.1.117.

Sims, A. C. (1980). Macroeconomics and reality. *Econometrica, 48*(1), 1-48. Available at: https://doi.org/10.2307/1912017.

Smith, A. (1776). An inquiry into the nature and causes of the wealth of nations. Available at: https://doi.org/10.1093/oseo/instance.00043218.

STATA (2019). Stata manuals 13 Vec Intro. Retrieved 5 12, 2018, from https://www.stata.com/manuals13/tsvecintro.pdf

Task Force on Measuring Human Capital. (2016). *Guide on Measuring Human Capital*. New York and Geneva: United Nations.

Teixeira, P. N. (2014). Gary becker's early work on human capital–collaborations and distinctiveness. *IZA Journal of Labor Economics, 3*(1), 1-20. Available at: https://doi.org/10.1186/s40172-014-0012-2.

United Nations. (2020, 2 8). Retrieved from https://www.un.org/en/

Vieira, F. H. (2013). Growth and exchange rate volatility: A panel data analysis. *Applied Economics, 45*(26). Available at: https://doi.org/10.1080/00036846.2012.730135.

West, E. G. (2020). The Political Economy of Alienation: Karl Mark and Adam Smith. Oxford Economic Papers, 1-23.

World Economic Forum. (2016). Skilling up: Human capital and Latin America. Retrieved from World Economic Forum: https://www.weforum.org/agenda/2016/12/skilling-up-human-capital-and-latin-america.

World Penn Tables. (2019). Retrieved from: http://datacentre2.chass.utoronto.ca/pwt/alphacountries.html.

Yate, F., & Fisher, R. A. (1925). Statistical Method for Research Workers.